Patty,

Thank you so much!

Stay RIGHT always!

Chris at the Tygrrrr Express

Ideological Idiocy

A Politically Conservative and Morally Liberal Hebrew Alpha Male Stumbles Upon Jihadists, Peace Activists, and Other Ridiculous Leftists and Trips Over Their Heads Located Up Their (redacted).

eric aka the Tygrrrr Express

iUniverse, Inc.
New York   Bloomington

IDEOLOGICAL IDIOCY
A politically conservative and morally liberal Hebrew alpha male stumbles upon jihadists, peace activists, and other ridiculous leftists and trips over their heads located up their (redacted).

iUniverse books may be ordered through booksellers or by contacting:

iUniverse
1663 Liberty Drive
Bloomington, IN 47403
www.iuniverse.com
1-800-Authors (1-800-288-4677)

Because of the dynamic nature of the Internet, any Web addresses or links contained in this book may have changed since publication and may no longer be valid. The views expressed in this work are solely those of the author and do not necessarily reflect the views of the publisher, and the publisher hereby disclaims any responsibility for them.

ISBN: 978-1-4502-1172-7 (pbk)
ISBN: 978-1-4502-1174-1 (cloth)
ISBN: 978-1-4502-1173-4 (ebook)

Printed in the United States of America

iUniverse rev. date: 4/6/10

Eric is the brilliance (God bless declining standards) behind the Tygrrrr Express, the 2007 Bloggers Choice Award for Most Passionate Fan Base.

He is also the author of the books Ideological Bigotry and Ideological Violence.

"The Tygrrrr Express" has been published in the Washington Times, Jewish Journal, RealClearPolitics Online, Commentary Magazine Online, and on the Web sites of Hugh Hewitt, Mark Steyn, Michelle Malkin, and Andrew Breitbart's Big Hollywood.

A sought after public speaker, he has addressed many chapters of the College Republicans, Young Republicans, Republican Jewish Coalition, and the most powerful people on Earth, the ladies of the Republican Women's Federated.

A radio host since 1992, his radio beginning was a sophomoric hard rock music program entitled "Hard as a Rock." Maturation eventually settled in (some disagree), and serious radio interviews with top politicos and other notables ensued. On the flip side of the microphone, the Tygrrrr Express has been a radio guest of Hugh Hewitt, Dennis Miller, and Armstrong Williams, in addition to being a frequent guest of Frank and Shane of "Political Vindication" on Blog Talk Radio.

The Tygrrrr Express has conducted print interviews of virtually every notable politician, although the Secret Service still will not allow a warm hug of President George W. Bush or Vice President Cheney.

Honors and privileges include sleeping for an entire week in a sports bar with full access to the beverages and pizza, in addition to meeting Miss Wilmington, North Carolina.

Often referred to as a "typical white person," the Tygrrrr Express will be editor of the yet to be created "Ordinary Average Caucasoid Monthly."

Rumors of his spending quiet nights alone with his Susan Boyle pinup calendar are not entirely true. Rumors of his preparing to duel to the death with Piers Morgan for the right to give her that first kiss are somewhat untrue.

About: The Tygrrrr Express is me. I am Brooklyn born, Strong Island raised, and currently living the good life in Los Angeles as a stockbrokerage and oil professional.

While Wall Street is forever in my blood, I am now on the speaking circuit full-time.

I like politics, the National Football League, '80s hard rock music, the stock market, and red meat. Blogging is a shameless ploy to get what I really want, which is to be sandwiched between a pair of Republican Jewish brunettes, and impregnate at least one of them. There will be a ceremony several months beforehand since my parents are NRA members.

The only political issue more important than killing taxes is killing terrorists. I do not sing "Kumbaya" with Islamofascists or leftists. Scorched Earth is my approach, with the grace and subtlety of a battering ram. The events of 9/11 fuel my emotions every day. Civilization must defeat barbarism, and my generation is up to the challenge. We will win the War on Terror, because we are Americans.

eric, aka the Tygrrrr Express

To every brunette who ever let me play with her yummy bouncies: Some of you were Republicans. Some of you were Jewish. None of you were both. Thank you anyway. If I did not thank you back then, I was distracted for obvious reasons. Thank you again.

Warning: This book was written between March of 2007 and December 31st, 2009. It was written under the assumption that liberal stupidity and gutlessness did not get us all killed on January 1st, 2010. If it did, either you have larger concerns, or no concerns whatsoever.

Contents

Chapter 0: A Moronic From the Get-go Foreword 1

Chapter 1: Ideological Idiocy 3

Chapter 2: Jewish Ideological Idiocy...............................12

Chapter 3: Pacifist Idiocy 27

Chapter 4: Palesimian Idiocy 39

Chapter 5: Media Idiocy 55

Chapter 6: Financial Idiocy 81

Chapter 7: Sexual Idiocy 109

Chapter 8: Sports Idiocy...129

Chapter 9: Hysterical Idiocy.....................................142

Chapter 10: Historical Global Idiocy.............................149

Chapter 11: Musical Idiocy 162

Chapter 12: Educational Idiocy...................................171

Chapter 13: Community Organizer Idiocy...........................181

Chapter 14: Religious Islamofascist Jihadist Idiocy..............212

Chapter 15: Religious Leftist Jihadist Idiocy....................225

Chapter 16: Rancher Idiocy 245

Chapter 17: 2012 and Future Idiocy 249

Chapter 18: American Idiocy 265

Chapter 0:
A Moronic From the Get-go Foreword

When I wrote my first book, I expressed that those wishing to learn all about me could buy my second book. Consider this my third book. If you are already monitoring me, you have seen me sit for hours on end watching ESPN and Fox News while railing about bad referees and all liberals. If watching me in this way excites you, then the lobotomy failed. Organ donors knocking at your door have been trying to tell you that you have been deceased for several years and nobody told you.

My family is so secretive and anonymous that even they are not sure who they are. They have so many questions about me that they cannot begin to ask about you. I would ask about you but I have a ton of questions about me as well.

I am also busy. Too much free time once had me waking up screaming that I was the child of the Pelosiraptor and Bidenator. The nightmare ended. Unlike them, I work.

Conservatives are busy trying to save the world. The world is going to heck in a hand-basket, and liberals are trying to figure out whether to hold angry peace rallies or celebrate the environment by leaving their signs on the grass for productive people to clean up. I only wish liberals knew how many trees and bunny rabbits were murdered on 9/11 by people unconcerned with carbon emissions.

Without love and laughter, there is no life. Nothing I do will change the world, but I am pleased if I can get a stiff person to lighten up and smile.

Whether your favorite charity is Guns for Conservative Tots or Tater Tots for Liberal Have-Nots (stuffing their faces with food is one way to briefly shut them up), the political spectrum of life has space for you. Relax, have a slab of deceased bull and some high-fructose corn syrup mixed in water, and enjoy what I have to say. You already bought the book, so you might as well read it.

This book is a compilation of columns ranging from the barely coherent to the depths of the intellectual chasm. This was done so that if you are too high-brow for what I am saying, in two or three pages I will be on to something even more beneath your dignity. For those that abhor salaciousness and scandal, skip chapter seven. For those that want to avoid anything that may expand the mind, skip the first six chapters.

So get on board and ride the Tygrrr's back to the finish line of this book. You'll be glad you did. Welcome to the 2007 Bloggers Choice Awards Winner for Most Passionate Fan Base. Welcome to the Tygrrrr Express.

eric

P.S. I sign my name with a lowercase "e." If this bothers you, take a pen and correct your own copy.

Chapter 1: Ideological Idiocy

Liberals like to declare every conservative on the planet to be either evil or stupid. This book is about their declaration of our being unenlightened dolts. This is ideological idiocy. Having liberals declare me stupid is like listening to members of the KKK call me insensitive. Conservatives must remember that our critics do not matter. Nobody listens to these crying children. For those that do not have a blunt instrument nearby, or are looking for a solution that avoids jail, humor is a powerful weapon. Use it against the left every moment they breathe. They may get offended, but that is the point.

Black Blood Cells, White Out, Ritz Crackers, and Vanilla Extract

Answer: Obama on Letterman, and the Emmy Awards.

(Either Johnny Carson or Alex Trebek gives us the question.)

Question: Things that are irrelevant. Now on to the news.

I have built a circumstantial case proving that President Barack Obama hates white people.

The initial evidence involves the water issue that has been decimating Central California. Actor Paul Rodriguez and Sean Hannity have been highlighting the fact that farmers in the San Joaquin Valley are starving. The drought has hurt the California agriculture industry, but the environmentalists have hurt more. A two-inch minnow fish has been declared more important than the farmers. The federal government has ordered the water turned off.

Obviously President Obama is doing this because the farmers are white. True, some of them are Latino, but given that Latinos supported his primary opponents, they are closer to white than black.

Then President Obama decided to surrender on missile defense. The man that wanted to get along better with our allies decided to throw Poland under the bus. Poland has always been a loyal ally of America. Liberals sadly respect the Polish people less than the French because Poland likes America. Poles also like Ronald Reagan, not leftist oppression. So why did Obama abandon Poland? He chucked them because most Polish people are white. If there are black people in Poland, I have never met them.

(I have never been to Poland. Let it go. Fact-check the "Jayson Blair" *Times* [*JBT*] instead.)

The third piece of evidence is the unending corruption of ACORN. Most ACORN critics are conservatives. Most conservatives are white. Therefore, Obama defends ACORN because he hates white people.

In further news, White-Out is a racist product. If somebody had invented "black-out," "Jew-out," or "Gay-out," there would be riots in the streets.

Ritz Crackers are another racist product. Imagine if a snack was known as "Ritz Darkies," or some other epithet.

The term "pure vanilla" is racist. All vanilla extract should immediately be replaced with chocolate extract to make up for America's past. They are both brown, but that is beside the point.

Lastly, all scientists and God are racist because black people have white blood cells but white people are not allowed to have black blood cells.

Everything is racist. Until milk is colored black, Selma, Alabama should be in every third sentence of every school textbook.

Okay, my point has been made as plain as black and white.

Barack Obama's indifference to the suffering of California farmers does not make him a racist. He truly is colorblind in his lack of regard for most people. He is every bit as insincere with many black people as he is with white people.

As for missile defense, Barack Obama is not a racist. He is just an appeaser and an apologist. He is willing to surrender to any nation run by any person of any color, provided that hurts America. He has tapped into the ideologically bigoted culture of today's American left. Since George W. Bush favored missile defense, Barack Obama has to be against it. If George W. Bush were to cure cancer, Obama would announce that the American Medical Association is outraged at doctors being forced out of work. If Bush says black, Obama says white…so to speak.

This leads to ACORN. President Obama is not going after ACORN's critics because they are white.

Conversely, critics are not going after ACORN because they help black people.

Critics of Obama are not going after him because he is black.

This is where the left gets confused. Aren't the people on the right racists, sexists, bigots, and homophobes, while those on the left are noble purists with beautiful intentions?

If somebody is a member of a minority group that has suffered greatly, shouldn't all members of that aggrieved group automatically be given lifetime immunity from any and all criticism for anything and everything?

If one is a liberal, then yes, absolutely.

Racism is poisonous, but conservatives understand that tossing out the race card at the slightest hint of unrelated and self-inflicted problems only makes things more difficult for victims of real racism.

Corruption and greed are colorblind. All humans are capable of sin.

Charles Rangel is a corrupt tax cheat. So is Timothy Geithner. Yet Charles Rangel continues to skate by.

David Patterson is the incompetent governor of New York. His race is irrelevant. His lack of effectiveness is the issue. It is called David Dinkins Syndrome. He wasn't tough enough for the job.

William Jefferson had $90 thousand cash in the freezer. His race was not the issue. His corruption was.

What do all of these criminals (Patterson was not accused of crimes) have in common? They blamed institutional racism for their own bad deeds.

Barack Obama ran as a post-partisan president. Instead he and his colleagues on the left play the race card when conservatives dare to disagree with him.

Nancy Pelosi and other guilty white liberals are willing to label conservatives as racists to win at politics. They are willing to pass a national health care plan by tearing this nation in half. They imply that people who sharply disagree with Obama are going to murder him in cold blood, despite that fact that it was liberals that burned President George W. Bush in effigy.

They don't care about anything but winning at all costs.

I will not be labeled a racist just because I want low taxes and dead terrorists.

I will not be afraid to criticize Barney Frank, Jim McGreevey, or any other gay politician that uses their sexuality to intimidate others.

I will go after any corrupt politician, even if they are black like Mel Reynolds.

I will also criticize white liberal corrupt politicians, be they Eliot Spitzer or Jon Corzine.

I will go after conservative politicians that are corrupt, be they Randy Duke Cunningham or Mark Foley.

I want to root out corruption from crooked black and white politicians.

This is known as chocolate and vanilla extract.

Racism must be stopped. So must racial grievance-mongers crying wolf, even if they are leading this country.

eric

Conservative vs. Republican

Election Day Tuesday, 2009, had the very closely watched race in the twenty-third New York congressional district.

For those not following, the district was described as "conservative" despite being carried by President Obama in 2008. The seat became vacant when the Republican occupant took a cabinet job. The Republican nominee was a woman whose name reminded me of Fozzie Bear from *The Muppet Show*.

(After less than extensive research, it seems her name is Dede Scozzafava or something like that.)

The problem is conservatives did not get a warm feeling from Scozzie. Scozzie Wozzy simply wasn't Fozzy, or fuzzy, or something like that.

As much fuzzy fun as it is to do that, the serious issue is that she was seen as a very liberal Republican. Given the Trotskeyite leanings of New York, this seemed normal.

Yet conservatives were so up in arms that they decided to throw their support behind Doug Hoffman, who until then was known for...well, nothing really.

Third parties usually quickly fade. Everything changed when Sarah Palin endorsed Hoffman. Fred Thompson and Sean Hannity lined up behind him as well.

Days before the election, Scozzafava dropped out. The conservative candidate knocked out the Republican candidate, as they both faced off against the Democrat, who is known for...well, nothing.

As a conservative Republican, I ask...

Is this a good thing?

The answer?

I really honestly don't know.

I have thought about this on a general level and specifically related to this particular race.

On a general level, it bothers me when somebody says, "I'm not a Republican. I'm a conservative." For one thing, many of them say this with a smugness that is normally reserved for liberals. Then again, you will not hear liberals claim they are a liberal or a leftist. They hide behind phony words like "progressive." At least the conservatives are bragging about who they are, rather than denying who they are.

Yet it still bothers me because in general I can't stand third party candidates.

I love these right-of-center people that brag about voting Constitution Party, Libertarian, or American Independent. These same people also voted for Ralph Nader in some cases. They like the attention of being "rebels." Ask a Ron Paul supporter why they are a Republican, and they have no idea.

We are a two-party system. It works. We don't have coalition governments. We are not like Israel or Italy changing governments every few minutes.

I am a conservative. I also believe in the Republican Party. It is the party committed to low taxes and dead terrorists. It is the party of individual freedom and liberty. The party has had people who have strayed from the ideals, but the ideals are still noble.

Most importantly, I am not interested in ideological purity. I am interested in winning. Conservatives that spend every waking night praying for the next Ronald Reagan fail to grasp that Reagan did not become Reagan until he was elected.

Winners get to govern. Losers get to obstruct. Republicans and conservatives are currently trying to slow liberalism. That is not the same as advancing conservatism.

When I speak around the country, I bring up what Rahm Emanuel did in 2006. He went around the country recruiting right-wing Democrats. He did not care if they were George McGovern or George Wallace Democrats. A "D" was good enough.

I don't care if somebody is to the right of the late Jesse Helms, or barely right-of-center like Susan Collins. If you have an "R" next to your name, I support you. We are a family.

California will not elect an Idaho Republican. Massachusetts and New York have had GOP governors, but they were not Alabama or Mississippi Republicans.

This is not to say that we throw out conservative principles. We just make sure to spend more time focusing on what unites us, such as low taxes and dead terrorists, and stop fighting over red meat social issues that split us apart. This angers many social conservatives, but anybody that thinks that a moderate Republican is the same as a liberal Democrat needs to have their head examined.

So what does this mean for the New York special election? Is this rise of Hoffman good or bad?

My initial response was, "Ask me on Wednesday. If he wins, it is fine. If he loses, it is a disaster."

That is it. There are no moral victories.

In this specific situation, I was originally fine with the developments for two reasons.

First of all, after Scozzi Fozzie (I can't help it, it's fun.) dropped out, she endorsed the Democrat. This was an act of spitefulness not seen since Betsy McCaughey Ross was fired as the Republican lieutenant governor and then became a Democrat.

I will stand up for moderate and liberal Republicans, but once they leave the party, like Arlen Specter, I am done with them. That is betrayal.

The second reason I was okay with Hoffman is because he did something that Ron Paul never did. Hoffman showed allegiance to the GOP even while running on the Conservative Party ticket. He stated that if elected, he would run for reelection as a Republican. He was willing to join the party. That is good enough for me.

There is a difference between being somebody who works from within and someone who is just an attention-seeking gadfly.

Ross Perot broke up the Reagan coalition and elected Bill Clinton. Before Perot, Pat Buchanan tore apart the GOP. Clinton signed many bills that bothered me. I vocalized my opinions. I also told those that voted Libertarian to shut up and stop complaining because they elected him by not supporting President George H.W. Bush.

The issue is viability. Doug Hoffman has proven his viability. Winning would truly help his credibility.

The same cannot be said of the governor's race in New Jersey. John Corzine is a socialist and a disaster, although those are redundant. In a two-party race he would get his clock cleaned. Yet a third party candidate with no chance of winning was hurting Chris Christie.

I disagree with Christie on gun control. Again, this is New Jersey. He is the type of Republican that can win. If Corzine won, it would have been because conservatives cut off their elephant noses to spite their puritanical faces. This is nuts.

Leftists blame Ralph Nader for George W. Bush defeating Al Gore. Conservatives would have been justified in slapping independent voters silly if they had inadvertently reelected Jon Corzine.

Some people say that it takes a Carter to bring about a Reagan, and that Obama has united conservatives. This is insane. I don't need to elect a liberal to know they will be dreadful. Football teams claim that they learn from losing. This argument is garbage. The goal is to try and win everything.

I do not know enough about any of the candidates in the twenty-third New York special election to offer much more. What I do know is that a Hoffman win may have caused conservatives to cannibalize Republicans around the country. If that happens, we will become an ideologically pure minority.

Ronald Reagan was a conservative, but he treated every Republican as a member of the family.

I rooted for Doug Hoffman to win that Tuesday, but I want "conservatives" to help fix the Republican Party, not destroy it.

(Hoffman lost. Some conservatives truly believe they sent a message. No, they sent a Democrat to congress.)

I am a principled conservative Republican. I am ideologically conservative, and the only viable place to pass a conservative agenda is to go through the Republican Party.

Right-of-center individuals can either fall off a cliff or fall into line.

eric

Chapter 2: Jewish Ideological Idiocy

Bill Cosby is going after cancerous elements in black America not out of hatred, but out of love. I love being Jewish. As the son of a Holocaust survivor, I am determined to weed out those that compare Republicans to Nazis. Jews have been victims of the worst bigotry known to humanity. Sadly enough, the liberal Jewish community engages in verbally dehumanizing behavior toward me and my ilk. Some call this madness. I call it Jewish liberalism.

Liberal Jews and Battered Housewives

Politically liberal Jews are like battered housewives, only with less hope.

Before the hags at the National Organization for Women send me another feminist Fatwa, I am not celebrating battered housewife syndrome. Even if a woman bothers me when I am trying to watch football, a simple, "Honey, I can take care of the trash later" is sufficient. Abusers are scum. While the woman's timing is terrible, the man could take the trash out before the game.

Nobody should be abused. However, there is a subtle difference between liberal Jews and battered housewives. Battered housewives really are innocent victims. Liberal Jews really do sow the seeds of their own pathetic weakness.

(Do not confuse battered housewives with *"Desperate Housewives."* In that show the husbands get battered in various ways.)

Only liberal Jews could create entire umbrella organizations designed to destroy their own communities and fight against their own interests.

An Arab Islamist-loving, Palesimian-appeasing, liberal Jewish handwringing and groveling organization has visited the White House. J Street claims to speak for all Jews. They speak for sane Jews as much as Armageddonijad in Iran does.

They arranged a self-hating Jew conference in Washington, D.C., to the delight of President Obama.

The key is not just to acknowledge the whining, begging, and sniveling of these and other Jew-lite (Jew? Where? Not me! Don't dare call me that!) organizations. What matters is how deeply pathological the self-loathing has become.

For non-Hebrews, some basic facts must be disseminated.

There is nothing in the Torah that commands anybody to be politically liberal (or conservative). Liberals who babble about things such as "social justice" and "being good stewards of the Earth" are simply manipulating the Torah to fit their own ideology.

(Conservatives Christians are accused of this. I am not Christian, and do not attend church. If this turns out to be true, liberal Jews should remember that two wrongs do not equal righteousness.)

The greatest Mitzvah (good deed) in all of Judaism is Tzedakah (charity). There are eight levels of Tzedakah. Anonymous giving is higher than gifts made aware. Giving cheerfully trumps giving angrily. The highest level of Tzedakah is helping somebody become self-sufficient by helping them start their own business. That is conservatism, not liberalism.

The Torah has nothing to do with liberal Jews acting the way they do. Many liberal Jews are simply liberals first and Jews second. More importantly, they are often secular liberal Jews. They are liberal and secular first and second (in either order) and Jewish third.

Some liberal Jews do care about Israel (many do not). The issue is that liberal, secular Jews care more about abortion, gay rights and environmental issues than they do about issues such as safety and security. They are no different than other secular leftists.

Why does this matter? Why can't they just be free to live their lives and believe what they believe?

Their lives encroach on my right to live. Their beliefs are dangerous. Their actions are preposterous and their collective analysis is naive and foolhardy.

This brings us to the 2009 meeting between President Obama and Jewish "leaders."

Barack Obama managed to fool most American Jews, but he has not fooled the Israelis. He polled only 6 percent approval in Israel. 6 percent! This means that Israelis believe that on Jewish issues (Israel is a main Jewish issue), the President of the United States is full of garbaggio. He is seen as hostile, bullying, meddlesome, and antithetical to all that Israel believes in. This is because Israelis look at results. Jewish and non-Jewish liberals look at intentions.

Imagine waking up one day and being forced to confront that everything you believe in is wrong. The painful but honorable choice at this point is to admit this and move forward. The other option is to live in a constant state of denial.

Liberal Jews worship Obama because he is liberal. Therefore, he has to be good on Jewish issues. He is their Messiah. They have pinned their hopes on him. The problem with this is that Barack Obama is less of a man than a brand and icon. He consists of whatever his supporters project onto him. They confuse their support of him with his support of them.

No matter how many times President Obama batters liberal Jews with the blunt instruments of his deeds, the snivelers and grovelers will blame themselves, explain why he really is supporting them, and blame evil Republicans for trying to use Israel as a wedge issue.

The evidence is in the gushing praise J Street and other apologists had for President Obama after meeting with him. Ordinary occurrences were treated as proof of kinship.

He "met" with them. He "listened" to them. He "empathized" with them. He "reaffirmed his commitment." He "understood" them.[1]

This is apologetic drivel. Only liberal appeasers could treat a meeting in itself as a victory.

Let me explain to liberals again for the Milli-Vanillionth time what conservatives have always grasped. Having a meeting is a means to an end, not the end itself. No matter how vigorous the handshakes, tasty the sandwiches, or comfortable the chairs, a meeting is a beginning, not an ending. Meetings prove nothing. What matters are actual tangible achievements coming out of meetings.

This is not only about Judaism. Liberals celebrate meetings with evil people that produce nothing. The United Nations is a giant slumber party of dictatorial madmen. They talk to each other, which is supposedly useful. Genocide takes place worldwide while pleasant meetings occur.

In addition to meetings, President Obama is a master at conveying agreement. The guy can nod his head as well as any middle manager. He is polite. He listens. Has anybody on the left noticed that when it comes time for concrete action, he completely discounts the views of those he politely listens to?

Barack Obama has turned Judaism on its head. Judaism is about questioning anything and everything. The expression about ten Jews in a room giving twelve opinions has validity. Yet with candidate and then President Obama, blind unquestioning faith is the norm. If he says something, it has to be true because he said it.

This reminds me of the old Eddie Murphy joke about a wife who catches her husband in bed with another woman. The husband responds, "Who are you going to believe, me or your lying eyes?"[2]

Barack Obama allowed Jews to enter the White House. That is what he is supposed to do. He represents the people. Jews are people. President Obama did not make any promises, guarantees, or assurances. He did not reassure the Jewish lefties. They reassured themselves. By being allowed to be in his presence, they felt the same gratitude that comes with being "allowed" to join an all-white country club rather than express anger that restrictions ever existed to begin with.

It is this desperation to believe that has the Jewish left twisting themselves into pretzels. It is how they can attack Republicans, even though most anti-Semitism in America now comes from the left. It is how negotiating with Armageddonijad when the Iranian people want to be free does not conflict with liberal support for human rights.

In mathematical terms, Obama is a tautology. He is truth, and truth is him. Any criticism of him is motivated by evil and lies, even when such criticism is not only part of rational Jewish debate, but based on a sincere desire to improve Jewish quality of life.

Liberal Jews stick up for everybody else. They defend blacks, gays, Latinos, and even Palesimians. They protest the death penalty for murderers, yet have hostility toward conservative Republicans.

If liberal Jews would at least be willing to look at Obama with the same critical lens that any intellectual or thinker would, they would see that his attitude toward Israel ranges between indifference and hostility. Israelis see this.

American liberal Jews are blind. The only question in months to come will be whether that blindness is innocent misguided naiveté, or a willful refusal to see.

I suspect the latter. Like battered housewives, the beatings will continue until liberal Jews start fighting back against their attackers and stop fighting their supporters.

Even worse, the supporters might get fed up and either join the attackers or just walk away.

I will not make any predictions based on predetermined opinions and emotion. Unlike liberal Jews, I will act like a conservative Republican Jew. I will look at the results, and let logical reasoning lead the way.

eric

Jewish Politicians to Attend Jewish Self-loathing Conference

We as Jews have survived the Holocaust, countless pogroms, and third-world genocidal lunatics that want to kill us all because we exist and breathe air.

While we have great survival skills when facing external threats, we are also the masters of self-immolation. With a 52 percent intermarriage rate, we are well on the path to cultural extinction.

With too many Jewish people becoming schoolteachers and social workers rather than stockbrokers and corporate executives, we are also on the way to economic extinction.

Now we have decided to complete the trifecta of stupidity with potential political extinction.

One mythical block from K Street, a politically toxic organization has formed in Washington, DC.

The Group is J Street. They are as helpful for Jewish interests in America and worldwide as Benedict Arnold was for America itself.

When I think of J Street, I am reminded of the (Dave) *Chapelle's Show* comedy sketch where he plays a blind black man who thinks he is white, is married to a white woman, and is a member of the KKK. After years of racism toward blacks, the character is forced to confront the fact that he himself is black. His response is to divorce his wife for her being married to a black man.

In the Jewish community, there was Groucho Marx, who once famously stated that he "would never belong to a club that would have me as a member."[3]

Yet Groucho was not self-hating. He was mocking the anti-Semitism of his day, and was rejecting the idea of joining an anti-Semitic club. He was standing up for his people.

J Street does not stand up for or stand for anything remotely positive for Jews. To make matters worse, these people used their constitutional right to assemble to hold a conference. Worst of all is that Jewish politicians gave this organization legitimacy.

Dianne Feinstein, Al Franken, Russ Feingold, Henry Waxman, Bernie Sanders, and Adam Schiff are among many that are determined to contribute to the stereotype that liberal Jews are liberals first and Jews second.

Liberal Jews that find my sentiments harsh should spend less time worrying about a Republican Jew typing on a keyboard and more time worrying over an anti-Israel organization getting its hooks into an eager White House.

For those not convinced, the J Street agenda is as subtle as a homicide bomber, and on an emotional level, just as destructive.

The J Street Web site is all the evidence one needs.

"Israel's settlements in the occupied territories have, for over forty years, been an obstacle to peace."

"J Street supports President Obama's call for an immediate and total freeze of settlement construction."

"It is important to note that J Street supports the concept of a security barrier as an important element of Israel's defense, but believes that the barrier must be located along an internationally recognized border."

"J Street believes that the immediate imposition of harsher sanctions on Iran would be counterproductive."

"We are strongly opposed to any consideration at this time of the use of military force by Israel or the United States to attack Iran's nuclear infrastructure."[4]

Nowhere on this dreadful Web site is there any mention of anything that Iran, Hamas, Hezbollah, or any other enemies of Israel have to do. J Street preaches a balanced approach to the Middle East but places all the responsibility on Israel.

In addition to praising multi-lateralism and diplomacy, a new nonsensical phrase has entered the liberal lexicon thanks to J Street. "Strategic Patience" is a fancy way of doing nothing and praying that baddy meanies decide to become goodie niceys.

Has anybody at J Street listened to Armageddonijad? The guy wants to wipe Israel off the map, not sit at the campfire with Jews, make Smores, and sing about what they would do if they had a hammer.

Like most liberal Jews, J Street loves to attack "Neocons" and other conservatives as bellicose.

Well J Street and liberal Jews everywhere need to answer some tough questions right now, or forever be denied the right to be taken seriously.

What specific steps must the enemies of Israel take in the name of peace?

Why should we make agreements with rogue leaders when they break every agreement they sign?

If we make an agreement with them, how can we enforce it?

What happens if they break the agreement?

Given that Israel has made concessions in the past, why not make any further Israeli actions contingent on the cessation of terror, as specified in the Road Map?

Israeli withdrawal from Lebanon and Gaza led to more terror. Why would any further withdrawals yield a different result?

If liberals become conservatives after getting mugged, why have they not reacted upon their Jewish brethren getting bombed, shot at, and murdered indiscriminately? How many Jews have to be killed by Islamofascist enemies of freedom and liberty before enough is enough?

On October 25th through the 28th, a conference dedicated to the destruction of Israel took place.

It called itself a "Pro-Israel, Pro-Peace" event, but as we learned in "Hamlet," for some people, "there is no right and wrong. Only thinking makes it so."[5]

Jews have given enough, voluntarily through hope and involuntarily through innocent bloodshed.

I just thank Hashem that my Holocaust surviving grandfather did not live to see Jewish politicians like Al Franken and Henry Waxman attend a Jewish surrender conference.

eric

Another Pathetic Liberal Jew

Slate Magazine, that leftist bastion of intellectual emptiness, has found a pathetic liberal Jewish apologist that believes peace in the Middle East will come when Israel is pressured.

Playing the role of "Kumbaya" surrender monkey is Jacob Weisberg.

I never care to meet this man.

The title of the column is as odious as it is misguided: "How to Lean on Israel."

This self-loathing lemming truly believes that the best presidents on Israel policy have been the ones that bullied Israel into submission.

Jimmy Carter gets credit for the Israel-Egypt peace agreement of 1979. The situation between these nations is not a true peace. It is a cold peace. Egyptian promises of bilateral trade have never been fully realized. Egypt cracks down on Palesimian arms smugglers only when international pressure gets too great.

George Herbert Walker Bush is lionized for the peace agreement between Israel and Jordan. This peace is not what the United States shares with Canada.

There is no peace in the Middle East. There are breaks between wars. The reason why there is no peace is because Israel is not allowed to do anything and everything necessary to defend itself. Now that George W. Bush has left the world stage, Israel is in trouble.

The notion that Israel's closest supporters have made matters worse is idiotic. Does anybody think that Jimmy Carter created peace? Israel winning military victories is what brought temporary respite. A permanent respite will occur when complete, total, and uncompromising brute force is met on Israel's enemies until they crack.

Jacob Weisberg should be talking about forcing Palesimians to keep their own promises. Asking Palesimians to maintain integrity is like asking Lesbians to marry men. The concept of Palesimian integrity is an oxymoron. Palesimians have been 100 percent consistent in breaking their word.

Ronald Reagan and George W. Bush are criticized as having "encouraged Israel's worst tendencies."[6]

Worst tendencies? The right to stay alive is a bad tendency?

This issue is so simplistic. Ask the Palesimians to recognize Israel's right to exist. Wait a few seconds until they refuse this request as unreasonable. Then let Israel go in and break these savages.

Peace is impossible when one side defiantly refuses the right of the other side to live.

Israel supporters do not "build up Arab resentment." Arab thugocrats build up Arab resentment. Israel is an excuse for them to deflect from their own failed policies. Yassir Arafat was offered a state. He chose terror instead. The Palesimians had a chance at democracy. They elected Hamas. They chose terror.

Benjamin Netanyahu is described as having a "dangerous fixation" on striking Iran.

What this liberal apologist calls a dangerous fixation is what normal human beings call a reasonable fear based on the behavior of the Iranian murderer Armageddonijad himself.

It is bad enough that Israel is surrounded by barbaric animals bent on wanton destruction.

We don't need to compound the problem by offering weak and pathetic surrender advice under the guise of tough love. Liberal Jews don't know a d@mn thing about toughness. Israel exists because soldiers defend the state. Soldiers mainly vote conservative.

My father did not escape the Nazis so that Jacob Weisberg could help our enemies repeat the process.

Thank God Benjamin Netanyahu is prime minister and not Jacob Weisberg. I have hope that Israel will continue to exist, despite the fact that too many liberal Jews are the best friends that Arab enemies could ever ask for.

eric

Another Liberal Jew in Need of Cranial-Glutial Extraction Surgery

Another liberal Jew has confirmed that cranial-glutial extraction surgery is necessary to pry the head of Judaism from the rumpus of liberalism.

This man is Rabbi Daniel Gordis.

For the sake of full and honest disclosure, I have always found him useless. In 1990 I was a college freshman. I was physically attacked by another student in a classroom. I defended myself in front of a room full of witnesses. Rather than investigate what actually happened, he declared the incident a "fight," and both parties were admonished. This frustrated the victim, myself, and emboldened the aggressor.

(If I met this guy from class on the street today, we might get in a fight. We are both pretty strong-willed. He would never admit it, but I broke him in half psychologically by letting him know I would go to any lengths to win. Everybody he knew was potential collateral damage. He saw I would never back down as long as I lived. He decided it was not worth it. He looked in my eyes, and decided I was serious. To this day, the Guns n Roses song "Welcome to the Jungle" applies. "If you've a hunger for what you see…take it eventually. You can have anything you want, but you better not take it from me.")[7]

In 2009, my mother sent me an article by this rabbi. It was awful. I emailed him my response.

My issue is not that this guy is a pompous liberal gasbag, or that he handled me badly nineteen years ago. I got over it. What bothers me is that the same attitude of moral equivalence that drove him to criticize a guy for defending himself is still inside of him. Palesimians are murdering Israelis. Arabs are murdering Jews. Liberal Jews, even the ones admitting that "Kumbaya" does not always work, cannot bring themselves to accept the fact that with regards to resolving conflicts, force works.

(Grabbing a bullhorn)

FORCE WORKS! FORCE WORKS! FORCE WORKS! FORCE WORKS! FORCE WORKS!

This should be piped into the eardrums of every namby-pamby until they become either less namby or less pamby. One out of two is an improvement.

In his article he expressed the positive aspects of an Israeli prisoner swap, where two dead bodies were exchanged for live Arab terrorists. He cannot understand why the Mideast surrender process might be an inferior alternative to actually winning the war.

The worst of his Kumbaya-loving column waxes poetic.

"Yes, in strategic terms, it was probably a mistake. But sometimes mistakes are worth making."[8]

His logic is that we learn from mistakes. If we can avoid making mistakes, that is learning as well. I don't want my learning experiences to come from dead Jews.

He claims that this learning will help shake people from the notion that peace is possible in the current climate. I understood this when I was an eighteen-year old student and he was my thirty-something professor with his head up his hide.

This is not about a fight in a classroom. It is about how a liberal views justice in an adult world. It is about applying moral equivalence to unequal moral parties. He was a young professor then. Now he is a middle-aged man, and he still doesn't get it.

How many liberals have to see their own families murdered before they become conservatives? I wish no pain on his family, but I care more about my family. My approach protects his family. His approach gets mine killed.

"Now we know that the right was correct – further retreats will only embolden our enemies. They'll demand more. And more. Until we're gone."

I knew this in 1990! Yet despite his admitting that his liberal beliefs have been a colossal failure, he remains a liberal. I can understand being a liberal when you don't know any better. He has seen the evidence, and still cannot bring himself to endorse force as an option.

"The challenge facing Israel isn't to win the war against the Palestinians."

Yes it is!

"The war can't be won."

It's like Harry Reid is Jewish. Of course it can't be won if we listen to people say it can't be won, and elect people who refuse to win.

"We can't eradicate them…"

Says who? I wish they felt the same way about us. If we got them to that point, they would stop.

"The challenge that Israel faces is not to move toward peace. Peace can't be had."

It can't be had because liberal Jews don't get it. Things were pretty peaceful when Ariel Sharon was the bulldozer in 1982. Had the prime minister at the time let him go to Damascus, we would not be in this mess today.

"We did the right thing. We gave Karnit Goldwasser her life back. We gave Udi and Eldad the burial they deserved."

(I met the brother of one of the kidnapped soldiers. I wore around my neck the dog tags of the three kidnapped men for two years, vowing to take them off when they returned safely. I took them off after the prisoner swap, but out of disgust.)

Had Ehud Olmert been a private citizen, Ariel Sharon would have burned every Palesimian village.

(For those who mention Sharon in the same sentence as the Gaza pullout, make no mistake about it. He was a lifelong warrior. This allowed him to be trusted to make peace.)

We did not do the right thing. While Rabbi Gordis is weeping, Hamas and Hezbollah are planning their next round of kidnappings.

"And we showed the next generation of kids who will go off to defend this place that this is not a country about calculus, but about soul. We showed them what it is to love. We showed them that we'll get them back. No matter what."

We showed them peace at any price, and how to surrender.

"I was proud, not ashamed. I wasn't ashamed to be Israeli. I wasn't ashamed to be a Jew. We proved to our kids once again that we're the kind of country that's worth defending."

24

Defending? What the hell does this liberal academic know about defending? Perhaps he defended a thesis once. I suspect the antithesis was correct.

We did not defend anything in 2006. Israel lost its power of deterrence. This is what happens when a liberal is sent to do a man's job. Shimon Peres is about one hundred-forty years old, and he finally figured out at age one hundred-twenty that the Arabs simply don't like us. I will never forget after his fifth loss for the prime minister position (fifth! Imagine Dukakis or Kerry getting five chances.), he asked, "Am I a loser?" Somebody in the crowd replied, "Yes!"[9]

"We lost. We knew that already. What we did this week is that we did right by the families who paid the price."

No. A few individuals were "helped" at the expense of the entire nation. These poor departed Israeli soldiers died in vain. They died for nothing. They died for a nation run by leftists that would not fight for them. Olmert did everything but blow up an abandoned building in the Sudan like Bill Clinton did.

"There will be other ways to get our deterrent edge back."

You keep smoking that peace pipe, rabbi. Perhaps it's a crack pipe, since that would be the only explanation for a man not to grasp that deterrence is about force.

"But in the meantime, we showed ourselves once again that this country is about soul. They won, and we lost. They celebrated, and we buried. They cheered, and we wept. And I'd rather be one of us, any day."

There is no "us." There is him and there is me. If an Arab were to come after me, Rabbi Gordis would sit there impotent, and let me die. That is what the left in Israel did for the kidnapped soldiers. If somebody came after him, his family would want him to actually do something.

Candlelight vigils do not bring people home. Raid on Antebbe worked. Benjamin Netanyahu, naturally a conservative, helped actually do something. The job got done, and done right.

Maybe the next time Rabbi Gordis has his prostate exam, the doctor can remove his cerebrum and reattach it above his neck. It is amazing he was able to bring children into the world at all given that I do not recall him ever having a pair.

It is too late for me to get a decent college education with regards to Jewish civilization.

It is not too late for Israel to take the Palesimians and break them.

Give the Palesimians seven days to return every terrorist on the watch list. On the eighth day, set Gaza ablaze. Let them burn. They have had every chance to show that they are civilized human beings and not animals. They have failed.

This is not aggression. It is self-defense.

When conservatives ran Israel, this was understood.

Fire involves smoke. Israelis like to smoke. Since liberal Jews have their heads up their hides, we should shove the peace pipes up there as well. That way they can smoke while fires rage around them.

Either Jews or Palesimians will burn. The Palesimians have not allowed for an in-between.

It is us or them.

Rabbi Gordis is a liberal. He prefers being morally superior.

I am a conservative. I am also the son of a Holocaust survivor. I prefer being alive.

There are no tears in my eyes or blood on my hands.

I may not be a hero, but he is worse than zero. He is Nero.

We know what happened to Rome. We know what happened in Germany. We know what is happening in Israel.

Never again.

eric

Chapter 3: Pacifist Idiocy

Between artists, hippies, hipsters, beat poets, and of course, activists, love will be in the air. Actually the smell of drugs will most likely be in the air, or as artists call it, "inspiration." I don't need a muse. I'm busy working. I don't have time to be hip or cool. I am productive. Some will say that there is nothing wrong about getting together and making a difference. There is plenty wrong if the difference is worse. Liberals clamored for change, not realizing that sometimes the status quo was less screwed up than their idealistic solutions.

Woodstock–Hippy Druggies Celebrate Forty Years of Being Hippy Druggies

The world would have been a better place had Woodstock been known only as the little bird that hangs out with Snoopy the Beagle.

The fortieth anniversary of a never-ending music concert got more coverage than the anniversary of the landing on the moon.

The disparity is staggering. One month after courageous men truly took a giant leap for mankind, a bunch of derelicts and degenerates took hits of acid so that they could leap out of their minds.

One small hit for man…one giant bong for mankind.

I was born in 1972, which means I grew up in the 1980s. I thank God for this. Lord knows how I would have ended up if I would have hung out at an event glorifying stoners.

It is long past time to dispel the myth that anything positive to human society came out of that event.

Some of the people involved did eventually shave, get cleaned up, and go on to lead productive lives. That was despite Woodstock, not because of it.

Woodstock was nothing more than hippy druggies celebrating their right to be hippy druggies.

Let us count the negative contributions of Woodstock to American society.

1) The glorification of drugs.

There is nothing positive about drug use. Drugs destroy lives. Anybody who thinks that doing drugs is "no big deal," should simply find another nation to drag down.

Drug use is not a harmless or victimless crime. My tax dollars go to pay for everything from prevention programs to rehab centers to more prisons. Those who want to legalize drugs forget or willfully ignore the fact that medical care is more expensive than necessary. One of these reasons is treating drug addicts.

I am not advocating refusing to treat these people. They are still human beings. However, they are also still screw-ups. They are redeemable, and I have yet to meet a person on drugs that was less enjoyable to know after giving up drugs.

I have a family member that is a basket case. I am convinced that drugs contributed to this.

2) The glorification of unprotected sex.

I am not puritanical when it comes to sex, but unprotected sex again kills people. Those that do not develop fatal diseases end up with less serious medical problems that again involve trips to clinics. This is not free. Taxpayers pay for the irresponsibility of others. The AIDS crisis that exploded in the 1980s, glorified by pious celebrities and their useless red ribbons, is a result of the sexual anarchy that these same moralizers created in the 1960s.

3) The glorification of uncleanliness.

I had limited access to facilities in 1985 when Hurricane Gloria belted Long Island. Facilities are good. They separate civilization from "Lord of the Flies." Nothing about going to a music concert requires slovenliness.

4) The glorification of the anti-war movement.

War sometimes is the answer. Those saying war is never the answer should either move to Europe, endorse slavery, or live under a world controlled by Adolf Hitler. This is before anyone ever heard of Saddam Hussein. The Vietnam War was absolutely winnable. We won on the battlefield and lost in the media. The only lesson of Vietnam should be that if a nation is going to go to war, they had better do whatever it takes to win. Scorched Earth is ugly, but it shortens wars and saves lives. Holding up peace signs doesn't accomplish anything except embolden enemies willing to fight to the death.

5) The glorification of cutting school.

I wish Joe "Lean on me" Clark had taken a baseball bat to these kids. Upside their heads might be excessive, but he could have cracked the bat against a pole to make his point. People skipping school to get high are not learning. I know that schools are a disaster, and home schooling is the only solution. Yet these kids were not learning anywhere during those days. They were wasting their parents' money.

Liberals love to romanticize Woodstock and show how these people matured and led positive change. They conveniently ignore that many people at

Woodstock ended up incoherent, rambling lunatics. They might have ended up that way anyway, but Woodstock could not have helped.

I have been to music concerts. It is possible to enjoy the music without LSD, hashish or any other mind-numbing stimulants, depressants or hallucinogens.

The genie that jumped out of the bottle in the 1960s will never be put back. Woodstock will no longer ever be the bird hanging out with Joe Cool on a dark and stormy night.

Woodstock should be remembered as a bunch of Joe Uncools trying to preach individuality and rebellion by looking, acting, and dressing the same. Woodstock was about mindless automatons preaching that they knew better than everybody else.

Now those people are bankrupting Medicare and Medicaid, many of them needing medical care in their early sixties for illnesses that do not affect clean living eighty-year-olds.

The Woodstock crowd didn't know anything.

Forty years later, many of them still don't.

eric

Unartistic Saturday

Every autumn, men should celebrate a new holiday known as Unartistic Saturday.

Men are encouraged to dress in ripped jeans and beat-up sneakers. They are to only eat foods that require the use of hands. Finger foods do not count. They should watch as much football as possible.

Because of a long since dead sexual relationship, I spent irretrievable hours of my life at the Palo Alto Arts Festival. I am not an arts festival type of guy. I do not have an artistic bone in my body, nor do I want one.

I am a hard-charging, corporate, Type A Wall Street guy. Yet I saw something at the arts festival that forced me to take notes. One painting exhibit had words from the author.

"Imagination is stronger than knowledge."

"Myths are more important than history."

"Dreams are more powerful than facts."

"Hope always triumphs over experience."

"Laughter is the only cure for grief."

"Love is stronger than death." [10]

These were described as the "Storyteller's Creed."

It was at this moment that an initially held belief of mine was reinforced.

I am now certain that I really detest artists.

The entire culture makes me ill.

"Imagination is stronger than knowledge."

This is true if one is five years old. I don't care what adults think. I care what they know and do. Corporate America has been destroyed by everything from diversity to multiculturalism to sensitivity training to "new" twenty-first century management.

Corporate America should be about delivering the d@mn profits. We are slowly producing a nation of creative imbeciles. We have children that ace arts and crafts and music but can't do multiplication tables.

"Myths are more important than history."

No, no, no, no, no.

Camelot is a myth. The entire Kennedy family is one big phony myth. Barack Obama is a myth. Myths are stories. I care about actual results.

The favorite myth in leftist circles is that Americans are a bunch of sexist, racist, homophobic pigs that oppress the rest of the world in pursuit of greed. The truth in conservative circles is that America is a nation of good people that feed, clothe, protect, and defend the world.

Only a leftist could prefer words to deeds and intentions to results.

"Hope always triumphs over experience."

This particular community organizer artist most likely misread the label on the shelf when sprinkling on colon scent instead of cologne scent. With artists, the scents are indistinguishable.

In the 1960s the left said, "If it feels good, do it." This brought us a generation of rambling drug addicts and incurable sexually transmitted diseases.

As conservatives are trying to save the world from terrorists who hijack planes and turn them into guns, the left responds with silly blather about "hope," "change," and "Yes, we can." These vacuous slogans accomplish nothing, mean nothing, and inspire people that find insipid rhetoric inspiring.

When Ronald Reagan ordered Mikhail Gorbachev to "Tear down this wall,"[11] it meant something only because the wall actually did fall. Abraham Lincoln's Emancipation Proclamation was followed by actions. Slaves don't get freed by burning incense and chanting "Yes, we can."

The entire artist image makes me sick, especially the glorification of the "starving artist."

Memo to starving artists: There is nothing noble about being poor. There is nothing romantic about being broke. Owning a private jet is more rewarding than making art out of literal garbage that the poorest of the artists call dinner.

I will leave artists alone when they shut up and stop criticizing corporate America.

Beauty can be found in individual works of art. I am sure there are museums and art galleries that offer value. As a kid I liked the dinosaur exhibit at the Museum of Natural History.

What I can't stand is the preachiness and pretentiousness of the art world.

Business is a necessity. Art is a luxury.

Forget the storyteller's creed. I have my own creed.

Go to school. Learn reading, writing and math. Learn about business. Get a job. Pay taxes. Balance a checkbook. Seek prosperity.

Ben Affleck in *Boiler Room* put it brilliantly when he said, "People who say that money is the root of all evil don't have any."[12]

There are some artists that do not inflict their entire world view and philosophy on society, but the majority of art festivals I have attended have been left-wing drivel.

In the same way that the movie *History of the World, Part I* had a depiction of the French Revolution where there were "beggars, begging from beggars,"[13] too many art festivals have artists railing against the wealthy while pleading with those same rich people to sponsor them and buy their works of art. If it was not for guilty white liberals, I truly believe artists would be forced to apply for government aid.

Another *Boiler Room* line applies here. "You think money won't make you happy? Look at the f*cking smile on my face."

Not all artists are poor, struggling and miserable. Not all rich people are tormented. Many of them are happy. The more money I make, the happier I am. I am also significantly more handsome when making more money. At the peak of my earning power I am downright gorgeous, as are the women paying attention to me. Money also makes a man's genitalia larger.

The secret to life is so simple. It is not about wailing about inequities, and using pastels and paint brushes to convey suffering.

The secret to life is to find rich and powerful people and get them to like you. That's it.

eric aka the Tygrrrr Express

To all the artists trying to feed themselves on hope, myths and dreams... learn about business. Take a marketing class. Be a lemming. Conform. Be like everybody else.

You may not be happy, but you probably were not going to be happy anyway. At least my way puts food on the table.

eric

The Pelosiraptor Attacked My Patriotism

In a *USA Today* column, The Pelosiraptor attacked my patriotism.

I could dismiss this as the rantings of a woman that is preparing for life as a permanent minority member of congress. That would let her off the hook.

I could say that the statements were meaningless simply because Nancy Pelosi said them. This is the Joe Biden defense.

Being clueless is not a defense.

At least Barack Obama won 52 percent of the vote of all voting Americans. Nancy Pelosi won a majority of votes from a few thousand people in the most wacked-out city in America.

So why is the leader of the Friscotics (oh cool, I think I invented what Rich Little referred to as a "sniglet.") full of Pelosi?

Pelosi knows that honesty does not sell when the product itself is not worth buying.

Political fights should be based on policy alone. That is exactly what the health care fight was about.

President Obama believed his health care plan was a net positive. I believed it was a net negative. We disagreed, and I supported those trying to defeat his plan.

Those claiming President Obama had a mandate to blow up the health care system because he won the election are grossly mistaken. His mandate was to fix the economy. He did not say anything about health care during the campaign except for the fact that he wanted "change."

Unlike his predecessor, who did what he said, Mr. Obama got elected by saying absolutely nothing. He got a lead, and ran out the clock. Disagreeing with the details was impossible because specifics were non-existent. The man is a human generality with a splash of bromide and several cups of platitudes.

Now he has to govern, and he has no experience running anything. One thing he does know how to do is community organize. He knows how to win blood fights. While conservatives are worried about taking down al-Qaeda, Obama and Pelosi are interested in taking down me and other mainstream conservatives.

Unlike Rahm Emanuel, I never mailed a dead fish to anybody.

Unlike leftist agitators, I never abused people trying to peaceably assemble. Unlike leftists, I never wrote or idolized a book about how to polarize and personalize.

I never questioned the patriotism of other Americans. Liberals see any disagreement with Barack Obama as an act of war.

They play the race card from the bottom of a marked deck.

When Barney Frank is shown to be a corrupt official, the left calls his critics gay bashers.

Howard Dean, whose very existence is synonymous with hate speech, heads the Democratic National Committee.

The issue is the same one that has infected the left in this country.

They are simply bullies.

Whether it is the anti-Semites at Code Pink or the terrorists that make up the Earth Liberation Front, the left is simply about the ends justifying the means.

When the right fringes speak, mainstream conservatives disavow them. When leftist basket cases act like…well, themselves…they get celebrated.

A conservative protester was beaten at a rally. The man was black, which would lead to charges of racism had he been a liberal.

I am sure there are plenty of liberals out there claiming they would object if an elderly lady was knocked over and her wheelchair broken. Would they loudly condemn the behavior, or would they make excuses?

I know what it is like to be subjected to left-wing violence. My hate mail inbox has been the recipient of some vile comments that I occasionally publish. Don't tell me that conservatives have a right to speak in this country. From my college days to too many synagogues, I have seen the leftinistras attack conservatism as morally repugnant.

The solution for conservatives is to hit back ferociously. I took on my college classmates. I take on synagogues, letting them know that their tax-exempt status is on shaky ground.

I take on monsters like the Pelosiraptor who dare to have the gall to criticize Americans for engaging in democracy.

Neither voters nor Republicans are to blame. The Democrats gained control, and they had the votes. What they lack are guts. They are more interested in placing blame than passing laws.

They are simply the same failed human beings that have watched America move to the right despite the occasional election hiccups.

They had the political numbers, but not the American people. Like two-year-old versions of Barbara Boxer (or sixty-two-year-old versions for that matter), they cry, kick, scream, and throw the mother of all tantrums, all because they can't get what they want. They scream at military leaders, play the race card against a Chamber of Commerce leader who happened to be black, attack police officers as racists for doing their jobs, and use thugs such as ACORN to steal elections when honest tactics fail.

This makes sense, since acorns are collections of nuts.

I never thought I would live to see the day when Hillary Clinton would appear to be more reasonable than anybody, but the Pelosiraptor is succeeding in this endeavor.

Attempts to portray conservatives as bad people will not stand up to reality.

I was at Sean Hannity's Freedom Concert. Some attendees were Democrats. They were treated in a friendly manner. I shook their hands, because I am capable of disagreeing with people without despising them.

I don't throw eggs or tomatoes at MSNBC trucks. I engage in civilized discourse.

Sometimes civilized discourse can get heated. Passions run high. Yet one would have to be a complete fraud or totally insane to think that senior citizens are political operatives. One would have to lack integrity or common sense to think that asking tough questions of elected officials is morally wrong.

Only a complete disgrace of a human being with no connection to reality would question the patriotism of me and my friends.

Welcome to the world of the top Friscotic (Wow, I really do like that word. Neato).

Like the forces of Augustus Caesar taking on Brutus and Cassius, our side has true beliefs while the left offers paid mercenaries. We offer ideas, and they respond with verbal suicide bombers.

We have senior citizens and veterans. They have agitators, union thugs, political hatchet people, college students, and radical professors. They are the mob. We are the people.

If the left wants to have a peaceful discussion, don't question my patriotism.

As for the Pelosiraptor, I will quote the words of President George W. Bush.

Bring it on.

eric

Chapter 4: Palesimian Idiocy

A non-Jewish former coworker once pointed out to me that he had evidence that the Jews were loved by God. He pointed out that only a loving God would give us the dumbest enemies on the planet. When Palesimians threaten to become suicide bombers, the solution is to take them to an area with no Jews or Americans, and set off the d@mn detonators. Somebody asked me if I was worried when Hamas and Fatah were killing each other. I was very concerned. I did not have any chips or soda in my house. Thank heaven for 7-11. Long live Tivo, which allowed me to pause live Fox News reports so I did not miss one minute of the greatest violence since Hillary last screamed at Bill. Enjoy my hate mail. I know I do.

Finally, Some Irrational Hate Mail, Courtesy of an Anonymous Palesimian

It seems I have touched a nerve. Who knew that terrorist supporters had feelings?

I finally received my first piece of hate mail, even though I go out of my way to emphasize ideas over vitriol. I am hard hitting, but I do not curse or use racism, sexism or any other kind of ism to make my points. Luckily, my feebleminded opponents have no such societal constraints.

The policy toward hate mail is to address it once in what I hope is a humorous manner. I do not address responses, depriving haters of their ill-informed (and often badly written) platforms.

I had the nerve to suggest that the Palesimians are a disaster as a civilization, and that they are entirely at fault for their own miserable lot in life. Hamas and Fatah are killing each other, yet some Palesimians still want to blame Israel, which to my knowledge does not have membership in either of these groups. Unlike Groucho Marx, we refuse to join any club that would have them as members, not us.

Now I offer the hate mail, from a brave soul who left an email address of anonymous@here.com. That is too courageous.

"jewish is a religion, NOT A SPECIAL BREED OF PEOPLE!!!!!!"

My parents actually think I am quite special, although they could mean the type of special that rides in the back of the little yellow bus.

"what is your origin? I bet its not even close to the middle east…"

I do not have to live next to homicidal lunatics to know what they are. I have never grown an apple tree, but feel comfortable identifying the apple and eating it.

"FACT: at least 10 to 1 is the ratio of palistinians dead people to israeli dead people because of the sh*t that happened in the region because of Israels existence, do you think that those people (palistinians and israelis) would've been murdered in the same way if Israel didn't exist?"

Absolutely! Of course they would. Jordan massacred one million Palesimians. Palesimians are Arabs. They outnumber Jews one hundred-to-one. A ten-to-one death rate is not an impressive achievement, although the current situation in Gaza is leading them to play catch-up.

"FACT: Israel are the one who broke the UN agreements and they took land that does not belong to them, kicked out it's native people, destroyed their houses, and even killed some natives in the way, and built settlements and cities in there, caused a couple of wars in the way, and whined and still whinning about being the 'victim'."

Wrong, wrong, wrong, and your houses could not be salvaged with help from Bob Vila. I agree Israel should stop blowing up empty houses. We should stop warning the people to get out alive before we blow up the house. We should stop dropping leaflets warning when the house is being bombed. We should just do what you do to us. Your objection is not that killing is wrong. You complain because the Israelis are better at it, and humane in how they do it. Maybe if you stopped hiding terrorists and munitions in the houses, we would not blow them up. Behaving like human beings seems a foreign concept.

"If israel has not been greedly eating land like a b*tch every couple of years, Israelis and palistinians would be living in peace today."

Apparently Israelis are not just dogs, but female dogs. Got it. Oh, and this fellow keeps misspelling the word Palestinians. Lastly, Israel withdrew from Gaza. There are no Jews there. Yet Palesimians are killing each other.

If Palesimians want to stop killing altogether, Israel would be happy to embrace them. Palesimians say this is not true, but they never tried the non-lunatic approach. You act normal and then get rewards, not the other way around. Since Palesimians refusing to kill is about as likely as children refusing to give up candy, I would strongly prefer they kill each other and not my people.

There is nothing like a good breakfast after a civilized debate among rational people. My favorite is burnt Gaza Strip and eggs sunny side down.

eric

More Hate Mail From Palesimians

A new civilization has been born, that being Palesimians.

Palestinians shall now forever be referred to as Palesimians.

For those who insist on creationism, I may have to rethink my view and lean toward the evolution side. After all, the hate mail I receive from Palesimians is significantly closer to descendants of baboons than anything a God who created me could come up with.

Spare me the "peaceful Palestinians" garbage. There are plenty of Arabs. Many of them are good people. The worst defective Arabs are the Palesimians.

I offer their version of reasonable discussion followed by my response.

The woman called herself Citizen Shelly. I recommended she change her name to Deported Shelly with a little help from some Israeli launched bazookas.

I cleaned up the language.

"Whoever you are, No way in hell would I sign up for your bullsh*t blog, so I'll send this to you directly.

I'm on the side of the Gaza citizens. You are a Zionist @sshole…The Israeli govenrment is racist and is universally hated around the world for what they did to Gaza in their recent "war". What a bunch of crap they represent.

Don't ever send me your spam racist sh*t again.

You're goddam right I think for myself. Israel sucks, and so do Zionist fascists and so do Aussie fascists. You're all racist pigs."

This is what Palesimians refer to as "thinkers."

I responded in kind.

"Thank you so much! I am now about to make you famous.

You should chill out and listen to disco music. My favorite song from the disco era is 'Burn Gaza Burn, Disco Inferno.'

Please give my regards to your homicide bomber friends. Oh wait, you can't. They blew themselves up.

I happen to agree with you about the war in Gaza. I am not happy about it either. Israel should have done much more."

These are Palesimians. This is who they are and how they behave. This is not an aberration. This is the norm.

Somebody throw them some bananas.

eric

More Irrational Hate Mail From Arab Terrorist Lunatics

I attended a symposium at UCLA entitled "Gaza and Human Rights."

I felt like I had infiltrated a terrorist sleeper cell. There was nothing human about the speakers or most of the crowd. For those wondering what savage barbarians look like, I am sure somebody took pictures.

Since then, one of the anti-Semitic speakers, Lisa Hajjar, had her terrorist mask ripped off. Her department has been shut down. Like cockroaches, anti-Semite Arab terrorist enablers are many. After publishing my column detailing the verbal genocidal atrocities committed by Arab terrorists posing as "academics," I received hate mail that only a Palesimian homicide bomber (or a UCLA professor) could love.

Some of the bile is below. I redacted the foul language. As with most "intellectuals," they cannot argue on substance. Instead they criticize spelling, grammar, and anything else that allows them to retain their rare combination of smugness and ignorance. Those are the qualifications for being a leftist professor, although supporting terrorism helps.

One email came from a guy named Jascha, who insisted he was male. Rather than address the substance of my column, he offered the following:

"Pity that (me, eric) does not know the difference between 'incredulous' and word he sort of had in mind, viz., 'incredible.' Jascha Kessler Professor of English and Modern Literature, UCLA"

I could have let that remark go, but letting it go is what supporters of Hamas say Israel should do. I did what any decent person would do with garbage…I removed it.

"Ms. Kessler,

I wrote a column explaining that a symposium on Gaza and Human Rights was the academic equivalent of a terrorist sleeper cell.

Your rebuttal was to criticize my not knowing the difference between incredulous and incredible.

Only an elitist gasbag, a terrorist enabler, or a college professor would offer that as a rebuttal.

I plan on making many more unintentional linguistic errors in the future. Your silence on the issue of Palesimian terrorism support at UCLA would seem to be a bigger error.

Feel free to correct the record, and if possible, do so with significantly less arrogance.

eric aka the Tygrrrr Express"

The response I got was perhaps not a Fatwa, but at the very least a leftist Palesimian screed. It was incoherent, but I am sure somewhere on the Web it can be translated from the original jihad.

"Rebuttal it was not! Schm*ck, you! I was helping your credibility, not your credulity or incredibility. Drop dead yesterday. Gasbag, indeed. Professor to you and your illiterate cohort. Stay off the Web for the public if you cannot distinguish between important words. And are you a misbegotten sexist? I am no Ms., and my name is male, all the way back to the patriarch Jacob. Toothless, cursing gnashing blogger. What you had to say was okay, but if you cannot spell in English, welll then, as the Brits say, F*ckall!
JK
As for my silence, I am anything but, brainless person. Here is a letter published in the FT before the UCLA event took place, which I have taken steps to oppose."

I deleted the link, because it was a commentary on Kublai Khan. I honestly never thought I would mention Kublai Khan on my blog, but if this professor thinks that the Arab-Israeli conflict relates, so be it. I responded for no other reason than I knew the response to me would be classic.

"Jessica,

You may claim to be a poet and a linguist, but like most Islamists, you resort to verbal violence and rage. Do you speak to your students with such foul language? I recommend you do some deep breathing exercises or some meditation from Deepak Chopra.

If you are the best UCLA can do, then enrollment at USC should increase rapidly.

I notice you won an award by George Soros. Perhaps you can win a Nobel Prize like Yassir Arafat to complete your inconsequential career. After all, those who can't do, teach.

I checked the terrorist watch list, and did not see your name. So before you criticize the spelling and grammar of others, if it was not for a misspelling due to your oddly spelled asexual first name, you would have already been captured.

I shall plant a tree in Israel in honor of your support of the Jewish state.

eric aka the Tygrrrr Express"

Sasha did not disappoint, although his/her responses would only reinforce the point of lunacy. At this point censorship would benefit us all. Besides, there was more hate mail.

Philip Andrew Jones was one of those fellows that started out trying to sound cerebral before eventually descending into the Palesimian city of Bonkersville. I have taken excerpts of his comments solely to reduce length, without taking them out of context.

"Dear Sirs/Madams,

Although I realize that you do not answer emails, however, I do hope that you would read the following:- I find it quite strange that the writers and promoters of 'Campus Watch', would charge UCLA with 'Jew - Hate'. I clicked onto quote, '…how best to spread…' End quote. Excuse me for any ignorance, but I did not sight any 'hate' in the news article on anti-Zionism, anti-Semitism or anti-Americanism.

As a very concerned person for the welfare of all human beings created equal under the LORD Thy God, I witnessed via main stream media and other news resources from around the world, the shocking scenes of high tech Israeli weapons raining death on civilian men, women and children trapped in the Gaza Ghetto. Although thirteen hundred human beings have been reported dead, further intelligence received is reporting that over four thousand have been genocide murdered.

I also have read concerning the 'violent' Hamas attacks on Israel - REALLY - but I suppose we could compare perhaps this Israeli atrocity to perhaps the British RAF bombing in Belfast, because of a terrorist attack in Manchester. That Israel can murder on this incredible huge scale, with the blind eye of Britain and America being totally despicable"

Okay, so he is not completely nuts yet. He needed another sentence to let the madness flow.

"It quite interesting that Tony Blair has of course revealed himself to be the usual puppet of the new world order banking elite, which is keen to stoke up the Israeli action to help divert attention from the global banking collapse."

There we go. The Zionist conspiracy to take over the world…those d@ng moneylenders. Tony Blair is in on it. He forgot to mention Kublai Khan. Luckily, he continued.

"While many are reticent about commenting, or being drawn into the debate about the 'Israeli / Palesimian issue', the brazen, wanton, criminal atrocities that have and will continue to be committed in this sick business by the superpower of the region are simply too heinous to be ignored. It is not enough for Israel to hide behind their historic suffering, when their actions are so vicious and unacceptable today, Jewish politicians and their lobbyists in the west, must be made fully accountable. No doubt, the smirking Mr. Blair has failed to stand and be counted due to US and home grown lobbying pressure. Just where did New Labour funds come from? No doubt also, that the United Nations has also failed to take action due to the powerful US/Israeli lobby."

With all those powerful Jews, I wonder why I never got a share of this money and power. According to these bigots, my time will come at their expense. I can live with that.

As for the gutless, useless, worthless organization known as the United Nations, I am not sure whether I should be happy or sad that their humanitarian relief workers were robbed at gunpoint by members of Hamas.

As punishment, the U.N. suspended aid to Hamas. That is talking tough. The U.N. is refusing to provide supplies and aid that were already stolen. Perhaps Hamas also stole supplies of Viagra, which could explain the impotence of the U.N.

As for the intellectual impotence of the blusterer, he continued misfiring on half cylinder.

"On a deeper level, what is it about the Israeli national political character, the 'siege mentality', that violence and murder against civilian populations can be pursued with such inhumane and calculated precision? How can a culture that who say they believe in God be so immune to the cries of the dead, maimed and dying - in the prison camp they have created, of what remains of the country they annexed from the Palestinians so long ago?

Could it be that one possible answer is to be found in the laws of the 'man - written' so called secret Babylonian Talmud, which documents the most racist, anti-Semitic, most anti-human writings ever written by the carnal mind of man."

Forget Kublai Khan. It is all about the Babylonian Talmud. As for killing with "precision," Israel should avoid punishment for not only defending itself, but doing so successfully. Conversely, Palesimians should not be rewarded just because they are the Inspector Clouseau of murderers. Stupid and incompetent killers should be killed with extra precision.

A third piece of hate mail was less serious. I have no evidence that the person is a bigot in any way. Since I contacted them first, and they responded to me privately, I will allow their name to be redacted.

My contact was polite. Leftists need to understand that incivility will be met with severity. I don't coddle verbal homicide bombers. The woman (I think it was a woman) was from Iran, and not sympathetic toward my support of Israel. She also did not think much of conservatives.

"Reading your incredibly stupid comments and completely ignorant analysis of world events literally makes me nauseous. I choose not to communicate with stupid people, and your emails qualify as this type of communication."

These people are the gift that keeps on giving, hence my using them for entertainment purposes in the same way that circuses utilize clowns and elephants.

"You claim you don't want to communicate with me, but yet you emailed me, which means you communicated with me. This makes you a liar.

You are also Persian, which means you are a guest in my nation. You should kiss the feet of George W. Bush every night. I bet you were not that brave in your insults under Ayatollah Khomeini.

You need a hug.

eric aka the Tygrrrr Express

P.S. I publish my hate mail so my readers can see what passes for 'intellect.'"

A fellow named Tanweer Mahmoodullah livened things up. Mr. Weird Dullard had his own screed.

"Hundreds of doctors and specialists have confirmed that Israel used White phosphorous and dime bombs on civilians. photographs, live and from Gaza do not lie! Israel has lied from day one. All its people, military and civilians should be tried for theft , murder, genocide, apartheid and crimes against humanity. hands up for Lisa hajjar and people like her who are brave and have a conscience. Israelis, get ready to be tried and persecuted! Your end has come!"

My time has come. Perhaps the fellow can sing "Time Has Come Today," [14] before detonating himself.

As for "hands up," perhaps he thinks this is a sporting event that required doing "the wave." His diatribe occurred the same week as the NFL Pro Bowl in Hawaii, which could be an explanation.

A better rationale would be that there is no rationale for those that are irrational.

These are Arab Palesimian terrorist enablers. This is how they behave and what they are. Notice I said "what" instead of "who."

These savages do not need a homeland. All of them, including the "English Professor," need some soap to wash out their mouths. As for soap, make mine a double shot of lava. I always need a good scrubbing to cleanse myself from the filth my "critics" leave behind.

eric

More Hate Mail From Leftists Gone Wild

It is time to open up the hate mail bag and expose some more liberals gone wild.

It is possible for somebody to be political liberal, or even leftist, without being hateful.

I know this seems hard to believe. Like Palesimians, liberals seem to be born angry, live that way, and die that way.

I received some more hate mail from a pair of leftists.

Some people have road rage or air rage. Others have telemarketer rage. With some people, it is email rage.

I do not expect everybody to agree with me. People have a right to be wrong. I just expect civility and politeness.

A pair of people decided to unload as only hateful people could.

Mr. Sean O'Neill needed expletives to get his point across. I altered his expletive ever so slightly since I abhor foul language.

"Who the f*ck are you…?"

I responded in kind.

"Your hostility, incivility, and cursing are not reasonable. I don't care how many emails you get. No excuses. Your attitude screws up the entire world… Be a better person in the future.

eric aka the Tygrrrr Express"

Naturally, he consulted his God of liberalism, and denied himself the chance for growth.

"'Be a better person'?? Am I supposed to fellate every clown on the Internet…? Perhaps you should step off your pedestal and go F*CK yourself. Meanwhile, I will happily continue screwing up the entire world with my bad attitude. Toodles! S, aka anti-Semitic commie socialist pinko leftist f*g-loving feminazi f*ck"

I do not recall ever asking Sean O'Neill to fellate me. I can refer him to Barney Frank. For those who think I took a cheap shot, shut up. Barney Frank is gay.

Gay guys fellate other gay guys. I am not condemning this, just pointing out that I do not fellate guys. Like many leftists, this one wore his anti-Semitism like a badge of honor. I never brought that issue up. He did.

Sean O'Neill was significantly worse than Robin27095, but she was nasty as well. The source of her anger was my spam blocker. She received a "no reply" automated response, even though I receive every single email. She was more animated than automated.

"You twit. Take me off…NOW!!!!!!!!!!!!!"

Angry leftists love capital letters and multiple explanation points.

I offered her my response.

"You overreacted and resorted to insults, which tells me you are most likely a liberal. Liberals look for any excuse or perceived slight to lash out at conservatives.

I don't expect you to apologize for your behavior. Again, you are a liberal, which means that civility toward conservatives is not necessary. Don't bother learning from this experience. Keep misjudging people. Otherwise you might accidentally improve the world.

eric aka the Tygrrrr Express"

Naturally she failed to learn from her rudeness.

"You are an @ss. You don't even know what 'no reply' (means)…"

I redacted the bad word, but let me assure the world that I know the meaning of "No Reply."[15] It is a song by Phil Collins.

Had this woman simply asked me something politely and let it go, there would have been no conflict. All she had to do was say the word, and I don't mean "Sussudio."[16]

Had she asked me to fellate her, I would have explained that I was in a relationship. Had she asked me one month earlier, I would have requested pictures first.

Another fellow named MaxNam did not curse, but he resorted to the typical tried and true smugness. Either conservatives are evil, dumb, or both.

"I read what you wrote. Nothing about what you said seems rational to me. Don't you realize that most of the citizens of the U.S. favor the positions taken by our new president and are thoroughly disgusted by what the conservative Bush administration did to our beloved country? You must be one who simply does not comprehend how pathetic your appeal appears to someone like me."

Because I view the world differently from this fellow, I am irrational. I cannot comprehend what he can. Also, my appeal is pathetic.

These people wake up in the morning unable to get through the day without hate.

For eight years, the entire existence of the Democratic Party was based on the hatred of one man, George W. Bush. A friend insisted that once President Bush left office, Democrats would calm down. They actually got worse.

Democrats cannot be for anything. They can only be against. Upon controlling all the levers of power, they desperately needed a conservative to despise. Rush Limbaugh filled the bill, but he has no policy role. Sarah Palin is a private citizen. George W. Bush is back at his ranch, and Newt Gingrich is long since retired. Eric Cantor is becoming a new bogeyman. Unless he wants to be seen as evil personified, he had better become ineffective in a hurry.

Hatred is all they have. It is easier to hate than focus on something resembling a policy.

These are liberals. This is how they behave.

eric

The Knesset Gets Bold

The Israeli Knesset voted on an explosive resolution.

Hardliners like me cheered, even though I knew that this was only symbolic policy that would never become law. I am constantly criticizing symbolism over substance. I know that saying is not doing, but at least I have a ray of hope that Israelis have had enough.

Israel voted on a resolution to give Palesimians their own homeland...in Jordan.[17]

Fifty-three out of one hundred-and-twenty members of the Knesset voted for this resolution. I am sure that many would have voted against it had it actually had a chance to pass, but fifty-three is still a staggering number.

This has angered Jordan, as if that should actually matter.

Jordan was supposed to be part of Israel. Israel was not created out of the Holocaust or the Balfour Declaration.

Israel goes back thousands of years before any Arabs or their defective Palesimian cousins ever existed.

Israel is finally uttering the phrase that tells me Israel has had it with these defective Arab misfits that support terrorism. Israel is pointing out that Palesimians are not a separate party like Norwegians would be. Palesimians are Arabs. The West Bank Arabs are Jordanians.

New Yorkers often flee to Florida for better weather and lower taxes. They are still New Yorkers. They can call themselves Nebraskans but that would be completely false.

There is no Palestine on the map. The Palesimians are not Israelis. They are Arabs.. They should live with their brothers. Those who object can say something as soon as Jews are allowed to live in Arab countries without being murdered for being Jewish.

There are twenty-two Arab states. Now Arabs want a twenty-third one. Israel owns 80 percent of one Jewish state, since 20 percent of the population consists of Israeli Arabs. Israeli Arabs are Arabs first and Israelis second.

This matters because Jordan murdered one million Palesimians. They drove them out. They should take them back. The United States should provide relocation assistance and ensure that it is not spent on guns and bombs.

Some say that it is wrong to drive people from where they live. Yet if somebody escapes from a looney bin and breaks into your house, you have every right to return them to the looney bin. That is a right of return I could embrace.

Palesimians are Jordanians. They are not being driven from anywhere they want to be. They want all of Israel. They want the Jews driven into the sea. If they wanted a homeland, they would not have attacked in 1948, 1956, 1967 (Israel technically attacked first, but the Arabs were preparing to launch a war), 1973 (On Yom Kippur, b@stards that they are), 1982, and pretty much every other day that ends in the letters d, a, and y.

Palesimians deserve the misery they face. They brought it upon themselves.

The Israeli government has finally decided to stop responding to Palesimian terrorism by groveling and begging for more terror.

There is no political or diplomatic solution with these savages. The only solution is overwhelming brute force.

The Knesset action will not provoke world war because it will not become law.

Yet psychologically, Israelis have finally accepted that Palesimians believe in peace as much as vegetarians believe in cattle ranches.

Israelis want Palesimians to shut up and go back to where they came from.

That would be Jordan.

eric

Chapter 5: Media Idiocy

Members of the media do have good qualities. Just kidding. America is on its way to becoming a nation of imbeciles. Our soldiers are trying to save the world, while Access Hollywood rolls out the red carpet for the wealthiest dregs in society. Rich and attractive garbage is still garbage. You can put a bow tie on a pig, but that does not make Hollywood celebrities politically astute. I believe in free speech. I exercise mine to tell those contributing to the intellectual decline of this nation to shut up, sit down, and keep the duct tape on their mouths until they can prove beyond a reasonable doubt that they know anything that matters.

How Can We Worry About Al-Qaeda When PHTV is the Only News?

Welcome to Paris Hilton Television, aka PHTV. It is all PH, all the time. Out of pure disgust, I will not mention her insignificant name ever again. Every time I think about creationism, I picture people like ANS (first name Anna) and PH. Then I think that the evolution people are right. Some people did descend from baboons, without much progress. How could the same God that gave us the gift of reason have created such wastes of empty space? If there was an air shortage, they would suck up every last breath.

This issue might be the one time where I sided with Kirsten Powers over Michelle Malkin. The normally tough-as-nails Ms. Malkin did not give PH a verbal lashing. Ms. Powers did, with superb rhetorical aplomb.

Ms. Malkin is deadly accurate when she lacerates the jackals masquerading as human garbage, our esteemed fourth estate. It is because of them that the day PH left jail was the ideal day for bad behavior by everybody else worldwide. I do not blame PH for this. She cannot help being worthless, but nobody makes the media smoke her crack lifestyle. It is not that they cover her with bated breath. It is that they ignore everything else.

If I were al-Qaeda, I would carry out as many diabolical attacks as I could every minute the media is inhaling PH's rumpus. What are a few bombs scattered in Iraq? Who cares about collateral damage? Execute all kidnapped journalists. Their colleagues will not notice. In fact, these soulless vultures might appreciate the reduced competition for PH interviews.

Fatah and Hamas should start an all-out war. Israel should join the fray. Anybody wanting to commit mass acts of war on a global scale without the annoying attention of reporters should have launched rockets the minute PH exited jail.

Domestically, politicians should pass as much harmful legislation as possible without debate. Pay raises, abortion bills, immigration, restrictions on the bill of rights…it does not matter. They can pass the Freedom of Choice Act and the Right to Life Amendment simultaneously just for fun and let the courts sort it out.

If ever politicians needed a day to drink, drive, and enjoy call girls (or boys, let's not discriminate), it should have been done on PH Freedom Day. Illegal campaign activities should be ratcheted up on future PH days. Fundraisers should be held in churches, synagogues, mosques, and of course Buddhist monasteries, since there will be "no controlling legal authority"[18] to monitor them at that time due to other news media desires.

Short of Natalie Holloway being found or ANS being resurrected, nothing will stop this lack of news deluging us.

America is winning the War on Terror, but not enough people know this because we are losing the war against nonsense.

Alan Colmes innocently asked a guest "What should we do, talk about nothing but Iraq and the War on Terror?"[19] Yes! That is precisely what we should do. Mr. Colmes is correct when he states that talking about PH is escapism from all the serious life and death stuff. That is justifying idiocy. If people want to escape, watch a comedy program. I enjoy *South Park*. Surf the Internet. Better yet, to quote my parents, "Read a book or go do something." The nightly news should never be the nightly nonsense.

Al-Qaeda and the broader War on Terror should never be relegated to "been there, done that." PH should never be news, whether she is PH balanced or PH unbalanced.

I pray for the safety of Americans. I also pray that we actually justify our existence on this planet by spending time on what matters. Wasted time is wasted life. We cannot and should not waste our time on a wasted life such as PH, especially when terrorists are too busy trying to end all our lives.

eric

Law and Order Nonsense Saturday

If ever a story deserved short shrift, this non-story is it. Here is my input.

Tiger Woods is the perfect spokesperson for golf. He is colossally boring, and so is golf. He is a great golfer, which does not make him remotely interesting. Somewhere out there a guy exists who manufactures ball bearings better than anybody else. Hooray. Tiger Woods is as far as Barack Obama from the Dos Equis guy on the interesting scale. Being boring is not a crime. Elevating boring people to interesting status is a waste. Stay thirsty my friends.

One serious news story was treated like a childhood prank. A scheming bimbo desperate to be seen as relevant crashed a White House party and managed to meet President Obama.

No, not Katie Couric, that ideologically bigoted slutty dancer shaking her badonkadonk while turning her nose up at other women. The other bimbo. If this event had any more useless wannabe flesh candy, it would be the Clinton White House.

As for Mr. and Mrs. Salahi, waterboard them. Better yet, beat the heck out of them in a private room. Burn them with cigarettes if need be. Just do something.

This was not a harmless prank akin to toilet papering somebody's yard. This was a serious security breach. I don't have to have voted for President Obama to pray for his safety. The idea that he was not in danger is ludicrous. Anybody that ever breaches his security potentially puts his life in danger.

I hope he privately bangs his fist on the table and demands that heads roll, whether it be resignations or more. What if this couple had anthrax or something else that would not be picked up by metal detectors?

They wanted to be on a reality show. I say make them *America's Most Wanted.*

It was funny when Vince Vaughn and Owen Wilson became *Wedding Crashers.* The Salahis are not funny. They are criminals.

I would have spent more time on this, but America was asleep from Thanksgiving Thursday, Black Friday, or Nonsense Saturday. It would not be the first time my words put people to sleep.

Too many people think *Law and Order* is just a television show.

This leads me into my next random segue in the great tradition of *Larry King Live*, an oxymoron if there ever was one (Thank you Evan Sayet for that joke).

Why is *Law and Order* so d@mn predictable?

I can save you all twenty years of watching this once-solid program that is now just liberal blather. A couple particular things sum up the show.

If there are three white suspects and a fourth black suspect, the black guy is automatically innocent. There is no way he did it. American crime statistics are wrong. 95 percent of all violent crime is committed by rich, white, Republican, investment bankers.

Wall Street has its share of greed, but men in navy blue suits with red and blue diagonal neckties are not out murdering people. For those who feel that they are killing society metaphorically, this show is about murders in the literal sense. Minorities are victims, as corporate white executives bludgeon minorities on the street during their three-martini lunch breaks.

More importantly, the severity of the crime is predetermined by the number of Powerful Bald White Guys (PBWGs) barking orders.

PBWG Level 1 usually involves the phrase "One Police Plaza is all over my @ss!" Then the guy storms off.

PBWG Level 2 has another guy show up with his military uniform on with all of his medals. He growls, "The mayor is all over my @ss!"

PBWG Level 3 is like Defcon highest level. At that point it gets kicked up to the governor (Donald Shalvoy is an Eliot Spitzer character played brilliantly by Tom Everett Scott. He is a Tom Hanks lookalike, only balder.) or Fred Thompson.

Law and Order worked when arrogant liberal gasbag Jack McCoy, played by Sam Waterston, was the number two guy. He would get bombastic, and Fred Thompson's Arthur Branch would calmly direct him to sit his liberal @ss down.

Even when the boss was a liberal, Stephen Hill as Adam Schiff was great. His answer to everything was "Make it go away. Offer him a deal." McCoy would ramble on, and Schiff would remind him that his job was to put away bad guys, not save the world.

Now McCoy is like any other raging liberal with unchecked power.

Without Fred Thompson, Angie Harmon, or even Dennis Farina doing his tough guy Chicago cop routine, the show is just another left-wing program. They should just bring in Dixie Carter and rename it "Designing Women."

No, wait. I take that back. May those ladies never be on my television again.

Some of you may think that Julia Sugarbaker is not worth discussing. Oh, and Tiger Woods is?

What the heck should I discuss? I live in a country where Saturdays are dedicated to commercials about a "Snuggie" for dogs. Anybody who bought that or bottled water for their dogs on Black Friday should face black and blue Saturday for wasting money when others are hurting.

Sunday is football and on Monday politics returns. Those days cannot come soon enough.

Some of you think I have a masterful ability to say so much and say so little.

That would be President Obama and Vice President Biden. At least I don't pretend to be important.

For them, every day is Nonsense Saturday.

eric

Jon Stewart Courageously Defends His Bottom Flank

It takes a big man to admit he screwed up and take a principled stand. It takes a phony liberal elitist to apologize for the sake of protecting his television ratings.

Jon Stewart makes Arlen Specter look principled.

Like Pee Wee Herman, Jon Stewart launched his intercontinental ballistic missile, and could not put the missile back on the launching pad. In his case, the only thing that seeped out was stupidity.

For those who are not "trendy," "hip," or "cool" (brie-cheese-eating-elitist-snobs), Jon Stewart has a nightly political television show where he presents the news with all the accuracy and fairness of the *Jayson Blair Times*.

He is slightly different from the *JBT*. The *JBT* wants to be taken seriously, despite being leftist, boring, and usually wrong. Jon Stewart wants to be taken seriously when it suits him, and as a comedian when that benefits him. He straddles like Bill Clinton, only with his trousers on. Stewart claims to offer intelligent political insight. Yet when challenged a couple of years ago, Stewart took the defensive posture that his show was preceded by "puppets making crank phone calls." [20]

This is not about *Crank Yankers*. This is about acting like a cranky wanker.

Jon Stewart had his CW moment when debating the absolutely brilliant Cliff May. I know Cliff personally. He is no partisan hack. He is a serious policy analyst with expertise in matters of national security. His lectures are brilliant.

Cliff May debated Jon Stewart on torture. The only thing that was definitely tortured was Stewart trying to keep up. Cliff May did not use coercive interrogation methods on Jon Stewart, but he certainly put him in an uncomfortable stress position. Stewart was twisted into a pretzel by the time the debate was done.

May asked Stewart if Harry Truman was a war criminal for bombing Hiroshima and Nagasaki. Stewart hemmed, hawed, and fumbled his words. For a man who lambasted President George W. Bush for malaprops and syntax fracturing, Stewart sure looked like the pot calling the kettle African-American. He looked like President Obama without a teleprompter.

He eventually blurted out that, yes, Harry Truman was a war criminal. [21]

The backlash came from the millions of people who understand that America is about the values of Jimmy Stewart, not Jon Stewart.

Jon Stewart apologized on a later show. It takes a tremendous amount of courage to apologize after a backlash occurs. After all, free speech is not free. Just ask Dr. Laura. Jon Stewart may have come to understand that some of his sponsors do business with Middle America.

This is about something deeper. Why does Jon Stewart give latitude to Harry Truman while skewering George W. Bush?

Ideological bigotry requires that liberals and Democrats be exalted while Republicans and conservatives are excoriated. Actual issues are irrelevant.

Jon Stewart realized that he criticized a Democrat. It is better to be a hypocrite and anger people that you already detest than to be consistent and anger people you love. It is not possible to unite everybody on your side, but it is possible to unite people against you.

Let me offer some common sense that will be self-explanatory to Middle America.

Harry Truman did the right thing. He made an impossible choice that none of us will ever have to make. His job was not, as some liberals insist, to save the world. His job was to save America. We were under attack. By killing many innocent Japanese civilians, he prevented millions of Americans from being killed. He did the one thing a president must do. He kept us safe. As an extra benefit, millions of people worldwide were saved.

George W. Bush also did the right thing. He also made the impossible choice. He also responded to an attack on our soil by going everywhere terrorists were harbored and protected.

We were attacked by Japan, but Harry Truman took the fight to Germany. Germany never attacked us, but they were part of the problem.

We were attacked by al-Qaeda, but George W. Bush took the fight to Iraq. Iraq never attacked us, but they were part of the problem. Iran and Syria remain problematic.

More people died at the hands of Harry Truman than George W. Bush. The numbers are not even close. Harry Truman took measures more brutal than anything George W. Bush ever did. Harry Truman ordered the most unimaginable response.

If Harry Truman was right, then George W. Bush cannot be a war criminal.

Jon Stewart knows this. To deny this is to be intellectually dishonest. Welcome to liberalism.

Jon Stewart once remarked that when George W. Bush was right about something, "My head may explode."[22]

Feel free to spontaneously combust, Mr. Stewart. George W. Bush got the biggest thing right that he was asked to do.

Jon Stewart has his right to free speech because George W. Bush protected and defended that right.

Jon Stewart allowed fear of being labeled a hypocrite to overrule common sense.

He then realized that nobody has a right to earn tons of money from "free" speech.

Jon Stewart was not protecting free speech. He was protecting very expensive, highly paid speech.

It is at that moment that he decided to "apologize" and defend his bottom (left) flank.

He had the courage of his "convictions," which was to defend his rumpus from financial harm.

Real courage would be Jon Stewart offering an apology to George W. Bush while he is still alive to hear it.

eric

The War Against Nonsense

Many of you over the last few years have gone onto the Internet or turned on the television and typed or heard the following words…

Natalie Holloway. Scott Peterson. Anna Nicole Smith. Don Imus. Rosie O'Donnell. Michael Richards. Al Sharpton. Jesse Jackson. Simon Cowell. Duke lacrosse players. Michael Jackson. Madonna's adoption. Bennifer. Brangelina. Tomkat. Vinnifer Vaughniston. *Inside Edition. Access Hollywood. Entertainment Tonight.* Barbra Streisand. Tim Robbins. Susan Sarandon. Sean Penn. Whoopi Goldberg. J-Lo. K-Fed. Britney Spears. Mel Gibson. Mike Nifong. Joy Behar. Joe Wilson. Valerie Plame. Paris Hilton. Sasha *Borat* Cohen. Tara Reid. Lindsay Lohan's father. Lady Ga-Ga (not to be confused with her twin Lady Blah-Blah). Howard K. Stern.

Now that I have your attention, if you care about any three of the items mentioned above, you are an imbecile. You are contributing to the decline of society. We are in the middle of World War III with Islamofascists, and you want to waste time with nonsense.

I am not concerned with Sanjaya. I am concerned with Bashar Assad and Armageddonijad. I am not concerned with Barack Obama in a bathing suit. I am not concerned with Barack Obama in any suit. Until he talks about what to do about Osama Bin Laden and worldwide terrorism, he is Barack Obama the empty suit. I do not care about *The View*. With apologies to Winston Churchill, never have so many…especially women…cared so much…about stuff that mattered so little. Barbara Walters once interviewed Menachem Begin. Now she is fascinated by Paris Hilton.

Even Fox News is not immune from the inane. Greta Van Susteren for far too long had an intelligent outlook on issues that meant zero. She improved when she began occasionally covering hard news. Even Geraldo gets it, for crying out loud. He was once ridiculed as the idiot behind Al Capone's vaults and the victim of a Bobby Knight-style chair toss. He now occasionally reports from Iraq. It is never too late at least try to be taken seriously.

While it is tempting to blame the above topics, some are blameless. Natalie Holloway did not deserve to go missing. The Duke lacrosse players did not deserve to be tried and convicted without going to court. Nevertheless, these people are not as important as Stephen Harper, Angela Merkel, or Nicholas Sarkozy. If you have no idea who they are, please leave this Earth. You are using up valuable air, and in some cases, television or Internet air time.

The American public has got to stop lowering itself. We can become intelligent human beings again. George W. Bush waged a Global War on Terror. We cannot do anything to help if we spend our time worrying about the fact that some Hollywood celebrity who won some award because he almost became president except he lost his home state of Tennessee tells us that in thousands of years after we are all dead it might become warm outside (while I suffer through a thirty-eight degree April Chicago).

Some say that escapism is a good way to unwind, and that we cannot focus on hard news all the time. This is a cop-out. People who spend their time on soft news usually know nothing else. I can watch Eva Longoria traipse around in her underclothing, but I would be embarrassed to see that reported as a news story while Nancy Pelosi is trying to undermine our government in a time of war.

There is a medical procedure I call cranial-glutial extraction surgery. People have their heads removed from their hides.

Some will say it is good that after 9/11 we have gotten back to normal. Worrying about possible hijinks on American Idol is complacency, not normalcy.

I enjoyed seeing Will Ferrell in *Anchorman*. Going to a movie is escapism. When I come home after a hard day's work, I want to know if the world I live in is about to be blown to Kingdom Come. I do not want *Anchorman*'s Ron Burgundy telling me about how a space alien and a baby panda mated and produced Al Sharpton, who is related to Strom Thurmond. This is about as important as my being the one hundred-sixty-four-thousandth cousin of Adam by birth and Eve by marriage.

Rather than start a debate about eugenics, I will ask my fellow Americans to either stop spending time focusing on nonsense, or voluntarily promise not to reproduce. It is important you learn where babies come from so that you can keep this promise. Otherwise, your children will be worse because stupidity is exponential.

We are at war. Iran is plotting to destroy the world. Bringing Anna Nicole back from the dead will not prevent this.

If we are to win the War on Terror, we must declare a war on nonsense. We cannot kill every al-Qaeda terrorist if our citizens are busy killing their own brain cells.

Americans are can-do people. We have the ability to be intelligent again. There is a place for nonsense, but it should be the exception and not the rule.

At night, I pray to God for America to win the war on nonsense, so that Americans can focus on how to help win the War on Terror.

eric

Charlie Sheen and the Truth About 9/11

I have been doing some research (okay, I am lying) about the tragic events surrounding 9/11.

President Obama needs to convene a blue-ribbon panel immediately to investigate things.

The truth is painful, but Jack Nicholson reminded me that I can't handle the truth.

It is time that we finally acknowledge what happened.

The clues were in front of our faces. I finally connected the dots.

Charlie Sheen was responsible for 9/11.

This is absolutely factual because I said so. Like global warming, the debate is now settled. The discussion needs to end. Disagreeing with me makes you a rude angry mob, even if you are a lone individual.

Think back to the California Achievement Tests. Now think about the following syllogism.

Premise 1: "All cats chase mice."

Premise 2: "Tony has a cat."

Conclusion: "Tony is a mouse."

This proves not only that California should abolish all public schools and allow for homeschooling, but that Charlie Sheen was responsible for 9/11.

For those still not convinced, let me paraphrase the rantings of conspiracy nut Louis Farrakhan. He makes others seem sane.

There are seven days in a week. There are seven letters in the word Judaism. There are seven letters in the word slavery. Therefore, Zionist moneylenders named JP Morganberg and Merrill Lynch Glassberg inflicted Africans with malaria. Malaria also has seven letters, as does the word disease, which malaria is.

For those still not convinced, the evidence can be found in the lack of coverage by the liberal media. Dan Rather, Katie Couric, and the *Jayson Blair Times* never bothered to cover the story. Given that they deliberately slant the news and get stories wrong, this story must be real news.

Keep looking. According to liberals, every Muslim is a good person, and every rich white male is an oppressor. The television show *Law and Order*, which Charlie Sheen is not on (part of the cover-up), constantly teaches this fact. Charlie Sheen is a white male.

Look at the similarities between Charlie Sheen and the Islamofascists from 9/11.

Charlie Sheen spent time with hookers. The day before the 9/11 attacks, the hijackers were in the casinos with hookers. Hookers are not monogamous. They have multiple clients.

Charlie Sheen has used drugs. The hijackers engaged in drug running.

The hijackers were human garbage. Charlie Sheen appeared as a garbage man in a movie that featured a guy who had Vietnam flashbacks. Vietnam was a war, which is what the terrorists are waging.

Charlie Sheen has been to Pennsylvania, New York, and Washington, DC.

The terrorists were considered brothers, even though they did not have the same last name. Islam, like other religions, teaches that all men of the faith are part of a brotherhood. Charlie Sheen is brothers with Emilio Estevez, who also has a different last name. In an even eerier coincidence, they have different first names. So did the hijackers.

Charlie Sheen's father was President of the United States. The terrorists tried to kill the president.

If you take the numbers from 9/11 and add them up, you get the number twenty. Now if you take the convenience store chain 7-11, which has been known to hire Middle Easterners, and add the numbers together, you get eighteen.

In early 1999, what was the score of the Atlanta Falcons playoff victory over the San Francisco 49ers? That's right. 20 to 18.

Eighteen is a lucky number in Jewish culture. Charlie Sheen is not Jewish, meaning bad things would happen. The terrorists were also not Jewish.

Eighteen and twenty add up to thirty-eight, which when looking into a mirror appears to be eighty-three.

Eighty-three consists of eight and three, which adds up to eleven. Eleven is the other half of 9/11 and 7/11.

Nine means no in German. The Germans were therefore not responsible for 9/11.

Seven brings us back to Farrakhan. Since he is always wrong, the Jewish slave masters could not have been responsible.

If the Jews and the Germans are innocent, and Arabs are always innocent, then what can we ascertain from this?

The words Saudi Arabia have eleven letters.

Does this mean that the Saudis were responsible?

Not entirely. The word Saudi has five letters. So does the word Sheen. The word Charlie has seven letters, as do the words Jewish, African, and slavery. Arabia does not, but Arabia is a country. The individual person is an Arabian, which does. Some would say they are Arabs, but that has five letters.

Half of five is two-and-a-half. Charlie Sheen appears in the television show *Two-and-a-Half Men*.

There we go!

Lastly, liberals criticize George W. Bush for being born to a famous father who guided his career path.

That would be Charlie Sheen, Al Gore and the uselessness that is the current crop of Kennedys.

Kennedy is an airport frequently targeted by terrorists. Charlie Sheen has been there.

He was even wearing a head covering, presumably to keep away the paparazzi. The terrorists also use head coverings to disguise themselves.

I am sure President Obama will engage in a high-level shrouding of the truth, which I still can't handle.

If Charlie Sheen thinks he will get away with being behind 9/11, he has another thing coming.

I did my part America. Now do yours.

Find Charlie Sheen, Rosie O'Donnell, and some Ron Paul supporters, and discover if scratching a dime on their foreheads yields either proof that fire melts steel, or at least a free Slurpee.

Oh, and Charlie Sheen has tasted a Slurpee in his lifetime (that is not a prostitute reference). Slurpees are sold at 7-11, which as we know comes right before…

Well, you know. 9/11.

eric

Limbaugh, Hannity, and Beck Caused 9/11

Here is a half-baked attempt, which means it will be up to my usual low standards.

I recently proved that Charlie Sheen was responsible for 9/11.

I now realize that he was a minor cog.

The evidence is overwhelming that 9/11 was caused by Rush Limbaugh, Glenn Beck, and Sean Hannity.

The left is constantly complaining that their patriotism is being attacked, and that they love America as much as conservatives do.

Most conservatives have never attacked anybody's patriotism, I have never done so. I simply say that the left is obsessed with nonsense while conservatives are trying to save the world. Until the left accepts the cold hard truth that trees and bunny rabbits were killed on 9/11, they will never see the light.

Yet if Limbaugh, Hannity, and Beck caused 9/11, then the left is absolutely right to spend every waking minute obsessing about them.

The Obama administration absolutely should spend a good part of their lives focused on these three individuals if it is a matter of national security.

I was under the impression that the Obama administration contained a bunch of thin-skinned crybabies that desperately needed a diversion to make up for their own inability to accomplish…well…anything.

The previous administration worried about Osama Bin Laden, Saddam Hussein, Armageddonijad, and other despots around the world. Maybe none of these individuals ever engaged in or sponsored worldwide terrorism.

Maybe the Obama administration is not full of garbage. Maybe they truly have evidence that any conservative that has ever been on Fox News is a true threat to our democracy.

Saudi Arabian Islamofascists may have knocked down the towers, but when homicide bombers fail to do their jobs and only end up wounded, they need access to health care. Conservatives tried to block Obamacare for the sinister reason that it was a dreadful idea. How dare they? The outrage is palpable. Therefore, Fox News is behind 9/11.

Limbaugh, Hannity and Beck also have issues with gay marriage. So did the 9/11 hijackers.

I rest my case. All conservatives are stupid and evil, despite those two characteristics being contradictory.

There is no way that people as intellectually brilliant as Mr. Obama and his cabinet of academics could possibly be spending much of their days focused on nonsense. They are good, virtuous, and noble. They would never waste taxpayer dollars on such stupid pursuits as waging war on television personalities when a real war is going on.

Of course, given that I am a conservative, I am always wrong.

Ignore everything so far, unless you already have.

Nobody at Fox News is connected to 9/11. Islamofascists were.

It would be nice if the Obama administration would just grow up and enter adulthood.

Their job is to keep us safe. If they fail, all the hollering about conservative media personalities will fall on deaf ears.

Beck, Hannity, and Limbaugh are not always right, but at least they are two things that the Obama administration wishes it could be…effective…and relevant.

eric

My Interview With Bernie Goldberg

I had the pleasure of interviewing Bernie Goldberg.

Bernie Goldberg is the author of several bestsellers, including "Bias," and "100 People Who Are Screwing Up America." He eventually added more people, and a reprint of the book upped the list to 110 people. His most recent book chronicled the mainstream media's open and unapologetic cheerleading for Barack Obama to win the White House. "A Slobbering Love Affair," is a must read.

I met Bernie Goldberg at the Nixon Library. He was very friendly, and agreed to an interview without hesitation. Although I was willing to do the interview by email to give him time, he liked the challenge of a rapid fire session over the telephone. It makes sense that a man who constantly criticizes journalists for shying away from tough questions and controlled settings would be willing to take a risk himself.

Bernie Goldberg is a proud Jewish Conservative. Like me, he does not shy away from controversy. The conversation lasted about twenty-five minutes, with none of it wasted. At no time during the interview did he mention that he has won nine…yes nine…Emmy awards for writing, journalism, and political coverage. The truly best do not have to announce their accomplishments. I only found out about his achievements because I did what people are supposed to do…research.

In the past he appeared with Jane Hall of American University on *The O'Reilly Factor* in a weekly segment. While Ms. Hall appears less often, Bernie Goldberg still makes periodic appearances.

With that, I present my interview with the wise, witty, and spot-on accurate Bernie Goldberg.

1) Does the media get anything right? Are they good at anything, and if so, what?

BG: "I am not making a blanket indictment of all journalists all the time. They are not engaged in a conspiracy. They are engaged in something worse, and that is groupthink. Groupthink is worse because it institutionalizes biases. Conservatives looking for a conspiracy will not find one.

Some journalists do or did a great job. Tim Russert of *Meet the Press*, rest his soul, was very fair.

The media are at their worst when it comes to social issues. Social issues are near and dear to liberals' hearts, so they don't see biases. They see their views as reasonable. Anything liberal is the center, and anything in the real center is described as being on the right."

2) Who are your three journalistic heroes?

BG: "I don't have journalistic heroes. I think heroes are for kids. As I said, Tim Russert was great. As hard as I am on him, what I give Dan Rather credit for is that he has covered every major story since JFK. He does have courage. He goes to the dangerous places to cover news. The reason he is not on this list is because of his problem. He does not take serious criticism seriously.

If we can expand the list beyond journalists, I like Charles Krauthammer. He is great. Brett Stephens of the *Wall Street Journal* does good work. For hard news, Jack Taperow of ABC News does the job well."

3) Since you put out the list, if you could add to it, who else is screwing up America?

BG: "Excellent question. I am glad you asked that. Right now, at number freaking one, would be the District Attorney in the Duke rape case, Mike Nifong. Race is way too sensitive to fool around with. He did it for the worst reasons, to get reelected. At the time I wrote the book, I had Michael Moore at number one. However, if I were writing the book today, he would not be number one. My lists are based on time periods, and Michael Moore would be lower on the list now. Mike Nifong is simply a villain. He is a major villain.

There is one guy on MSNBC...I don't want to mention his name, but he is angry and mean-spirited. He brings people down when they see him, whether it be in real life or even on television. As I said, I am sure you can figure out a clever way to mention Keith Olbermann without me having to mention his name. It is not about being liberal. He is just plain nasty."

4) Who are some people that are good for America?

BG: "People we don't know. One man I admire is Aaron Feuerstein. He is an Orthodox Jew that owned Malden Mills in Massachusetts. When a fire burned Malden Mills to the ground, he kept the plant open and kept all of his employees on the payroll.

There is a Jewish group that collects money for Scandinavians who helped save lives during the Holocaust. Imagine being an elderly person, and then finding out that people you helped a half of a century ago are helping you in your golden years.

There are many good people. We don't know them, but they make the world a better place."

5) When Hamas and Fatah are fighting, I find it very difficult to take sides. I want them both to lose. In the same vein, who are you siding with between liberal Democrats Jon Stewart and Jim Cramer?

BG: "Jim Cramer. Cramer got a big call very wrong. Yet even many big conservative financial institutions got it wrong. Lots of people got it wrong. I know plenty of people who got it wrong. Cramer is one of them, but he is public.

Also, this was a cheap shot by Jon Stewart. Stewart waited until after Cramer criticized Barack Obama. I have met Jon Stewart twice. He is very polite, very civil, and very liberal.

Cramer is one of many that got it wrong, but because he is public, he takes it between the eyeballs."

6) Who are your three political heroes, be they American or global?

BG: "Tony Blair is one. He was courageous. He spoke eloquently, especially on saying that it was impossible for people to say that with regards to Muslim terrorists, even though they disapproved of the violence, that 'they understood.' That is contradictory, and Blair pointed this out brilliantly.

Newt Gingrich is one of the smartest people with regards to his ideas, but he could not win election to the presidency. He has too much baggage. However, he is a real thinker.

Bill Bennett is another one. I like smart conservatives. I like the ones that are civil, decent, and listen to the other side. Charles Krauthammer, who I have mentioned more than once, is fabulous. He was a licensed psychiatrist, and he was the one who coined the term 'Bush Derangement Syndrome.'"

7) If you had five minutes to talk to President George W. Bush or Vice President Dick Cheney, what would you say to them or ask them?

BG: "I would ask President Bush, with regards to the Iraq War, 'Was it worth it? Could we have contained Saddam?' We have four thousand dead Americans, and President Bush's popularity fell so low that it allowed Democrats to take over and shove their liberal agenda down our throats. If we could have contained Saddam Hussein, that might have been better for us economically, and President Bush would have had higher popularity. He would have been more beloved, which would have prevented the loss of congress and the White House. So I would ask him today if based on everything, if he felt the Iraq War was worth it."

8) Where do you see the media in twenty years, and what role will the blogosphere play? Will the *Jayson Blair Times* even exist in twenty years?

BG: "The mainstream media will continue to become less and less relevant. Their problem is that they refuse to be introspective. I have said before that the guys at 7/11 selling Slurpees and Camels to insomniacs are more introspective than the mainstream media. The Internet and cable television are killing newspapers and broadcast news.

I would be amazed if three evening newscasts even existed in the future. Newspapers in their current form may not exist in two years, much less twenty years. This is mainly due to technology, but also due to ideology.

As for the Web, the best and the most vile journalism can be found on the Web. The bad part is that people think that they can be nasty and vile, and that they do not have to do any research. If the worst of the Web takes hold, it will be like hell. It will be the dark corner of a lunatic asylum.

I hope that growing pains allow those relying on anonymity to grow up.

As for the *New York Times*, Bill O'Reilly thinks it will be gone in a year. I am going to boldly say that they will still exist in twenty years. They may not exist in the same format, but to the consternation of conservatives, I am predicting that they will survive."

9) Given that all conservatives must be categorized as either evil, or as complete imbeciles, with President George W. Bush somehow being both, I want to know about a conspiracy that might involve you since at some point you might become a target. I will just ask. She has not been on *O'Reilly* lately. What have you done to Jane Hall?

BG: "I will answer that off the record. I will tell you the story, but off the record."

(What I can say without revealing anything Bernie Goldberg told me is that Jane Hall is alive and well. Therefore, I will not be sending Angela Lansbury or Andy Griffith to his house to investigate. At the risk of being almost as lazy as a mainstream journalist on the nightly news, I am exonerating him and declaring this matter closed.)

10) How would you like to be remembered 100 years from now? What would you want people to say about Bernie Goldberg the person?

BG: "I was an honest critic of the profession that I spent my entire adult life in. I had courage. I wrote things that put me in jeopardy.

My advice to people is to do something you believe in just once in your life and you will feel better about yourself. You don't have to do it every week, or even twice in your life. Just do what you deeply believe at least once in your life.

In 1996, I wrote an op-ed about media bias. It changed my life, thankfully for the better.

I was an honest reporter who gave both sides a fair shot. I was an honest critic as well. I was a critic whose criticism of the media showed more than anything else how much I cared for my profession.

I meant well, and tried to do the right thing. I had courage. I hope people say that I stood up, did what I thought was right, and made the profession better for it."

I would like to thank Bernie Goldberg for his time. I am occasionally in his stomping grounds of Miami, and at some point I look forward to meeting him again.

Until I am a regular guest on *O'Reilly* myself, I will happily declare his best guest segments to be the ones where the mainstream media is given their castor oil by Bernie Goldberg.

They may never learn, but he is absolutely right to keep speaking out.

My friends and I will also be extending an invitation for him to join our unofficial group, the Zionist Crusader Alliance For World Domination. We don't actually do anything but sit and talk politics and football, but we are nominating Sir Charles of Krauthammer to lead the group.

Regardless of whether or not our membership increases by 33 percent, I will say that Bernie Goldberg is good for America, and great for his industry.

I wish him well always.

eric

The Academy Award Goes to…Oh, Who the Hell Cares!

The Academy Awards came and went. The Oscar for best insignificant narcissist goes to…some insignificant narcissistic. Who the hell cares? Not me.

I spent a weekend at the California State Republican Party Convention. There were no Hollywood celebrities present. It was excellent. I got to meet politicians that make decisions that affect many people. I prefer to talk to people that actually matter.

My flight did get me home in time to watch some of the Oscars, which of course I did not do. It was bad enough that *Desperate Housewives* was preempted. Fox News had reruns. Thankfully the NFL Network had the NFL Combine. Normally I do not watch that, but it was not the Oscars.

I was debating whether or not to put on the last ten to fifteen minutes of the broadcast with no sound on, like I do with the ninth inning of the seventh game of the World Series when there are two outs.

I am sure I could have just read whether or not Bill Clinton showed up to play the saxophone while John Kerry gushed about the heart and soul of America in a building filled with people that have neither.

Some say it is unfair to indict every person in Hollywood. After all, like Palesimians and liberals, why blame the 20 percent of entertainment industry professionals that are not drenched in toxicity? After all, 80 percent is not a majority. Let it go.

The reason why the industry is so disgusting is because left-wing politics long ago replaced quality.

The first thing that all Academy voters should be required to do is sign an oath declaring that they watched every movie that they voted on. If they are caught paying their relatives or others to watch the movies and report back to them, their voting privileges should be permanently revoked.

The Oscars are boring, predictable, and disgusting. Voters have a formula for what they like.

One way to get nominated is to play a homosexual. It cannot be just any homosexual. It must be a homosexual activist, and the activist must be a hero. If it is played by a left-wing activist, all the better. Personally I would like to see a movie made about Sean Penn. A conservative actor would play him, and make sure to show the part where he engages in domestic violence against his wife and assaults cameramen.[23] For "dramatic effect," he can be shown praising Alec Baldwin while a tape runs of Baldwin verbally abusing his daughter. I personally thought *Milk* was a movie about lactation. The same people that praised the *Vagina Monologues* as "groundbreaking" must have thought that a movie about breast milk would be "courageous."

Another way to get nominated is to play somebody that is dying from a politically correct disease. AIDS is a good choice. Cancer is not. After all, many homosexuals and drug users get AIDS. To really stir the emotional pot, the person has to suffer from discrimination, either from an evil corporation, vile Republican, or both.

Another option is to play a retard or a "handicapable" person. It works. They are politically correct. Overcoming a physical or mental illness, provided that the story tilts leftward, moves voters. Anti-war activists injured in battle make great Oscar nominees.

When the academy runs out of generic movies of leftists as heroes, the next option is to find an evil conservative villain. The actor playing the lead role should have a hostile attitude in real life toward Republicans. Anything attacking Republicans works. *Frost-Nixon* is a movie that takes place three years after Nixon resigns in disgrace. Talk about kicking the dog while he is down. A conservative bellowing, "I told you I didn't want to take any questions on Watergate!"[24] makes Academy voters cream their undies.

The last step is to ignore the movie altogether and find somebody that died "tragically" and "way too young."

The 2008 "Batman" movie was outstanding. It should have gotten nominations in every major category. Yet the movie was politically conservative. That is a non-starter for the Academy. Also, the Academy snobs would not think of deigning to let a "comic book" movie win where it counts.

The Dark Knight was a stunningly brilliant movie that should have given Oscar nominations to Morgan Freeman (Lucius), Michael Caine (Alfred the Butler), Christian Bale (Batman), and especially Aaron Eckhart (Harvey Two-Face). Another almost certainty behind Eckhart should have been Gary Oldman (Commissioner Gordon). Michael Caine has been praised in the past by the Academy, but that was for playing the lead role in a movie that pushed a pro-choice activism on abortion. The movie was marketed as a sweet movie about children in an orphanage, but the agenda was clear.

Heath Ledger deserved his nomination. He was excellent as well, although not as brilliant as Oldman or Eckhart. Yet he got the nomination because he died too young, and tragically. The Academy said this loudly.

Forgive me, but Heath Ledger was a dumb (redacted) who killed himself, either accidentally or in a suicide. That must not have any impact on the voters. If anything, it cheapens his nomination because had he lived, he would have been worthy of a nomination anyway.

I am tired of people who die this way being glorified, whether it be Janis Joplin, Jimmy Hendrix, Kurt Cobain, or Heath Ledger. Death should have no bearing on Emmys, Grammys, or Oscars.

When all else fails, foreign love stories are the answer. Anything foreign appeals to the Academy.

Whether it is Asians crouching about tigers and dragons, or some people from India falling in love, foreign lovers are all the rage. If there is no love story, political activists are a global sensation. One year it is Irish revolutionaries. The next year it is Tibet. The less the story matters in the real world, and the fewer the number of people that watch it, the greater the chances for a nomination.

The worst part of this fiasco is the self-congratulatory left-wing blather. In very tough economic times, the Academy tries to scale things down. They then congratulate themselves on how spectacular they are at scaling things down.

For those that truly care about the self-indulgent spoiled brats that make up the Academy, just walk outside. There will be people bent over just enough to treasure the aroma of their own rumpuses. If that does not work, follow the trail of cocaine powder.

At least the event eventually ends. Then the industry can get back to its day job of putting out left-wing cr@p and calling it art.

eric

Chapter 6: Financial Idiocy

I like my taxes the way I like my terrorists…dead and buried in the ground. Liberals claim that their mix of high taxes and excessive regulations actually works. This is why people are leaving New York and Michigan in droves and moving to Texas, Florida, and other areas where the tax rates are low. If liberals truly believe in their own solutions, they should be forced to continue living in their areas. Nobody wakes up in the morning and demands the right to move to Massachusetts.

The Capital Gains Tax Is Unethical

Mitt Romney came up with a sound policy proposal that all other Republicans should immediately embrace. I could care less where good ideas come from, provided that they are implemented.

Mr. Romney proposed to abolish the capital gains tax for anybody making less than $200 thousand per year. Good for you Mitt! Well done sir!

The capital gains tax is unethical. It is immoral, and should be killed outright.

The first myth is that people who receive income from financial markets are not actually "working." This is nonsense. Investing takes guts, character, and a very strong stomach. It is about taking risks, which is what this nation was founded upon. Investing is hard work. An entire financial services industry consists of professionals who are as vital to a person's financial health as a doctor or clergy person is to their physical and spiritual health.

The next myth is that a capital gains tax cut is a sop to the rich. This is sheer folly. Cutting taxes on everybody benefits everybody. The rich do not need to "give back." They already give back in the form of producing thousands of jobs. To quote the brilliant economist Dr. Thomas Sowell, "It is the thieves and criminals that should give back because they produce nothing."[25] If I am given a $1 thousand tax cut and a multi-millionaire is given a bigger tax cut, how does that hurt me? It doesn't.. I still benefit.

Republicans are scared to cut the capital gains tax for fear of being labeled as friends of the rich. I agree that the capital gains tax should not be cut. It should be eliminated altogether. Enter Mitt Romney. Mr. Romney realizes the need to disarm the criticism that cutting taxes benefits only the wealthy. He is proposing to eliminate the capital gains tax cut for those making under $200 thousand. I would prefer that he eliminate it for everyone, but this is still a major step in the right direction because it can actually be accomplished.

Buying stocks, commodities, or any other investment outside of treasury bills is risky. If I lose money, the government does not bail me out. Why should I be penalized for winning? We already have a graduated tax system.

In 2006, the Indianapolis Colts won the Super Bowl while the Oakland Raiders finished last. To try and redistribute success means that when the NFL Draft comes around, the Raiders pick first and the Colts pick last. That is sufficient. To require Colts quarterback and Super Bowl MVP Peyton Manning quit the Colts and join the Raiders would be insane.

The Democrats are socialists when it comes to taxes. They believe in Robin Hood economics, which has never worked anywhere. The pilgrims experimented with socialism, and it failed then as well. Societies function properly when people are given incentives to work hard. Human beings by nature are incentive driven.

One other fact that often gets overlooked is the concept of charity. Rich people give more money to charity because they can. Poor people cannot give to charity. It is not their fault. They just don't have enough by definition. Rich people can either tighten their belts or loosen them, and antagonizing the rich is a good way to hurt those that need rich people to survive. On December 31st, rich people often sell stocks in their portfolio that they believe will never recover. By creating these losses, they can reduce their capital gains, leaving more money in their pocket. Why should I object if 90 percent of their extra money is spent on themselves if the other 10 percent goes to charity (number picked by example)? I can't. If people are helping others, we should thank them, rather than condemn them for not giving more.

Nobody is guaranteed victory in the game of investing, or life. Punishing the lucky (skillful in many cases) winners by confiscating their profits through taxes only provides a disincentive to investing. Contrary to what liberals think, the stock market is investing, not greed. What the left calls investing is what most human beings call "spending." It is not the same thing, and using phony words does not turn a cat into a dog just because it is declared one.

America ceases to be a moral nation if we hurt those at the top out of sport, vengeance or jealousy. Low taxes benefit everybody. High tax environments cripple societies. Those who disagree should listen to French President Nicolas Sarkozy. Liberals admire the French. He wants France to emulate America from a tax standpoint. That should scream volumes.

Opponents of Romney will come up with their own plans, and he might unfairly lose some credit. I personally am less interested in who changed the world than the fact that it was done. Romney's opponents had better get on the ball. This policy proposal is one of the soundest ideas to come about in years. It must become a reality, regardless of who wields power.

The left wants to spend your money. To do this they have to steal it. They will call it taxing and investing, but it is stealing. I worked hard to build an investment portfolio. I will hold onto my investments for decades if I have to do so. I will not be able to take profits, but what is the point of taking profits if they will just be confiscated anyway?

The capital gains tax is a vile, horrible entity. Like liberalism itself, it must be crushed into nonexistence and wiped from the face of the Earth.

eric

Who Regulates the Regulators?

America is Litigation Nation.

One of the most insulting movies ever made was Oliver Stone's *Wall Street*. A young stockbroker played by Charlie Sheen cuts corners to achieve success. He becomes crooked. He is rightfully punished, and near the end of the movie lets his father know that he is about to begin a jail sentence. So far, so good. The father, played by the ever pious Martin Sheen, says something to his son that every financial professional should find deeply offensive. Rather than criticize the specific behavior of his son, he instead remarks that when his son gets out of jail, he should, "get a real job instead of living off of the buying and selling of others."[26]

In one fell swoop, an entire profession was indicted, at least verbally. In this warped view of the world, financial professionals are all thieves, crooks, and liars. Those that regulate them are pure white knights in shining armor. Yet the regulators are often more dangerous than the financial professionals. The financial professionals have to answer to the regulators.

Who regulates the regulators?

Financial firms are under attack from three different sources of regulation. The first source consists of fly-by-night operations in the form of "lawsuit firms" that operate outside the legal system. The second source consists of self-regulatory agencies and government agencies. The third source consists of self-aggrandizing politicians. All three of these entities have abused their public trust.

There was a time when the financial services industry needed to be cleaned up. Regulators came in, did their jobs effectively, and helped put crooked firms out of business. At some point regulators became victims of their own success. The firms that survived realized that they had to play by the rules to stay in business. Playing by the rules is exactly what most of them did. They hired Compliance Departments. They taught ethics. They helped combat money laundering. They fired their own bad apples to protect their reputations.

Most people would see this as positive. To regulators, this is a disaster. Regulators exist to get rid of the bad seeds. When too many of those bad seeds are removed, regulators then lack things to actually do. They become less necessary. Rather than fire themselves, they need to create problems that they can then solve.

Problems such as insider trading, churning, and unauthorized trading are simply less common among firms because they know that those infractions are potential death knells. Talk to any Wall Street firm that is being harassed because one customer order might have three time stamps instead of four, or that a form is filled out with a fine point blue pen instead of a medium point black pen. Then concede that the regulatory system is out of control.

The first group of unchecked regulators that are causing problems are firms specifically set up to sue financial services firms. A firm that my company regularly did business with came under attack from the stockbrokerage equivalent of ambulance chasers.

I personally spoke to one of the employees of this "stockbrokerage recovery" firm. I asked him if he was an actual attorney. He said that did not matter. I asked him if he had a Series 7 stockbroker's license. He said that was also immaterial, and became irritated with such probing questions. He made it clear that he wants to settle every single case. He has no desire to ever go to trial. He knows that big companies roll over (he used stronger language), and he freely admits targeting companies that have a history of paying.

This fellow criticizes organizations that engage in "cold-calling" to find clients. Yet the business model of this stockbrokerage recovery firm is cold-calling people. They buy leads, call people up, and actively try to solicit them into suing their stockbroker. The firm takes the case on contingency. One client confessed to me that the firm receives 50 percent of any judgment. This is significantly higher than what most attorneys receive.

In speaking to this same employee, I pointed out that the statute of limitations on his case had already passed. I also pointed out that the firm he was suing had virtually nothing to do with the client, and that he was suing the wrong firm. I additionally pointed out that the client never purchased stocks in the account in question. He purchased options on commodities, which is a completely different financial product outside the jurisdiction of FINRA (formerly NASD). Therefore, he was trying to sue in the wrong court.

The employee seemed uninterested and uneducated as to how commodities worked, and made it clear that going after the stockbrokerage firm with deeper pockets in the hope of a settlement made more sense than going after the commodity brokerage firm that held the actual account. When I pointed out these facts to the client, their response was, "I am not paying any money for this service, so I don't care."

Lastly, this supposedly successful firm is located slightly away from Wall Street, in a place known as Coney Island. Coney Island is great if one wants to ride the Cyclone, walk on the Boardwalk, or eat a hot dog from the original Nathan's. It is not a business district. The "office" of this stockbrokerage recovery firm was the equivalent of a shack. It had a paper sign on the door, which was partially obscured by the much larger sign of another company that apparently sells kitchenware.

What is most troublesome about this firm is that they do not appear to answer to any professional organization. Attorneys and stockbrokers answer to the ABA and FINRA, respectively. Various stockbrokerage recovery firms such as this seem to have unchecked power.

The best way for firms to handle these firms is to refuse to negotiate with them. Once the person representing the firm filing the claim declines to state that they are an attorney, all conversation by the stockbrokerage firm being sued should cease.

If unlicensed stockbrokerage recovery firms are ants, then regulatory organizations are elephants. I have dealt with many regulatory agencies over the years, and they have truly become victims of their own success. Several examples of claims or suggestions that regulators such as the National Futures Association (NFA) have made are below.

1) My firm was told to have procedures in place for selling a specific type of financial product. Our firm explained that we do not transact in the type of financial product in question. We were told that this was still a "deficiency." We had to have procedures in place so that we could regulate a financial product that we had never sold, and most likely would never sell. Imagine the reaction from the medical community if heart surgeons were told to have plastered on their office walls the solutions to all medical issues concerning podiatry.

2) My firm was told that they overheard a broker discuss a goal of doubling the client's money. The regulator then explained that they specifically heard the phrase "50 percent." We explained that doubling is 100 percent, not 50 percent. As sheepish as regulator Melissa Glassbrennner was at this point, she included the error in her final report.

3) One branch office of my firm was told that we were in violation because we did not have a manager or supervisor on site.

Employees must be monitored. We explained that the manager was in the bathroom. The regulators including Ms. Glassbrenner acknowledged this, and yet included it in their report as another deficiency.

4)   One regulator asked loaded questions of our employees in an attempt to deliberately trick them into incriminating themselves and the firm. English was not the first language of some employees. They were quite scared at being taken into a conference room with no windows. One broker was asked if he had ever been "disciplined," meaning had he ever been found guilty of a regulatory violation. The broker answered in the affirmative. The regulators then tried to go onto the next question, but I intervened. I explained to the broker that only compliance and regulatory issues mattered, not human resources sanctions. The broker then explained that they had been disciplined by the firm for tardiness, which is not a regulatory or compliance violation of any kind.

5)   One client wrote a check to our firm that bounced. This caused the broker's commissions to be taken away. The stereotype of wealthy stockbrokers with golf clubs and putting greens in their office taking advantage of poor elderly people on Social Security is not always the true picture. Often it is multi-million dollar clients on their own private golf courses trying to cheat rookie stockbrokers who are trying to survive on less than $24 thousand per year. The particular wealthy aforementioned client kept promising to pay, and kept reneging. My firm sued in small claims court and won a judgment. Only after this occurrence did the client then retaliate by going to regulators and claiming malfeasance by the firm. The regulators were aware of the facts in front of them, because I proactively discussed this with Ms. Glassbrenner herself. The case was allowed to proceed. Facts did not matter.

6)   Some clients in the financial services industry have been actively solicited by regulators to file complaints. On more than one occasion, a client informed me that they filed a complaint because a regulator called them and told them that they should. As an inducement, the client was given information regarding the company that was false (The client mentioned Ms. Glassbrenner by name, but she is only one cog in a corrupt NFA machine). A thirty second trip to the Internet would have verified this. As for why regulators do this, complaints require both sides to pay

filing fees. These fees go in the pockets of the regulatory agencies. The regulatory agencies have a direct financial incentive to have more complaints. Lastly, the client was given information by the regulators regarding other clients, which is at best irregular, and possibly illegal. Firms know never to discuss a client account with another client without written permission. Regulators especially should respect this privacy issue.

I could write hundreds of pages alone on the examples listed above. When my firm needed help from the regulators, such as having them review a one page document to make sure that it was in compliance, this often took several weeks. When the regulators had a document request from us, they demanded an answer in seventy-two hours. This can be crippling to a financial institution from a productivity standpoint.

People who work on Wall Street should be trembling in fear at this. It is the equivalent of a slow-bleed strategy, death by a thousand cuts. Some would say that FINRA and the NFA are regulated by the Securities and Exchange Commission (SEC) and Commodity Futures Trading Commission (CFTC), but this oversight is minimal. The SEC and CFTC do answer to congress, but firms will not bring a claim before congress out of fear. Regulators are the good guys, corporations are the evil bad guys, and if the claim against the regulatory agency is unsuccessful, the regulators will come back even more determined. This is analogous to trying to "kill the king." If you only wound the king, he will come back after you with his entire regulatory army.

If regulatory agencies are elephants, then crusading politicians are Godzilla. One example of this would be former New York Governor Eliot Spitzer.

Mr. Spitzer wreaked havoc on Wall Street when he was the attorney general of New York. He rode in on his stallion and built his career around the evil enemy of Wall Street. There was some corruption. Like any other organization, Wall Street had bad apples. Those regulating and enforcing laws still must stay within the confines of those very laws themselves.

Mr. Spitzer was alleged to have threatened Wall Street executives over the telephone. Either they "played ball," or he would sue them. One CEO of a large insurance company finally had enough of Mr. Spitzer's bullying.[27] He went public to the newspapers regarding Mr. Spitzer's heavy-handed tactics. His company stayed intact.

Too many companies roll over because they are scared to death of a governor who is using his crucifixion of them to become President of the United States.

The fact that Mr. Spitzer was brought down by a financial scandal (it was about possible money laundering, not sex) does not change the fact that for too long he was unregulated, unchecked, and unrestrained. On a federal level, the United States government harassed IBM and Microsoft until both companies caved. Only when Intel fought back hard did Attorney General Janet Reno back down.[28]

Wall Street must start fighting back. The regulatory climate in the financial services industry has gotten out of control. I am not arguing that we stop regulating the industry. Regulation is necessary. I am advocating that more oversight be given to those providing the initial oversight. Bernie Madoff was regulated, but the regulators overseeing him were as bad as he was.[29]

The regulators must be more regulated themselves.

Financial services firms actually produce goods and provide services. They are the economic engine that drives America.

Stockbrokerage recovery firms, regulatory agencies, and government officials do not produce anything. They exist solely because corporate America exists. They play an important role in society, but without corporations there are no regulators. Destroying corporate America would destroy America itself. Productive people understand this. In tough economic times, corporations have to lay off employees. It is unfortunate, but a necessary evil of the business cycle. Regulators should be required to do the same. They should not be allowed to have bloated budgets pursuing frivolous and open-ended investigations about non-matters just to stay employed.

To paraphrase Oliver Stone, many of these regulatory employees need to get real jobs in the private sector learning how business benefits society, instead of living off of the buying and selling of others.

Guilty firms can and should be punished. No innocent person should ever be put in prison. No falsely accused corporation should ever be put out of business. Firms that are innocent of accusations trumped up against them should fight back tooth and nail.

Otherwise, firms can roll over and continue to end up black and blue because they filled out a form in blue when it should have been filled out in black.

eric

Celebrity Apprentice–Donald Trump Gets It

A *Celebrity Apprentice* was chosen. After six seasons of contestants scrambling to win the right to work for Donald Trump, the seventh and eighth seasons of *The Apprentice* contained only celebrities playing for charity.

I have always admired Donald Trump I like his reasoning. He likes top talent, and merit does matter. He likes people with advanced degrees. He likes people that are driven to succeed. In determining who to keep and who to fire, his rationale is usually brilliant. I have become a stronger employee. When I am in the boardroom, I will argue tooth and nail for what I believe in, and not give a single inch when I am right.

Most importantly, while I am a decent human being, I am not interested at work in being liked. I am interested in getting the job done. As I said to a receptionist once, "I am not warm and fuzzy. I am effective."

Donald Trump is effective. Yes, he likes to do things in grand style. Yes, style is a major part of everything he does. Yet my admiration for Mr. Trump is because when the rubber meets the road, substance wins. In Donald Trump's world, it is all about merit. He wants the best and brightest. He also wants the toughest and those who work the hardest.

I praised him for selecting Piers Morgan to be the original *Celebrity Apprentice*. Piers was not the most likable (although I thought he was fabulous). He was simply the best. The whole point of *Celebrity Apprentice* is to raise money for charity. Piers Morgan raised the most money.

Piers took a bruising to his humanity from a woman named Omarosa, whose only skill until her stint on *The Apprentice* seemed to be bungling her way to the top. She was even fired from the Clinton administration for incompetence. I did not know it was even possible to be too incompetent for that group.

Omarosa made fun of Piers Morgan's family, his teeth, and even his sexuality. Mr. Morgan just kept raising money.

The 2009 version of *Celebrity Apprentice* was even more vicious. The villain role vacated by Mr. Morgan was filled by World Poker Champion Annie Duke.

I admit bias. Every time Annie Duke is mentioned in the same sentence as the words "poker," and "branding," I imagine what it would be like to use the instrument to imprint my initials on her (redacted).

Now about cattle prods…oh wait, wrong column. Back to Annie Duke. She is gorgeous, smart, and a mother of four children. She is thirty-eight, looks twenty-eight, and runs circles around weaker candidates on the show.

Joan Rivers referred to Annie Duke as Adolf Hitler. As the son of a holocaust survivor, I find that deeply offensive. Joan and Melissa Rivers are not known for their grace and dignity.

The feud started when Annie Duke decided to align herself with *Playboy* Playmate (not literally, unfortunately) Brandy Roderick against Melissa Rivers. The logic was that Brandy was seen as the weaker player. By getting Melissa Rivers out of the way, Annie would have a smoother ride to the finish line.

There is nothing illegal about this. It's a game for crying out loud. Joan screamed at Annie, bellowing that she was a "poker player,"[30] as if that was supposed to mean something bad.

What Joan and Melissa Rivers were actually complaining about was that Annie Duke was playing the game better.

That is merit. That is why Donald Trump fired Melissa Rivers and kept Annie Duke. Like Omarosa before her, Melissa Rivers went into a tirade that would make the late baseball manager Billy Martin proud.

Tossing around f-bombs as if she were Rahm Emanuel, she spent several weeks whining and complaining that she was not popular. She kept saying that watching Annie Duke and Brandy Roderick freeze her out "reminded her of high school."[31]

While she was complaining, the other two women were raising money.

In an act of desperation, the crying Rivers Joan and Melissa actually thought that Donald Trump would frown upon Annie Duke being "unladylike." She cursed people out over the telephone when she felt they were trying to screw her out of a victory.

So what? She was successful. This is about merit, not methods. Does anybody in their right mind think that Trump cries in the boardroom in real life? Sometimes he has to rip into people. The only thing that matters is results.

I looked at Melissa Rivers explaining over and over how unfair life was, and wondered if she understood that most people do not have fame and fortune thrust on them at birth.

The real bitterness of Melissa Rivers was that she could not accept the cold, hard truth. Annie Duke and Brandy Roderick were better than she was. They are better looking, better acting, and better at raising money.

Raising money is what Trump wants. Despite notions when the show started several years ago that he would simply reward the hottest women, this did not happen.

Every once in awhile he does appear to leave the reservation. He has a bias toward conflict. Despite the fact that executives praised model Carol Alt as being basically perfect, he fired her solely because he wanted Piers Morgan and Trace Adkins to face each other. They disliked each other, which made for more drama.

Clint Black seemed to be the beneficiary of being a troublemaker. He would have been fired weeks earlier, except that other candidates raised less money. T from TLC and Chloe Kardashian were fired for suspect reasons.

Yet most of the time, Trump gets it dead-on right. Melissa Rivers yelled, yelped, griped, screamed, cursed, whined, and adjectived.

Annie Duke simply looked Trump in the eye and explained that she was the best.

All the hate speech by the Rivers hydra could not alter the numbers.

Men who don't follow the show, if given a choice, would rather paddle Annie Duke over Melissa Rivers.

Adolescent male fantasies aside, even Donald Trump does not factor that into his decision-making.

His criteria is simple. Can you do the d@mn job?

In a world where every minority group claims victimhood, there are still places where merit matters.

Past *Apprentice* winners ranged from the brilliant Randall Pinkett (black), to Kendra (woman), to Bill Rancic (white male). They won because they were the best. With Randall, you could tell in the first episode that he was far better than everybody else. He was also the most likable.

Donald Trump is not against diversity, but diversity can be accomplished without sacrificing skill and talent.

It is about being the best. Those who are not the best get sent home.

That is why Annie Duke kept racking up chips and why Melissa Rivers was cashed out.

Neither Melissa Rivers nor her Hitler-spouting mother got it.

Annie Duke gets it.

As for Donald Trump, he absolutely still gets it.

In a world where emotions trump (small t) quality, Donald Trump reminds us that merit matters.

Meritocracy. That is worth celebrating.

eric

Markets Drop, Liberals Celebrate

The stock market dropped eight hundred points in one day, the biggest one-day drop ever in terms of points. It did recover to finish down three hundred-seventy points, but eventually dropped over 50 percent from its high. Ordinary Americans were concerned. Liberals were popping champagne corks in celebration.

For liberals, success requires failure. Bad news for ordinary Americans is splendid news for liberals.

Republicans controlled the White House, and if it would have helped get Barack Obama elected over John McCain, liberals would have cheered the stock market dropping to zero.

I personally am not worried. I am well diversified, and thankfully young enough to be able to wait twenty to thirty years. Not everybody has that time horizon, but those with fifteen years or more of earning power should calm down. This is not 1929. It is not the Great Depression despite what the *Jayson Blair Times* says.

Before getting to the politics of this situation, let's start with some hard-core finance. Wake up. I can try and explain this without being boring. This problem was caused because people tried to remove risk from the markets. This always fails, and increases the damage in the long run.

The 2008 bailout package was a terrible piece of legislative garbage. It deserved to go down in flames as Lehman did. The entire rationale for the package was that without it, financial markets would collapse. This argument is... (grabbing a megaphone)...

GARBAGE!

Doing nothing was the right thing to do. It is what George Washington and the founding fathers wanted. Governments cannot affect supply and demand or strong-arm financial markets. Markets do what they want, regardless of whether governments need to get reelected. Perhaps Barack Obama can call the situation "unacceptable," and simply tell the markets to be more polite, as he wants to do with Armageddonijad in Iran. Even John McCain fell victim to the notion that "doing something" meant doing something helpful.

Presidential candidates can be allowed the occasional pander bear moment. Congress aggressively pushed the bailout package. Every member who voted yes should be pushed out of an airplane without a bailout package of their own.

How did we get in this mess? Was it conservatism and deregulation? Absolutely, if one has no grasp whatsoever of facts.

Some think that because they "read stuff," that they "know things." I do this for a living. I have been in the industry for fifteen years. My opinion matters. Yours…well…enough said.

This problem was caused by excessive regulation. Companies like Fannie Mae and Freddie Mac should not even exist in America. They are like every other liberal parasite in America, from PBS to NPR. Leftists despise the private sector, and wanted government in the home lending business.

Businesses have criteria, and they exist to make money. They are not laboratories for social experiments. Fannie and Freddie were ordered to make loans to more minorities, particularly blacks. For some reason, even though Jews are a true minority in terms of world population percentage, they never get "minority" benefits. Perhaps we have not suffered enough, but that is for another time.

Leftists concluded that not enough blacks owned homes. America was therefore a racist nation as long as Republicans were in charge. To avoid having Jesse Jackson and Al Sharpton marching in the streets (before Jesse threatened to castrate a black man who wanted to succeed without preaching racism and victimhood), bad loans were made.

President Bush allowed this to happen, and he ironically never got the credit when black home ownership was at an all-time high. He naturally got the blame when the housing bubble burst, even though every bubble bursts by sheer definition alone.

Irresponsible buyers were allowed to buy due to political correctness. Some would argue that helping more blacks own homes is positive. Those people ignore the end result of forced equality of outcome instead of opportunity. Once again the left helped blacks reach levels of financial misery not seen since before conservatives passed welfare reform in 1996.

1996 was also the year that Phil Gramm, a politically incorrect former senator and economics professor…one of the few people that actually does know what he is talking about…led the repeal of Glass-Steagall. Repealing this law is not why we are hurting. It was what prevented financial Armageddon. Bank Of America could not have bought Merrill Lynch if this law still existed.

Liberal do-gooders figured out that even if black Americans suffered, a bad economy hurts everybody. At least we are now closer to equality.

There is a more sinister reason why liberals love shared misery. George W. Bush was president, and the entire Democratic Party platform was hatred of George W. Bush.

This is a man who freed millions of people and gave two nations in the Middle East a chance at humanity and dignity. This is a man who healed the nation after the worst terrorist attack on American soil.

This is a man who was gracious to people who wanted to destroy him and grind him into dust. His own supporters are frustrated by his refusal to verbally bash their skulls in.

The left hates him. They would rather destroy this economy than risk giving up the chance to destroy him.

They would rather lose a winnable war than allow George W. Bush to win anything.

They would rather lose an American economy and a war than lose an election.

Am I saying that many on the left do not care about what is best for America?

I do not have to say this. They say it themselves.

Ask conservatives what they want for America. They want to win the War on Terror. The left wants to end it. The right wants to win it.

Conservatives also want to lower taxes for everybody, regardless of race, religion, gender, or sexual orientation. Whether one is gay, black, or Jewish, tax cuts help them all, especially if they are small business owners.

What do liberals care about? Mainly abortion.

Without taking sides in the culture wars, ask most feminists in this country if they truly care about anything besides abortion. They will try to think of something else, but that is what they care about. Occasionally they care about animals and trees, provided that those animals and trees do not bring new animals or trees into the world.

For those who care about more than just trees, bunny rabbits and zygotes, here is the plain truth.

An economic collapse hurts everybody. This means fewer abortion doctors. If terrorists attack and kill everybody in a multi-hundred mile radius, they may end up blowing up abortion clinics, animal shelters, and even innocent trees (Although I maintain the trees and animals may not be innocent, and had it coming).

Liberals live in a black and white world where everybody on the left is virtuous and everybody on the right is evil.

Kwame Kilpatrick extends the misery of Detroit for decades, and the left blames George W. Bush in between bouts of blaming Ronald Reagan.

Ray Nagin and Kathleen Blanco fall apart in New Orleans, and the left blames George W. Bush.

Black home ownership rises, and President Bush gets no credit. The bubble bursts and he gets all the blame.

Perhaps the left might want to blame Franklin Raines, the former CEO of Fannie Mae and advisor to Barack Obama. He is an advisor, despite protests to the contrary.

Then Nancy Pelosi and Harry Reid tried to ram the mother of all disasters down American throats. House Republicans tried to stop it, but did not have the votes.

What did the market do? It dropped anyway solely because it wanted to drop. Markets care about functioning properly, even if it affects elections.

The left needed to win the 2008 election. Optimism was not allowed anywhere. Once Barack Obama was elected, everything became fine. The markets recovered and he got the credit, even though he contributed nothing. This is the 1992 Bill Clinton economic plan. Be in the right place at the right time, get lucky, and take all the credit.

Obama's win ended homelessness in America. It might exist, but the media will not write about it. According to a chart I read, homeless people disappeared in 1993 and reappeared in January of 2001. They will return again upon Republicans winning again.

If the stock market had risen with John McCain as president, it would have been because of the bailout package that Democrats claim is theirs and theirs alone. After Obama's election, the market rise (after a violent crash) was solely because of him. A market collapse under John McCain would have been because he is George W. Bush's twin brother. The market collapse under Obama was because he inherited a mess. The market hit an all-time high under George W. Bush, but that gets discounted.

The left controls the cultural institutions in America, including the schools. They teach that George W. Bush destroyed America. They cite Oliver Stone, Michael Moore, and the *Jayson Blair Times* as evidence. Children will not learn that those who use government to control markets are repeatedly wrong, and those who let free markets reign benefit.

Truth is not what motivates the left. They want to win elections. That is the end, not the means. Even if what they create fails, such as the Great Society, they just claim success anyway. Even if Ronald Reagan creates an eighteen-year bull market thanks to lower tax rates, the left says he is wrong anyway.

The left blames Ronald Reagan, George W. Bush, Dan Quayle, Sarah Palin, and John Ashcroft, who has nothing to do with economic policy.

As the market drops, liberals can take comfort in knowing that they now have more reasons to convince people about the evils of George W. Bush. Who cares about making society better when the left can invest their money in voodoo dolls of Republicans?

The left will hold hearings to determine how to blame President Bush for a crisis that the left perpetuated. The left will rail in front of the cameras about greedy CEOs and crooked lenders, when the truth is that Christopher Dodd and Barney Frank should be investigated thoroughly, and possibly given jail time.

The rage that has engulfed the left has spread like colon cancer, or as we call it in failed neighborhoods, community organizers. Now they will have to destroy Sarah Palin the way they did Dan Quayle to distract from their own perpetual failures.

The left will have to destroy this economy and cripple us militarily because American success cannot be allowed if conservative Republican success comes with it.

Conservatives benefit when we all benefit.

Liberals benefit when people remain trapped in a downward spiral of dependency on government.

This is why liberals cannot govern, win a war, or help an economy.

They cannot fix things, because they only know how to destroy. Their existence depends on destruction.

I would rather crush liberalism than crush America itself.

eric

The Krauthammer Index

In the middle of a speech, I pointed out that nobody knows everything. Then out of nowhere, unscripted, I fliply added, "well, except for Charles Krauthammer." The audience laughed, and most of them nodded in agreement.

I think about this not just because I have too much free time, but because I find myself admiring those that do things better than everybody else. I marveled how basketball player Michael Jordan played the exact same game by the exact same rules as every other player, but somehow produced far superior results. Wayne Gretzky did it in hockey.

While sports are entertainment, intellect can help improve the world. There are many bright people, but for some reason a select few are just astonishingly brilliant. I am in awe of them. I went to good schools and have an advanced degree, yet do not see myself approaching them by the intellectual equivalent of a country mile.

I keep hearing that nobody knows everything. When I listen to Charles Krauthammer I think, "Maybe this guy really does know everything."

When I met Sir Charles of Krauthammer in 2008, I recommended that he be knighted by the Queen. Given his humility, perhaps he should share the official name of my newly created intelligence index. Most indexes contain at least two parties.

It was not easy finding a worthy partner, but the thinkers at the *Wall Street Journal*…they know everything. I used to say that the *Wall Street Journal* is never wrong, but then somebody would cherry pick a column, most likely written by a token liberal.

Learning is about access to information. Some sources are so accurate that once one sees the name at the front or the back of the article, the content can just be accepted as fact.

For those who think the Goldman Sachs, JP Morgan, or Morgan Stanley indexes are what should be traded, I would add only one item to one's intellectual portfolio.

It is in that respect that I present the *Wall Street Journal*/Charles Krauthammer Index, or *WSJ*/Krauthammer Index. For short it can be referred to as the Krauthammer Index.

As the self-appointed manager of this index, I will now roll out the initial holdings, with their percentage correlation.

Using Mr. Krauthammer as the standard scale of one hundred, others that have high correlation are added to this non-diversified portfolio. With intellect, diversification is not desired. Barack Obama has low correlation with this index, but Nancy Pelosi and Barbara Boxer have perfect negative correlation. They know virtually nothing.

Here are some more holdings.

Dr. Thomas Sowell knows virtually everything. He has about a 99 percent correlation with the overall portfolio. He should be read in abundance.

Larry Kudlow also has sky-high correlation. Follow his lead.

Dr. Walter Williams is brilliant, but he needs to take a higher profile. Being right is important. Communicating it to the masses spreads the rightness.

Although he is too young to have the silver hairs that Cicero possessed, age should at some point allow Capitalist Pig Jonathan Hoenig to be on this list.

Alan Greenspan would have been higher in this portfolio, but he admitted he was wrong when he was not wrong. He did not stick to his convictions, allowing the pressure to get to him.

Goldman Sachs could have been on this list years ago, butt any company run by Jon Corzine is disqualified. The company deserves points for firing him, but they still haven't learned.

On military matters, three people are worthy of being part of the Krauthammer Index.

In no particular order, when Colonel David Hunt, Colonel Ralph Peters, and General David Petraeus speak, just sit there and take notes. One can fact check in the beginning, but that will soon grow tedious. These people simple know what they are talking about.

From a politics standpoint he could rate higher, but as a private citizen advocating policy, Newt Gingrich has a solid grasp of history and domestic issues.

If there is a member of the media that merits being on this list, I have not met them. Bernie Goldberg can be considered.

In addition to the *Wall Street Journal*, the *New York Post* has high correlation with the Krauthammer Index.

Norman Podhoretz has well over 90 percent correlation with the Krauthammer Index.

I am not sure that a single politician merits inclusion, but Rudy Giuliani, Benjamin Netanyahu, and Vice President Dick Cheney are worth some consideration. If one measures them in a relative strength chart against Joe Biden, they rank higher.

From a legal standpoint, Chief Justice John Roberts has about a 99 percent correlation with the WSJKI. Justice Antonin Scalia also has a significantly high correlation. Sonia Sotomayor, whose entire career by her own admission has been mediocre, ranks higher than Boxer and the Pelosiraptor, which says little. She also ranks higher than Biden, which may mean even less.

There you have it America. Own as many shares as possible in these intellectual titans. Read and digest their newspaper articles. Spread them to the four corners of the Earth as gospel.

Although I have a long way to go, I am convinced that I will be a brighter individual once I place my entire intellectual portfolio in the WSJKI.

Do not diversify. Just stick with the Krauthammer Index.

Think and grow rich.

eric

Power and Pressure

Before getting to football, I am thinking about what it all means. I am not talking about Fort Hood, Texas or the Virginia Tech massacre. I will never make sense of those. I grieved like everybody else.

I certainly don't mean health care because most votes mean nothing. President Obama speaks, as if that results in real news.

Between all of this and the unemployment rate, I am treasuring solace and thinking about what it all means, in my own little way.

I am thinking about power and pressure.

I had the extremely good fortune awhile back of spending time with a brunette whose brains were matched only by a set of (redacted) and (redacted) that I eventually got to play with.

(Hence the words "extremely good fortune.")

She was over forty, but was no cougar. If anything, it took a decent amount of persuading on my part. As I was trying to explain to her through my actions that she needed to remove her clothing, she made some comments that led to a deep conversation.

When the conversation was over, I finally did get to play body bongo drums with her (redacted). While that memory will stay with me for some time, the conversation will stay with me much longer.

(Or at least almost as long.)

She remarked that I lived in a very nice place. She lamented that so many people like me got to live in nice places while so many like her struggled.

While I have been accused (justifiably so) of letting anything a hot woman says go unchallenged, on this night substance would trump style. Her comment bothered me. It needed to be challenged.

I live in America, the wealthiest nation on Earth. I live in Los Angeles, one of the most glamorous cities. It has poor parts, but I live in the nice area of LA. The very street I live on is the dividing line that everybody asks about. When a girl wants to get to know me, they ask if I live north or south of this street. I tell them I live on it.

They react with pleasant surprise as they make me reiterate that I do live right on the street that divides the city. I am three blocks from Beverly Hills, but Beverly Hills is rich people that want to be seen. Three blocks away means my postal address says Los Angeles. This is for wealthy people who desire anonymity.

I live in a high rise condo building. The penthouse people have a view of the city. I have a great view of others who have a better view. I wish the mayor would get rid of the building across the street. I am facing the city, and do have a good enough view.

At no time has this ever let me lose perspective. This is a wealthy area, but I was never wealthy. Like many people, I was broke when I graduated college.

When I moved into this area in 1996, I did not even have my own bedroom. Four guys lived in a two bedroom apartment. I could have gotten a studio apartment (the equivalent of a "loft" that only starving artists could glorify), but I wanted a big living room. Sharing a bedroom was a non-issue, even though I had my own room my whole life growing up and in college. The apartment was like a fraternity house, which I never experienced.

The building has a heated pool, a Jacuzzi, and tennis courts. It has twenty-four-hour security guards. Yet I was broke. When one of the guys had a girl come over, the other three guys would scatter. A woman would come over, see one guy in a two bedroom condo, and be impressed. My having a Jacuzzi allowed me to entertain women far more beautiful than I ever had a right to be around.

Somebody once asked me if it was wrong to use my place to attract women. I remembered advice from my Orthodox rabbi grandfather (rest his soul). He used to sell indulgences. When asked if it was unethical for him to sell passes into heaven, he responded, "No. It is unethical for people to buy them." I miss him. When asked if it was shallow for me to use my place to attract women, I would reply, "No. It was wrong for them to be impressed."

I still live in the same building fourteen years later, although in a bigger place on a higher floor. I have my own large master bedroom with closet space that makes women envious. It never occurred to me, but in the stockbrokerage industry, the phrase "fake it until you make it" is common. My friend remarked to me two years ago that somewhere along the line I "really did become that guy living in the high rise condo."

Until he said it, it did not hit me. I was not faking it any more. I had actually achieved the status I was striving for.

It did not come easy. I worked hard. When I started out as a twenty-two-year old stockbroker, I arrived in the office at 5:00 AM and stayed until 7:00 PM. Four days of fourteen hours was followed by a half-day on Friday, which was still eight hours. Come 1:00PM, we were out for the weekend. I had the whole Friday to play, which I spent sleeping before going out.

Like many, I scratched and clawed. If it was not for the Jacuzzi, I am not sure I would have gotten a single date, certainly not from the caliber of women that came over. The security guards were incredibly kind to me. It made an impression when the woman would arrive in her car, and the guard would say, "Ms. (name redacted) is here." Nobody came up without a phone call. That gave me a few extra minutes to make sure the place was spotless clean.

One time a woman that I was pursuing for two years finally came over. The guard called up and said, "Ms. (name redacted) is here…and she is very beautiful. You are one lucky man." She was in a great mood before she even reached my door.

Yet this is not about women.

It is about life, and what it takes to live in this area.

It costs a high price. Everything comes at a price.

At any minute, anything and everything could be taken away from me. It can happen to any of us.

The greater the power, the greater the pressure.

The stock market collapse of 2000 did not wipe me out, but it could have. I was lucky. The collapse of 2008 was even tougher, but through a combination of luck and skill I am still in the game.

I have always kept my expenses low, but financial time bombs hit all of us. I have loaned money to friends and borrowed money from them. Everything was paid back.

I have had the same friends my whole life. When we are sitting around the dinner table at a restaurant, some make more than me and some make less. It is impossible to tell us apart, which is how it should be.

Spending money does not mean wasting it. I bought a $2 thousand black leather sofa set for $6 hundred. The couple getting rid of it was simply too rich to care. One person in my building threw out a gorgeous marble table. One man's trash is another man's treasure. I still can't believe they got rid of it. My big screen television was worth $3 thousand at the time. I bought it for $8 hundred factory refurbished after doing plenty of research and getting a warranty.

I do not have anything remotely resembling millions of dollars in the bank. Yet I am surviving, and at times, thriving. More importantly, at the risk of excessive rhyming, I am always hard-driving. Sometimes I am too hard-driving.

Fear of failure drives me to succeed. I do not want what I have taken from me.

When I explained this to the forty-plus woman in my condo that night, we reached a very clear melding of the minds. She had a rough life, and knew what it was like to struggle. It does get easier, but it is never easy.

When we were done tasting the sweetness of life, she got up, straightened herself up, and went to the balcony to look at the view. I stared at her to look at the view. She said that what she saw was amazing. Still staring at her, I let her know that I thought she was amazing.

She gave me that look that told me to focus on something besides her fabulous (redacteds).

At this point I was staring at her because I did not want to look out the window. A few weeks later I would finally look outside and get some perspective. On this night I did not want to think about it.

Playing with her body brought me a brief respite from my worries. I wanted to just enjoy the moment, but as I told her, in forty-eight hours I had business to handle. I regretted having to wait two days to get started.

I just can't go back to being broke. When one is older, it is harder. I am only thirty-eight, but it all goes by rapidly.

As I kissed her goodnight, we both realized that what had overwhelmed us an hour earlier was just another metaphor for life.

The greater the power, the greater the pressure.

I have little relaxation, but zero regrets. This is the life I chose.

Everything must be earned. I am still learning and still working.

If I stop, the view and everything that comes along with it will be fleeting.

Getting it is tough. Keeping it is tougher.

She saw power. I felt pressure.

eric

Chapter 7: Sexual Idiocy

For those who appreciate a mature discussion of adult issues, chapter eight is only a few pages away. The bottom line is that Democrats use sex to sell their policies. Would it kill the Republican Party to have girls in red, white, and blue pasties running around with "support our troops" written on their bellies in edible crayon? I make so many sacrifices for America. Maybe I don't, but for the sake of argument let's pretend I do. Women can be sexy and politically liberal, provided they have laryngitis. I am proud to be the party of Sarah Palin and Michele Bachmann, and not the party of Madeline Albright and Helen Thomas.

eric aka the Tygrrrr Express

Republican Party Animals

This is not your Father's Republican Party.

An event in Los Angeles felt like Las Vegas, or at the very least, Sodom and Gomorrah with tax cuts.

It was fabulous.

A new "political" group has formed. Welcome to the world of the Republican Party Animals.

I would like to thank Scott Edwards and David Stein for bringing this group to several places in America, including Los Angeles. I would especially like to thank my friend Leo Bletnitsky for informing me of the event.

Several rock bands performed, including my friend Eric Porvaznik. He has previously done a takeoff on Neil Young's "Rocking in the Free World,"[32] with lyrics to "Blame Barack, It's Not a Free World."

This time he went after the liberals and their excessive lust for our tax dollars with the Georgia Satellites song, "Keep your hands to yourself."[33]

He then sang the standard versions of "I won't back down"[34] by Tom Petty before blowing the lid off of the place with a pair of AC/DC classics. "Dirty Deeds Done Dirt Cheap"[35] was perfect for this gathering, and "TNT"[36] had the whole crowd chanting "Oy! Oy! Oy!," which some thought was either 1980s Australian football star Jacko or Hebrew complaining. It was neither, since the "oy" was not followed by a "vey."

Scott Edwards described the people perfectly.

"We represent the smoking, drinking, cursing, gambling, and screwing wing of the GOP."

"Democrats enact smoking bans. Republicans say 'light 'em up.'"

"Democrats offer frigid feminists. Republicans have smart sexy women. They have Hillary. We have Sarah Palin."

Although I do enjoy traditional Republican rallies, the trapeze artist was a nice touch. So were the pole dancers, including the one with the delightful underclothing slogan "Got Pole?"

110

A "firedancer" named Angeldust dressed in pink and black. I used to think fire was made by rubbing two rocks or sticks together. She managed to rub other things together. Her skills with fire were incredible.

Comedy acts included my friends Evan Sayet and Ari David, in addition to myself.

Yet how do you follow that stuff?

My opening line summed it up.

"The Democrats have medicinal marijuana, but we Republicans have Angeldust."

I am a proud member of the debauchery wing of the GOP.

This is my kind of political party. The drinks and cigars flowed, the miniskirts of the ladies were hiked up, and the cleavage was barely contained.

(Social Conservatives might not like this, but if it gets young people to vote Republican, I say get them drunk and sexed out, and wheel their happy bodies into the voting booth to pull that lever. Leftists wheeled nursing home patients like my grandfather into the booth to vote Democrat, and my grandpa did not even get to have the fun first. We can always preach family values and morality after we win the election.)

If this is what we stand for, we should and will win in 2010, at least among the youth male vote. Heck, we will carry the entire male and non-uptight flaming feminist vote. There is no way the politically correct left is having this much fun.

All hail the Republican Party Animals!

eric

No More Grievance Summits

Now that President Obama has held a beer summit on race that was complete and utter nonsense (If it was truly important, Joe Biden would not have been invited), liberal *New York Post* columnist Kirsten Powers wants to hold a sexual summit. I was excited until I was informed that it was just a summit on sexism.

Lady Pandora, your box is wide open and waiting to be penetrated by men (and women apparently) bearing gifts in the form of stupid ideas.

Every activist group in the country is now gearing up for the next Yalta. Lesbian Vegans for Libya have already begun printing the flyers.

By left-of-center standards, Kirsten Powers is reasonable. She is not a wild-eyed leftist nutcase. She can be quite thoughtful and sincere. Yet in the end she is still left-of-center, and her arguments are still fatally flawed.

She expressed dismay over an article that described Hillary Clinton as a word that rhymes with witch. What really dismayed Ms. Powers was that the article was written by what she considers to be a "respected" (translation: liberal) publication. The *Washington Compost* was the offending rag, with Dana Milbank the offending liberal.

"This isn't some random blogger or even an opinion columnist expressing vile views. This is a reporter at one of the nation's top newspapers making a sexist joke about a woman he covered during the presidential race."[37]

Oh those bloggers, those low-class plebeians incapable of quality journalism. They always get the story wrong. They don't have the training and pedigree of the *Jayson Blair Times* or Dan Rather and Mary Mapes of *60 Minutes*.

I could generalize in the same way that Kirsten Powers does and point out that liberal snobbery is redundant.

So is blaming sexism against an entire gender on what may be contempt toward a particular individual who happens to be a woman.

"Conservative commentator Alex Castellanos defended this on CNN saying that Clinton deserves to be called a 'bitch.'

For what? Running for president? How dare she!"

No. She is one for being a nasty individual that has built her entire career on the success of her husband while claiming the mantle of feminism. She is one for helping her husband destroy the reputations of other women and blaming his philandering on a vast right-wing conspiracy. She is one for claiming that she has thirty-five years of experience when basic math says that she is simply adding thirty-five to the year she graduated law school to reach what was her present age at the time she ran for president. She is one for being, as one conservative columnist put it, a "congenital liar."[38]

This is not about her right to lie her way into the Oval Office. This is about being criticized for calling a woman one when she acts like one. Is it a nasty word? Sure. Is Hillary a nasty woman? Yes. Perhaps Ms. Powers can explain why other political women are not referred to this way.

She implies that she expects bad behavior from heathens and conservatives. When a liberal newspaper columnist says a politically incorrect word, intellectual Armageddon is upon us.

At least Ms. Powers is consistent in her own way. She is willing to do what most fake feminists would not dream of doing. Ms. Powers defends Sarah Palin.

"The only thing worse would be running for vice president. Just ask Sarah Palin.

I'm no fan of the former governor of Alaska, but as a life-long feminist I can't ignore the endless stream of sexism directed at her."

Then criticize the people actually doing it, Ms. Powers. They are called liberals. They are the same women that claim to care about the rights of women while ignoring the fact that Bill Clinton was abusing them. George W. Bush was liberating them from brutal beatings in Iraq and Afghanistan.

A few conservatives attacked Sarah Palin, but most of them are connected to McCain campaign consultants that need to place blame away from McCain. They know that if Palin gets the nomination in the future, these same consultants are finished. The bulk of the vitriol is not conservative rational self-interest, but irrational liberal ideological bigotry.

"Friday on MSNBC, guest host Donny Deutsch… was adamant: 'The only reason we are so fascinated, the American public has never seen a woman that looks like this in power. That's where the fascination starts.'

Where was this insightful analysis when the vapid JFK-wannabe John Edwards and his silky hair ended up as the Dems choice for VP in 2004? Or was everyone too dazzled by his completely undistinguished one term as a senator?"

Where were you Ms. Powers? You were supporting the Kerry-Edwards ticket because you put style and partisanship over substance. John Kerry stood for everything and nothing, yet you supported him and his even less substantive running mate.

Ms. Powers really goes off the track when she blames the behavior at the wrong culprits.

"There is something profoundly juvenile about adult men in the media grouping powerful women by crude stereotypes like 'bitch' or 'hot chick.'"

Women are far more abusive to their fellow sisters than men ever could be. Men could never get away with such boorish behavior without the tacit approval of women. Many women find brutes sexy, and nice guys boring.

Blame for attitudes toward women lay virtually solely at the feet of women. They sexualize themselves, and then blame men for being guilty of enjoying eroticism. They put on the tough guy gloves and then try to play the girly girl routine when men defend themselves.

Either women are clear thinking individuals that have the power to say "no" when they choose, or they are mindless automatons.

Ms. Powers is better than most liberal women. Yet make no mistake about it. Being reasonable compared to other liberal women is like Fatah being less murderous by a small degree than Hamas.

In the same way Palesimians wake up and blame the Jews, liberal women blame white, conservative, male oppressors for everything from world hunger to shooting Santa Claus.

White male conservatives are not the culprit. If anything, we are scared stiff of being called racist, sexist, homophobic bigots the minute we walk out of our homes and breathe air within fifty feet of an aggrieved victim group.

It is politically correct liberal hypocrites that cannibalize their own when they run out of conservative flesh to tear to pieces and devour.

Ms. Powers is totally right to demand that women be treated with respect.

She is totally wrong in understanding the cause and the solution to the problem.

We don't need a summit for grievance-mongers. We need grievance-mongers and the people using the offending words to shut up.

Jews call gossip Loshon Hara. Loshon Hara hurts the speaker of the words, the person receiving the words, and those overhearing the words.

Everyone should stop it.

Then again, what do I know? I am just a white, male conservative blogger with a fabulous smile and (by the grace of God) good hair.

eric

My Craigslist Personal Ad—When Eroticism Meets Laziness

I posted this ad on Craigslist. Women are making tons of money selling their talents, so I decided to advertise mine. The results have been less than stellar. Here is my solicitation to the women of the world.

DEUCE BIGALOW

Inspired by the movie *Deuce Bigalow*, but too tired after a hard day's work to do anything about it, for only $50, you will be allowed to WATCH ME WATCH TV.

That's right ladies, WATCH ME WATCH TV.

Some of you out there might wonder why any woman would pay me to WATCH ME WATCH TV. Here are some reasons:

1)   Your own TV is broken or you have roommates who monopolize it.

2)   You are doing a research paper on primitive male primate behavior.

3)   Your existence is even more exciting than mine.

4)   You want to make your man jealous without doing anything regrettable.

5)   I can be highly entertaining when watching TV, especially when news commentators say something dumb or referees make bad calls.

From 7:00 PM to midnight, I will watch news, sports, and *Law and Order* reruns, capping the night off with either a late night comedian monologue or more news and sports.

If you have sexual needs that you want fulfilled, I can brag about what I would do with you if I was not so exhausted from work. I have an intense desk job.

I can surf the Internet while watching TV. You can watch me stare at women I would invite to my home, except that they would distract me from TV. You might even be one of the women on the Internet I am ogling.

I have two video game systems, a Sega Genesis and an Atari 2600. I have a DVD player, and at some point plan to buy DVDs. I have a VCR as well that plays videotapes. It is modern, in the sense that it plays VHS, not Beta.

If you feel the need to do a striptease for me or just roll around on my carpet scantily clad, all I ask is you do it during the commercials unless the program is being Tivoed. You can hold any remote you want except for the one that actually changes the channels.

INCALLS ONLY! If I wanted to leave my apartment and actually do things, I would not have bought a big screen.

$50 per night, but if two women come over, I charge only $100. You will both be allowed to watch me watch TV. You may take notes, but not pictures. NO PAPARAZZI.

Ladies, email me your pictures and your phone numbers along with a signed "vow of silence" form that will allow me to watch TV without idle chatter.

WATCH ME WATCH TV! Ask for Deuce. I mean you can ask for Rachel, but she does not live here. I have a thousand channels, and will watch them with or without you.

eric

Gorgeous, Naked, and Totally Useless

Despite being a creature of radio, I decided to allow the world to see my fine quality mug. I bought a webcam. After seeing my smiling face and waving at myself for about ten to fifteen seconds, I realized that the purpose of this device was so that others could see me. Given that my chances of figuring out something technological on my own are about as likely as sleeping with all the *Desperate Housewives* at once (more likely once I buy the *Housewives'* doll figurines), I searched for someone to help me set up my webcam so that others could view me.

My friends fell into two categories...technologically challenged and available, and technologically brilliant and busy. These brilliant technophiles (not to be confused with pedophiles, technophiles stick their hardware into computer inputs for a technical sensation) kept asking me if I was aware my webcam came with a CD. I said I did. They then shrugged.

While watching the game with a friend, one of those brilliant (read: bizarre) ideas came to me. Since I needed help installing a webcam, why not contact people who were experts specifically with webcams and obtain their help? This led me to the erotica section of Craigslist, which apparently contains the largest supply of women using technology to benefit society.

While sifting through the ads, I had to find the ones that specifically understood webcams. Most of the women were hookers, masseuses, dominatrixes, phonesex operators, and other women that make me pray my future wife will only give birth to sons. These women were gorgeous and naked, but they were at that moment totally useless to me. Besides, they slowed up the process because five to ten seconds of gawking time was added to each ad sifted through. One of the reasons I have never been into cybersex was because I did not have Norton Anti-virus virus protector, and I did not wish to catch a computer virus. Phonesex seemed dicey because I did not exactly know where the phone was supposed to go, and did not really wish to find out.

I finally found webcam girls. I sent them each a simple, pleasant message stating that I would happily pay them for the price of a "show," but that they did not have to do the show. This confused them, MIT scientists that they were (They probably make more money than me, and can figure out how to set up a webcam. If Henny Youngman were alive, he would ask them to wash his car and paint his house). I told them that I just wanted help setting up my webcam, and the price of their show was cheaper than calling in the Geek Squad from Best Buy.

Some were threatened by potential competition until I stated that I was a heterosexual guy who only wanted to use his webcam for g-rated purposes (time will tell if that last part was truthful). Others offered me a monthly pass to see hundreds of girls. Between JDate, Eharmony, and Republicansingles. com, I really did not have time to view any more women, even if they were naked. I just wanted help setting up my webcam.

I always assumed that hot naked women could not be useless. The irony was that women who make a living using their webcam were willing to take my money to view them naked for two-and-a-half hours, but unwilling to let me see them fully dressed for the fifteen to thirty minutes it takes to explain five minute concepts. This was mind-boggling.

My political career is in ruins, assuming these women save instant messages. I could just picture being in a senate hearing room being grilled by Democratic drunk drivers, Klansmen and plagiarizers, and explaining to them that I was not seeking Internet sex from women whose sole business purpose is to deliver Internet sex. I could wag my finger at America and say "Yes, I contacted Internet sex providers, but I neither sought nor had sex with any of them." Besides, Internet sex is not sex…unless it is.

Later that night one of my friends pointed out to me that the problem was not my technology, but the technology of my friends. They did not have the updated AOL Instant Messenger that allows for video viewing. We chatted by computer for five minutes. He saw my face and heard my voice. It was spectacular.

My next goal is to be able to get my webcam to be viewable on my blog, which I think has something to do with Web sites and servers. While I have no idea what I just said, it is apparently doable. Hopefully the world will one day soon see me on my webcam and ooh and ahh at my ability to wave hello at people while watching TV and drinking soda.

All I know is that when I need help with something that requires intellect and technical know-how, I will not bother asking hot, naked women offering hot, steamy sex. They are simply totally useless for anything outside their skill set.

As the night wound down and I got ready for bed, I noticed that I spent so much time getting my webcam up and running that I did not devote enough time to my favorite pursuit…women. It is so hard finding a hot girl to get me (redacted). Where does a guy find hot girls looking for someone? I could only think of one place…JDate!

I may not have learned anything from this experience, but I have something that only hot, naked and useless women are talented enough to have…a working webcam.

eric

Happy Passover Shannen Doherty

On April 12th, 1971, Shannen Maria Doherty entered the world.

April 12th, 2009, came and went, and she and I are still not back together.

The rumors that we are a couple have to stop, and they have to stop now.

If the social conservatives ask, it is because sex before marriage is a sin.

If my parents ask, of course I know she is not Jewish.

Deep down I know the truth. She is Jewish.

One only has to play the game "Six Degrees of Kevin Bacon" to grasp this.

In fact, the trail is much shorter than that.

She was on *Beverly Hills, 90210*. Beverly Hills is approximately 70 percent Jewish. In college, 70 percent is the lowest passing grade. She is therefore just barely Jewish, by the skin of her (redacted).

She has me so confused that that I am now redacting the word "teeth."

It has been fifteen years since we were together. Thanks to Bill Clinton, the word "together" can mean whatever I want it to mean. Well we were together. I worked in a retail store, and she was a customer. We did speak.

It started out innocently enough in 1994. I saw her walk in, nearly fainted, and calmly went into the back room to talk to the owner. All my coworkers knew what was up. The owner saw her and knew.

"Sir, please clear all of the customers out of the store. I want Shannen on top of the jewelry table right now."

Like a block of ice from Antarctica, the owner was offering discounts on brutal reality.

"Oh, I am sure a woman making $100,000 a week is going to go out with a guy making $5 per hour."

(Laugh all you want, but only weeks later I got a raise to $5.50!)

I tried to explain to him that honor and integrity are important. In the same way liberals believe in an evolving Constitution, I believed in what I call "flexible morality."

"Sir, just tell her I am the owner of the store."

He then turned into the love child of Socrates and Abraham Lincoln.

(Actually my boss was a Sikh. I think every guy with a long beard has an emotional connection to Abe.)

"Eric, don't you have a girlfriend?"

Come on! That is not fair. I hate it when people take cheap shots by injecting a situation with the poison pill of facts.

I had a girlfriend, but this was the hottest Republican brunette on the planet. There had to be an exemption somewhere.

I went to help her with her merchandise. My intention was to compliment her brilliant speech at the 1992 GOP Convention. That was really my only major familiarity with her work.

"Ms. Doherty, although I have never seen a full episode of '*90210…*'"

She immediately cut me off and said, "Oh I don't blame you. It's terrible. That's why I am leaving. You didn't miss anything."

Wow. Maybe God does protect the dumb. I scored points by sheer accident. I continued.

"Like I said, I don't know your acting, but your speech at the 1992 Convention was great."

She smiled and asked, "Oh, are you a Republican?"

After that she was very friendly. We talked politics for about 20 minutes. She really knew her stuff. Her analysis of the 1996 race was as solid as that of any pundit.

As I prepared to ask her out, my boss from the other side of the room whispered the word "girlfriend."

Had I asked her out, even though this was Hollywood fantasy, even if she had said no…that would have been cheating. When you have a girlfriend, and you hit on somebody else, that is cheating.

(I know. I'm a moron.)

I finished helping her with her merchandise. As she prepared to leave the store, she said, "I enjoyed this. I'll come back again."

As she walked out, after the door closed, I exclaimed, "Wait, Shannen…you forgot the wedding and the kids. Come back."

I never saw her again.

I still own the note she wrote me. No, it is not laminated on my wall. It is buried somewhere in my walk-in closet beneath old midterms from classes I barely remember. To the best of my knowledge, the note reads,

"Something-or-other, blah blah blah, etc, etc. Stay Republican. Love, Shannen Doherty."

I could say that every April 12th I lament this situation. The truth is that it was sheer coincidence that I learned her birth date for the first time on April 11th, 2009, leading to a hastily cobbled together column that made as much sense as (insert senseless simile).

From 1997 through 1999, I worked in zip code 90210. I never saw her.

On January 3rd, 2009, I became single again. I wanted to reach out to her, but I got distracted by the NFL playoffs and the last seventeen days of real American leadership.

On January 9th, I celebrated my birthday. She did not pop out of a cake for me. I will therefore reciprocate her non-gesture.

She came back on "*90210*," but I was in a relationship.

The timing was never right.

Ms. Doherty, we are both politically conservative and morally liberal. I would be happy to deck a paparazzi guy for you provided he was a liberal and you have connections with the judge.

Happy birthday, Shannen. Until overwhelming evidence of wrong that only Janet Napolitano could ignore comes to light, I will wish you a Happy Passover.

eric

Yummy Bouncie Medical Saturday

There comes a time when a man has to do the right thing for the wrong reasons.

I have decided to become a champion of women's rights.

The Democratic Party has been pretending for decades that it cares about women. In 2009 it decided to take them back to the dark ages of…well, whenever that was.

A liberal wack job in Florida got elected to congress by claiming what most liberals claim, that Republicans want people to die.[39]

At least Democrats are now willing to tell women that they can go ahead and drop dead.

The issue deals with those phenomenal creations of God known as yummy bouncies. When not thinking of hamburgers and football, my attention turns to one of the loveliest, titillating aspects of the human female.

(It is impossible to discuss this topic without the word titillating.)

Breast cancer kills women. Early detection and prevention saves lives. The first signs of health care rationing and death panels have arrived. Women are being told, in the immortal words of Gilda Radner as Roseanne Rosannadanna, "Never mind."[40]

What possible reason could the government have for telling women to forget about breast cancer before age fifty? Why get tested every other year instead of annually?

(Harry Reid said something in a press conference that I am deliberately and completely taking out of context because it sounds hilarious.

"We have plenty of provisions for women. We are going to make them better on the floor."[41]

Who knew that C-Span was turning into the *Playboy* Channel?)

What is it about saving lives that is so objectionable?

More importantly, why should I care?

I care because I like yummy bouncies. If women shouted out that they loved my (redacted) and wanted them to be preserved and healthy, I would be appreciative.

Some guys take yummy bouncies for granted. I don't. Too many of us do not appreciate what we have, or are allowed to temporarily have, unless it is taken away from us.

The last time I got to play with a girl's yummy bouncies was awesome. Even though we did not make it as a couple, I thanked her for the recreational game of sexual volleyball.

Could I do this if she no longer had them? I don't think so.

Some women will label me a male chauvinist oinker looking for an excuse to talk about women's yummy bouncies.

These women should shut up and be grateful that I am talking about this subject. Beneath all the sophomoric lusting is the fact that women will die if they do not get educated on the facts.

Tom Green once wrote a song dedicated to men called, "Play with your balls, or else you'll get cancer."[42] If that gets people to spend intimate moments with themselves in the name of medicine, I say keep singing.

Ladies, even if I never reap the benefits of getting to see, touch, or taste them, make sure to rub and bounce those things for your own sake.

Do it for yourselves. You want to live.

If you won't do it for yourselves, do it for me.

For those of you who will be on spring break in Florida, I look forward to seeing you happy, jiggly, bouncy…and most importantly, alive and healthy.

There is no need to thank me for this public service announcement. The pleasure is all mine.

Happy Yummy Bouncie Medical Saturday.

eric

No Man is Safe

"Jilted Bride Awarded $150K After Wedding Called Off

POSTED: 12:53 pm EDT July 23, 2008   UPDATED: 6:44 pm EDT July 23, 2008

HALL COUNTY, Ga. — The jury has awarded a Hall County woman $150,000 after she sued her former fiance for calling their wedding off. RoseMary Shell sued her ex-fiance, Wayne Gibbs, after he broke off their engagement in 2007. Shell argued her fiance's promise of marital bliss amounted to a binding contract. She said she left a high-paying job in Florida to be with Gibbs and she said she has suffered financial losses since their break-up. She also said she has suffered emotionally.

Gibbs testified that he had taken Shell on trips and paid $30,000 of her debt while they were engaged. He said when he found out she had even more debt, he canceled the wedding by leaving Shell a note in their bathroom. Closing arguments were heard Wednesday morning and the jury awarded Shell $150,000 by Wednesday afternoon. 'People shouldn't be allowed to do that and hopefully he'll think twice before he does it to someone else,' said Shell.

Copyright 2008 by WSBTV.com. "[43]

No man is safe anywhere in this world.

I do not know if the judge in this case was a woman. What I do know is that this woman should have her face plastered on every dating site in America, along with this article. She should be blacklisted, blackballed, or whatever the new term happens to be.

Casinos have lists of cheating gamblers. Stockbrokerage firms have the names of crooked clients.

Men need to know who this woman is so that she never gets another date ever again.

A promise of happily ever after is not a binding contract. It is a goal.

I had an ex who got upset because I promised to always "be good and take care of her."

How many men, upon breaking up with a woman, find out that the woman is telling her girlfriends that the man was bad in bed? Should the man sue the woman for lying either during the relationship or after the breakup?

I know some people will want to hear the woman's side of the story. She has no side.

Somebody sterilize this woman immediately. If we don't, she will bring a daughter into this world (most likely through in vitro fertilization) that will be as screwed up as mom.

She said that the breakup caused her emotional pain. Breakups do this. It is called disappointment.

Luckily for this woman, there are judges whose parents were also not sterilized in time.

Unless this case is reversed on appeal, it will do for romance what the KKK did for race relations.

We now live in a world where a woman can sleep with a man, have regrets the next day, and file charges.

If a man uses alcohol or drugs to influence a woman, that is…and should be…a crime. If a man uses sweet talk, and is what used to be referred to as a "cad," that is not a crime.

Unethical behavior is not necessarily illegal. It is not a crime to be a "meanie," a "not-nice-nik," or a "baddie."

What happened to women who would just eat chocolate ice cream, gab with their girlfriends, and be done with it?

The NOW, Gloria Allred, and every other female activist need to condemn this ruling.

Perhaps they could care about relevant issues, such as honor killings and other third-world savagery toward women.

Instead some white-collar woman eases a broken heart by seeking revenge.

What if she coarsens society? What if this causes some men to delay married life until ten prenups are signed in triplicate? She feels better, consequences to others be d@mned.

I am not blaming an entire gender for this crackpot. However, the feminist movement helped shape this female train wreck. The American culture of lawsuits also contributed. Liberal judges more concerned with feelings than codified law are ripping at the fabric of this nation.

There is nothing for men to do in this situation except to hide money, keep offshore bank accounts, and run at the first sign of lunacy.

Some of my exes were basket cases. I did what any man would do in that situation. I ran. I also let them know why. I told them flat out that I don't date basket cases. That may seem ice cold, but it is not my job to solve the problems of others.

If a woman I marry develops an illness, I would empathize.. Yet when a woman starts crying over the Ozone Layer or the Wetlands, a man has to have the spine to let them know that he just does not care.

Nothing is guaranteed. People who promise to love each other should keep that promise.

However, things happen. This is life.

Men should be more gentlemanly. Women should stop being basket cases. Terrorists should stop blowing things up. Lots of things should happen.

Judges should follow the law.

I have no answers at this point. I have only questions.

I am sure of only one thing.

No man is safe.

eric

Chapter 8: Sports Idiocy

Everything in life people need to know can be learned from sports. Most people do not even know what defines a sport. People who think that chess, checkers or marbles are sports need to stay indoors and avoid anybody that still has hope of a normal life. Also, if America is bad at it, it is not a sport. If it snows, and people run indoors, it is not a sport. If crowd noise is banned, it is not a sport. If it requires a pretty outfit, it is not a sport. Liberals can count complaining and crying as skill sets, but they are not sports. Lastly, if it is on Lifetime or the Oxygen Network, it is not a sport.

The 4-Ever Man Does It Again

Some know him as the Iron Man. Some know him as the Gunslinger. Some know him as # 4, his jersey number. His name is Brett Favre. In 2009 he quarterbacked the Minnesota Vikings.

The Vikings defeated the Packers 30-23 on Monday Night Football. Yet this is not about football. This is a celebration of the human spirit. Football is just the backdrop.

Brett Favre began playing football in 1991. He joined a losing Green Bay Packers franchise in 1992, won a Super Bowl in 1996, and reached another one in 1997. From 1995-1997 he was the NFL MVP three straight years. He holds the all-time NFL record for touchdown passes and yardage thrown. As of October 5th, 2009, he became the only player in NFL history to defeat all thirty-two NFL teams.

In his later years as a player, he became known for offseason drama. He did not get in trouble with the law, disgrace his family, or disrespect football. He simply took forever every offseason to decide whether or not to retire. Every year his body was one year older and had more wear and tear. His mind and heart would battle it out with his body to see if he could still play.

In 2005, he was introduced with the song "Forever Man"[44] by Eric Clapton playing in the background. The television screen showed his image with the caption "4-Ever Man." That year the team went 4-12. What made this amazing was that it was his first losing season. He had been in the league fifteen years! He decided not to retire, saying he could not leave the team in shambles.

In 2006, after a 4-8 start, he willed a team light on talent to four straight victories and an 8-8 season. Then the annual Favre retirement watch reached a fever pitch matched only by Punxsutawney Phil on Groundhog Day.

He went to his farm in Kiln, Mississippi, which had been devastated a few months earlier by Hurricane Katrina. He sat on his tractor, mulled, and pontificated. He kept the entire team and Green Bay management waiting. In June, four months after the Super Bowl ended, and just before the start of preparation for the following year, he finally announced that he was coming back.

All he did in 2007 was lead the Packers to a 13-3 record, and one game short of the Super Bowl. They lost at home in overtime to the eventual champion New York Giants.

Despite the success on the field, management was tired of the annual guessing game. Coach Mike McCarthy and President Ted Thompson were relatively new to the organization. They wanted to put their own stamp on a franchise that was doing just fine without them. They pressured Favre to make a quick decision on his future after the 2007 season ended. In March of 2008, Favre announced his retirement.

Within days, he already regretted his decision.

He tried to unretire, but the Packers no longer wanted him. He gave them sixteen years, and they wanted to move on. Football is a business, but he as a player had accomplished success. Management had not. He was told he could compete for the starting job, but would not automatically have it handed to him. He left and went to play for the New York Jets.

In 2008, the Jets began 8-3, but faded down the stretch, finishing 9-7 and missing the playoffs. Favre received much of the blame, as his arm wore down along with the team. He retired again. He still could not stay retired. From the moment he announced his retirement, he agonized. Not even a presidential race could lead the news in Green Bay, where Favre was tossed aside, and archrival Minnesota, which wanted him to play. On July 26th he announced that his retirement was "final." Four days later, on July 30th, he unretired and came back *again*.

On October 5th, 2009, on Monday Night Football, the Minnesota Vikings defeated the Green Bay Packers 30-23. Favre was magnificent. This was only one week after Favre threw a miracle touchdown to win a game on the final play. The Vikings improved to 4-0, and finished the season 12-4.

Those who do not care about football may ask why this matters. Why should a plumber, a carpenter, or a homemaker care about Brett Favre?

Again, this is not about football. It is about something that will affect every human being at some time in their lives, if they are lucky. It is about being considered "too old," in a nation that puts people out to pasture as if they were horses going to the glue factory.

America is a beautiful nation on so many levels, but it is also a nation obsessed with youth, beauty and sexiness. Old people are targeted the least by advertisers, despite the fact that they have most of the money.

At age forty, Brett Favre is hardly old enough for an AARP card. Yet in the world of professional sports, he is old. Old people cannot, and should not, be seen as useless. Old people should be revered, not passed over. Outside of giving them the front seat on buses, old people are relegated to the back of the bus in most aspects of life. In business they get a gold watch, and if they are truly lucky, a golden parachute. What they do not get is to keep working.

Some people like my parents wanted to retire early. At fifty-five and fifty-two, they did. This was voluntary. My grandfather, while "retired," ran a synagogue until his health at ninety-one forced him into the hospital. He still lived another six years, constantly telling me in our weekly phone call that he had things to do. Every day spent in the hospital was a day he could not attend a meeting.

My other grandfather may have been less ambitious in his later years, but he enjoyed sitting outside with his friends. At age one hundred, a brutally cold New York winter forced him to stay inside. He rapidly declined due to dementia. Even at one hundred, the decline was mainly due to the fact that he went "stir crazy." He had nothing to do.

My grandmother also lived to one hundred, and she cooked for me until she was ninety-four. The day before her death, her appointment book had her "to do" list. She was busy. She had a hair appointment and financial matters to handle with her CPA.

People need dignity. Taking away dignity is like taking away oxygen.

Who are we to tell corporate CEOs to take mandatory retirement? If Sumner Redstone can still run a company at ninety, then let him. Don Pardo is ninety-one, and he flies every Thursday from Phoenix to New York to be the opening introductory voice of *Saturday Night Live*.

Bob Dole and John McCain were told that they were too old to be president. They were younger than Nelson Mandela.

While America is a charitable nation of charitable people, we should not confuse respect for the elderly with charity. Most reasonable people would agree that if a heart surgeon is ninety years old and shaking from arthritis, he should no longer be holding the scalpel. As long as somebody can continue to do their job, we should let them. More importantly, we should encourage them.

Youth is overrated and experience is underrated.

I take the Favre situation personally because I am in a very similar situation.

I am thirty-eight years old. I play in a coed touch football league. Even though it is not tackle, it is still strenuous. I am one of the older players (the league caps out at forty), and while I am certainly not the star of the team, I am a role player. I am productive. I contribute.

I played the season before last with an injured foot. I toughed it out. We won the championship, and I retired after the season. A few days later, I was already waffling.

Just before the deadline to finalize my decision, I reversed myself. The season started October 10th, and I played again. That season was even tougher, but we went unbeaten and won the championship again. I retired again, this time a two-time champion who wanted to go out on top.

I am already waffling again. I should retire, but I want to play. I love football.

Whether it is Michael Jordan in basketball, Wayne Gretzky in hockey, or a corporate CEO that does not want a parachute of any kind, people should be able to contribute to society, not be sent to the glue factory.

The youth can wait their turn. The experienced people deserve their due.

Because I refused to retire from the game I love, I now have one more championship than Brett Favre.

When I walk away, it will be on my terms. My body may not be fully intact, but my mind and heart will be.

Keep playing Brett. Well done # 4.

eric

2016 Olympics…ZZZZZ

Rio Di Janeiro (somewhere in Brazil) defeated Chicago (somewhere in Midwest America) for the right to host the Olympics. The decision was made by Copenhagen, which I believe is similar to Skoal Bandit. World leaders gathered in Copenhagen, which most likely means that they agreed that chewing tobacco causes global warming. Major League Baseball will therefore be abolished because excessive spitting hurts the planet.

Zzzzz

A chewing tobacco contest would actually be slightly more watchable. We could be the champions of chaw.

Barack Obama, while likable, is politically completely irrelevant.

To prove otherwise, he and David Axelrod will be ordering military strikes against Brazil. Rahm Emanuel sent a dead fish to the Brazilian president.

I made that up, but research showed that Brazil does have a president.

Axelrod basically claimed that the process was corrupt, and that the International Olympic Committee was an old boy's network. The pot again has called the kettle African-American.

Even though the lights have been turned out, Mr. Obama is still talking.

If Obama speaks in the forest, and nobody is listening, does he still make a sound?

I wonder what sport Rod Blagojevich is preparing for.

Okay, enough political fun. This is about sports.

My indifference is not sour grapes. Quite the opposite. I am delighted that Chicago did not get the Olympics.

I was rooting for Rio. Anybody except Chicago would have been fine.

(I did root for New York the last time, but was thrilled when London upset Paris.)

Chicago is a dreadful city. I travel there frequently on business. It is awful.

The weather is horrid. Chicagoans wear frostbite like a badge of honor. I would rather sit in my Jacuzzi in Los Angeles. Chicago is freezing cold in winter and more insufferable and full of hot air than Barack Obama in the summer.

Had the world never heard of Obama, I would still dislike Chicago due to snowstorms, and thirty-eight degree weather in April. It is for animals, not people.

New York also has better pizza (Chicago is very good on hot dogs and steaks).

I have also already experienced decadence with naked Chicago women. I have never even seen a naked Brazilian woman, much less touched or tasted one. Think vacation spots, people. I have done Mardi Gras in New Orleans, but never experienced Carnival. Like a sorority party when I was younger, Carnival seems like a good way for a guy to feel his way through the crowd.

Okay, enough bawdiness. There is a major reason not to want the Olympics here.

The Olympics are boring.

There is virtually nothing interesting about the Olympics. Sports programs piece together the best highlights, but that obscures the fact that those seventeen days of competition lead to maybe thirty minutes of watchable moments.

Michael Phelps was amazing, and the Olympic Gold Medal hockey team at Lake Placid was spectacular. Most Olympic events are dull.

The opening ceremonies are inspiring, but they are the pre-game show. The actual game does not measure up.

Americans only care about sports where we play a major role. That is why World Cup Soccer should never be played here either. I don't care if we lose to Iran in soccer. I care that we can defeat Iran in the game of bombing to smithereens.

Now I only wish America could get rid of golf and baseball, two sports that I think are in the Olympics.

Golf is about hours of walking in ghastly pants to spend a few seconds hitting a ball. Baseball has hours of spitting and scratching between eventual actual plays. For every winning putt or play at home plate, there is plenty of inaction.

eric aka the Tygrrrr Express

When the Olympics include American Football, then it will be worth watching.

At the very least, ban all professionals and go back to letting only amateurs compete.

At the very least, have a drug testing program that does not make baseball look honest.

At the very least, choose a nice location people would actually want to visit, someplace with jiggly, bouncy, scantily clad brunettes.

At least they actually did that.

Congratulations Rio.

The games may be useless, but at least the right city got them.

As soon as I figure out whether these are the winter or summer games, I will go back to sleep.

If I have trouble sleeping, I can always watch either past Olympic Games, or news coverage of the 2016 games.

eric

Olympic Sized Irrelevance

It took some barely relevant people on this planet to finally expose America's First Gasbag-in-Chief.

It is one thing to be scoffed at by Armageddonijad and Kim Jong Il. When one is not important enough for the International Olympic Committee, one truly ceases to matter.

Before getting to my own commentary, I received an anonymous Top Ten list on the matter that is priceless.

Top Ten Reasons Obama Failed At Winning The Olympic Bid

10. Dead people can't vote at IOC meetings

9. Obama distracted by 25 min meeting with Gen. McChrystal.

8. Who cares if Obama couldn't talk the IOC into Chicago? He'll still be able to talk Iran out of nukes, right?

7. The impediment is Israel still building settlements.

6. Obviously no president would have been able to accomplish it.

5. We've been quite clear and said all along that we didn't want the Olympics.

4. This isn't about the number of Olympics "lost," it's about the number of Olympics "saved" or "created."

3. Clearly not enough wise Latina judges on the committee

2. Because the IOC is racist.

1. It's George Bush's fault.

Some runner ups:

"Tough to win elections without Acorn."

"We saw Obama throw a baseball."

"Global warming will destroy Brazil first - best to see Rio now."

"IOC refused to re-distribute gold, silver, and bronze medals to those who come in 15th, 16th, and 17th."

"The IOC is the committee of 'No.' "

"The IOC 'acted stupidly!'"

Now we come back to our First Gasbag-in-Chief.

In past years I would say that Barack Obama would be starting to look French, but Nicholas Sarkozy has shown that real change can make a positive difference.

I could care less about the colossally boring Olympics. President Obama's trip to Copenhagen is not the issue in itself.

The argument of wasting taxpayer dollars is criticism that goes too far. Presidents take trips all the time, and pursuing the Olympics is a legitimate undertaking. Yet presidential prestige should not be squandered recklessly.

There are plenty of reasons why a reasonable person could have expected Rio De Janeiro to win the games. South America has never hosted before. America has many times. Holding the games in a new and pleasant location is sensible, and certainly fits in with the liberal notion of fairness and global equality. The issue is not that Chicago was a terrible choice, but that Rio was an exceptional one. Mr. Obama cannot and should not be faulted for this.

What he should be faulted for is his narcissism. There is no way he would have taken the trip to Copenhagen if he thought Chicago would lose, especially so badly. He is so in love with the power of his own words that he actually believed he would carry the day.

Remember that he prostrated himself before the world and apologized for America ever existing with George W. Bush at the helm. Some blamed animus toward President Bush for New York previously losing out to London.

In an all too common theme, Mr. Obama is liked but not respected. He is irrelevant. He doesn't matter. As the gulf between soaring rhetoric and meager accomplishments widens, Mr. Obama simply declares victory.

Chicago loses the games, so he declares his presentation a success.

Economic trouble abounds, so he states that things are getting better.

The CBO says his numbers do not add up, so he states that they do.

He announces talks with Iran and that the Iranians promise to be nicer. The next day the Iranians break their word because that is what they do. Obama claims that things are moving in the right direction.

A couple of girls are kidnapped in North Korea. They are then released after we make concessions. Obama calls it a diplomatic success.

Mr. Obama is not a stupid man. He just thinks that everybody else in America is stupid. He declares things to be truthful, with no backup except that he said them. His entire rationale seems to be that if George W. Bush said or did something, it is automatically bad. If Obama does it, it is automatically noble and virtuous.

By trying to show that he knows everything, people come to the conclusion that he knows absolutely nothing. What he should be seen as is a man who knows some things and listens to others when they know more.

President Obama is becoming more and more like Julius Caesar every day. Up until the moment Caesar is stabbed by Casca, he is convinced that everybody loves him to the point of worship.

Despite endless setbacks, Mr. Obama does not allow humility to enter his lexicon. His speech to the IOC was not about the beauty of America or even about Chicago. It was about him personally. Michelle Obama spoke about her own father and her husband. Barack Obama basically said that Chicago deserves the Olympics because Chicago gave us him.

The world is finally waking up to the fact that our president cleanses himself with Obama Ego Scented Shower Gel.

Their is no there there. His speeches are 45 percent platitudes, 30 percent bromides, 25 percent meanderings, and 5 percent nonsense. That adds up to 105 percent, which in Obamaworld adds up perfectly because he says so.

If Barack Obama is irrelevant, why does all of this matter?

The President of the United States must not ever be irrelevant. People thought it was okay for Bill Clinton to be irrelevant, because the 1990s was a decade where nothing really happened. Sleepy decades are frequently followed by turmoil, often avoidable turmoil. Inaction is not "peace." It is complacency, which threatens peace.

The world is a tinderbox. Iran is ready to explode. North Korea is selling bad stuff to worse people.

The issue is not that Mr. Obama went to Copenhagen when so many other problems are occurring. Had he won, the trip would have been worth it.

The issue is that the world is not taking him seriously. Anywhere. On anything.

Illinois Senator Roland Burris, a product of Chicago corruption himself, actually blamed George W. Bush for Mr. Obama's failure. This is getting ludicrous. Does any sane person think that George W. Bush is to blame for Chicago not getting the Olympics?

Barack Obama as a candidate was elected because enough people wanted change. He needs to stop campaigning, stop blathering, and stop being irrelevant. In short, he needs to get off of the television, sit down at his desk, stop showboating, and just do his job.

He needs to stop responding to defeats by just declaring them victories.

Liberals all over the world respond by saying "Well George W. Bush did (X, Y, Z, etc)." That doesn't cut it.

Even if George W. Bush was responsible for kitties and puppies crying at night, that does not change the fact that Barack Obama needs to deal with these issues now. If all he can do is assess blame, how is he useful?

The answer at this moment is that he is useless.

What about health care? The Pelosiraptor is handling that. How about Afghanistan and Iraq? Bush was responsible.

I want Barack Obama to matter. I want him to drop his "too cool for school" attitude and actually do the work.

The entire world is watching, If he continues to abdicate his role as leader of the free world, others will be happy to take his place. Nicolas Sarkozy and Benjamin Netanyahu are already filling in.

He needs to stop being that coach on the sidelines that stares with his arms folded. He needs to pound his fist on the table, knock over a water cooler, and show people he means business (behind closed doors).

Some point out that he very well could be doing all of this in private. If that were the case, there would be results.

If he manages to successfully deal with third-world genocidal lunatics threatening to destroy western civilization, then nobody will remember his failing to get the 2016 Olympics. The deck was not in his favor. His failure was not in losing, but for failing to come to grips with the fact that he even could lose when most bettors saw the handwriting on the wall as clear as a Rio beach.

Mr. Obama, I don't even care if you have to get tough with Republicans and ram bills I disagree with down our throats. I will be disgusted from a political standpoint, but at least your manhood won't be in question.

Trust me, sir. Having people dislike you is no big deal. It comes with the job. Right now I and many others worldwide like you personally. You are affable, or as our enemies see it, harmless.

Your likability is just not translating into respect.

Likability is not the ends. It is the means.

The end is winning, which means victories for America.

Barack Obama will most likely never read these words. Even if he does, as with any opinion he disagrees with, he will ignore them.

I can handle him ignoring me. What cannot be accepted is the world ignoring him.

It is not the world's responsibility to adapt to him. It is he who must "change."

This must start now. The tinderbox is ready to blow.

eric

Chapter 9: Hysterical Idiocy

Liberals are the gift that keeps on giving, or to some, the curse that keeps on taking. The choice is to laugh or cry. If we cry, then we are liberals. That is what they do in between bouts of screaming and foot-stomping. The only solution is laughter. After all, the more conservatives smile and laugh, the angrier liberals get. They cannot handle anybody being happy. Since they like being miserable, let's at least be bipartisan and give everybody what they want by laughing at their misery. Now that is compassionate conservatism I can believe in.

Nationwide Comedy Tuesday

There are many serious issues going on in this world. Between constant nationwide travel and news stories exploding and just as rapidly dying, a day of levity is a welcome respite. If something tragic happens on that day, leave me alone. Such is the risk of pre-written sentiments.

On Nationwide Comedy Tuesday, I offer my remarks to various audiences.

"It's great to be here in Arizona. Before getting to politics, I want to go over some football happenings. When talking to a women's' group, the best way to keep them enthralled is to start talking about football."

"The Arizona Cardinals had a great week. As a Jewish person, I have always felt that the Cardinals were the Jews of the National Football League."

"They wandered all over from place to place, from Chicago to St. Louis before finally finding a home in the desert."

"They suffered endless defeats for decades until a hero finally emerged to lead them to the promised land. We have Moses. You have Kurt Warner."

"On offense last week, Kurt Warner had five touchdown passes. On defense, Janet Napolitano had four quarterback sacks."

"Actually, I apologize for that last remark. I should never use 'Janet Napolitano' in the same sentence as 'defense.' She can't defend anything."

"Arizona is being overrun by undesirables. They drain the state of services. They demand new services. They don't work. They contribute nothing. They are pure parasites on the Arizona economy. Of course, I am talking about AARP liberals.

Some of them might be Mexican. I have no idea."

"It's great to be here in Texas. I am not going to take sides in the battle for supremacy in Texas. Rick Perry vs. Kay Bailey Hutchison? No, no, I meant the Texans vs. the Cowboys."

"I have always felt a bond with the Texans because they are like the Jews of the National Football League.

They were minding their own business as the Oilers when they were cruelly uprooted from their homeland."

"Everything was peaceful until they were driven from their land by an evil dictator named Bud Adams. Whether it is Egypt or Nashville, it is not the true homeland."

"Bud Adams wanted to come to Houston with his team when the Titans played the Texans. I say to Bud Adams exactly what I say to the Palestinians. There will be no right of return."

"Thank you for welcoming me to North Carolina. It was a pleasure to meet Ms. Wilmington. Some of you asked if I was willing to buy her dinner. Have you seen and spoken with her? I would be willing to buy her a third-world. nation."

"I hope she likes Laos. $6 should cover it."

"Your North Carolina military base near the airport is very impressive. As Veteran's Day approaches, let me say to all the veterans in the room, 'Thank you, and welcome home.' I know something about war zones. I did two tours of duty as a student in a New York public school."

"It is great to be here in Baltimore. I know you are all concerned about Barbara Mikulski, but don't worry. Next year she will have a new job playing defense for the Ravens alongside Ray Lewis."

"For those of you complaining in Maryland about Barbara Mikulski, I offer no sympathy. I am from the People's Republic of California. We have two of the three worst Barbaras in the country, that being Boxer and Streisand."

"At least Boxer spells it correctly."

"I recommend we put San Francisco on eBay."

"Don't worry, I am sure there are people in Seattle or Boston willing to overbid for it."

"Once the Earthquake hits and we float away, we will become part of Russia. This will be fine, since living under Vladimir Putin will be less oppressive than living under Barbara Boxer or the Pelosiraptor."

I have to admit it is pretty cool getting paid money to tell people what I think and hopefully make them laugh.

Best of all, wherever I go, I make friends I will have for life.

There is nothing left to say, but plenty more to do.

On to the next adventure.

eric

Governor Corzine, Please Vacate My Swimming Pool

Things have really gotten desperate for New Jersey Governor Jon Corzine. Politically, he is sunk.

I just wish he would stop trying to avoid his troubles by fleeing to Los Angeles and hiding in my swimming pool.

If he wanted to drive New Jersey into the ground, as a New Yorker living in California I could care less. Besides, I have never thought of New Jersey as an actual state. It is a province of New York, with some of it belonging to Philadelphia.

(Rangers rule, Devils suck, because I said so.)

A joke I heard as a kid was that the famous inscription written at the bottom of the Statue of Liberty read, "New Jersey sucks."

Childish humor aside (until the next moment at best), it is one thing to arrogantly treat your state like your own entire Six Flags Great Adventure amusement park. It is one thing to be a politician in Free Fall (a great ride there) tying your words up like the Ultra-Twister (an even better ride).

There is no excuse for Jon Corzine to seek refuge in my swimming pool.

Several months ago I went poolside for a Jacuzzi soak before bedtime. As I prepared to relax, this middle aged, bald, white male with an incredibly sinister looking beard appeared lurking in the shadows. Perhaps he was plotting his next evil move, although he seemed harmless enough drying himself off with a towel. I should not have been staring anyway.

I knew he was a man of influence because of his lack of a crop on top. He was definitely a PBWG (Powerful, Bald, White Guy, similar to a character on any of the *Law and Order* franchises).

I was going to let Governor Corzine know that he was the second coming of the wretched Jim Florio. I wanted to ask him how a guy could be the head of Goldman Sachs and end up a socialist. Goldman Sachs did fire him, but he must have learned something, anything.

I hoped he did not eat a big meal before getting in the pool. He does have a penchant for reckless behavior, including his ninety-one MPH car crash.

I was still mostly curious as to why the leader of the garbage state was in my d@mn swimming pool.

I was about to ask him about it (and then criticize his budget policies), but a couple other people approached him first. The woman stood behind the man. The man then greeted Governor Corzine warmly. In fact, he greeted him a little too warmly. He kissed him on both cheeks.

What the heck? Is this a New Jersey thing or something? I knew Jim McGreevey was gay, but I was convinced that Jon Corzine was straight. I clearly remembered him getting caught putting his lover on the payroll, which did not cost him his job because the lover was female. I could not understand why this man was kissing Governor Corzine.

I had to eavesdrop at this point, as the man began to speak to the governor.

"Mr. Jamshidian, it is always good to see you my friend."

"Likewise my friend."

"Mr. Jamshidian, this is my wife. Honey, Mr. Jamshidian runs the local pharmacy where I buy my prescriptions."

Now hold on. Is the governor a drug dealer? Also, why does this other man keep calling him Mr. Jamshidian?

Things got even more confusing when they started speaking in a foreign language. I thought that perhaps his tenure at Goldman Sachs caused him to learn Chinese for international business purposes. It seemed the language spoken was similar to Hebrew and Spanish. It was Farsi, which is spoken by Persians, who apparently are from Iran.

I am not sure why Governor Corzine was pretending to be some Persian pharmacist named Mr. Jamshidian, but if he has a condo in my building to hide his mistresses, I will find out about it.

I could have sworn I saw police then show up, perhaps to indict him. It turned out that they were security guards for the building. It was time to lock up the pool for the night.

Mr. Jamshidian said goodnight to the man. "Goodnight, Mr. Goldman."

Mr. Goldman? Could Mr. Sachs be far behind? This was definitely a code.

So far neither LAPD nor NJPD want to investigate this situation, especially since there was no crime. The gate was not forced open, and everybody left when they closed the pool for the night.

I am not sure what Mr. Jamshidian is trying to pull, but my building really needs to install more security cameras.

Meanwhile, Governor Corzine, stop this nonsense and leave my swimming pool alone for good.

I need rest. Well, not quite yet. A homeless guy seems to be by the barbecue area. He should not be there. This is private property.

Never mind. It's just Denver Pyle from Dukes of Hazard. For a guy who has been deceased since 1997, Uncle Jesse does not look half bad.

Now if only Catherine Bach would show up wearing her Daisy Dukes. That would be a poolside hallucination I could live with.

eric

Chapter 10: Historical Global Idiocy

In Iran young people protest for the right to be free from the terror of the mullahs. In Iraq women protested for the right to not be beaten for wearing dresses that reveal their ankles. In America people protest for...well, everything. Whether it is too hot, cold, black, white, up, or down, every action has an equal opposite reaction and every occurrence is counterbalanced by liberal protesters.

This Column Was Written Under Protest

It should be legal to hit the accelerator pedal when entering a protester zone.

Each day brings another protest. I have had it.

My favorite holiday is "Shut the heck up and go to work Day." Every human being should celebrate it. It should cross every racial, gender, and religious line. We can even make the official ritual a duct taping of dolls representing the ten biggest protesters.

Conservatives have attended rallies at various tea parties. They assembled peaceably despite attempts to demonize them.

Make no mistake about it. Being a protester when one is a liberal is as natural as breathing oxygen. They wake up in the morning and complain about something. Even winning an election did not stop them. They are still bitter over the 2000 election and the fact that their right to protest is countered by our right to see them as useless.

I just want to get from point A to point B without being bothered. I don't mind liberal protesters when they throw temper tantrums in their own homes behind soundproof doors.

It is not the liberalism. It is the traffic congestion. I live near UCLA. Every week brings another cause that nobody outside of UCLA cares about, resulting in one hour drives to travel one mile.

One protest at UCLA came in the form of enraged students protesting fee hikes.

Students were unhappy about having to pay more for education, which is not a right to begin with.

Memo to these self-absorbed students: California is broke. There is nothing. Everybody is feeling the pain. Either fees get hiked, or professors get fired, leaving nobody to teach.

(That is a delightful notion for so many reasons. I will resist the tangent temptation.)

The student protesters had signs that read "California: # 1 in prisons, # 48 in education."

I prepared a contra sign that read: "California Students: # 48 in learning, # 1 in protests."

Look at some of these protesters really closely. Of course we need to build more prisons, in order to house these future criminals. Disruptions on campuses are not "peaceful." Shouting and harassing people is not "non-violent." It is thuggish behavior.

At a healthcare rally, some liberal student protesters had signs that read "We can't afford to wait." Other supporters had the Obama platitude signs that read "Yes we can." These people were standing next to each other. They don't need a healthcare plan. They need Barbara Bush's literacy program.

At another leftist rally I was called a "Donkey, Zionist, Aggressor Infidel" for trying to cross the street to my own home. Apparently I was a colonizer. These people do not need a homeland. They need a thesaurus. They told me "Jew, go home." I responded, "This is my home. This is Los Angeles. You have Gaza. You're not getting Wilshire Blvd."

Where do they find these people? Oh yes, on college campuses.

I sometimes bring fake signs to campuses and take delight in seeing that the students think my causes are real. Some of them asked me how they could help combat obesity in the transsexual community. I explained that the solution was to eliminate trans-fats. They can be either one, but not both. Persian environmentalist supporters were curious about global shawarming.

Uniting the white supremacists and the radical feminists was easy. Repressed women like chocolate. White supremacists like the vanilla inside. Getting them to stop talking and share dessert came together under the slogan "What would you do for a Klandyke bar?"

(God help you if you start to research this.)

Even real organizations are getting ridiculous.

Falun Gong? I have nothing against these people, but this is the United States. Students should not march on behalf of a group if they can't tell me in less than eight billion words what the group actually cares about.

One protest rally had people chanting "Free Uighurs." This would have been fine except that most of the students thought that Uighurs were things, not people, and that they were being given away. Liberal college students, like most liberals, drop everything for free stuff. Some of the students thought that free Nintendo Wiis were being given away. One aging hippie revolutionary demanded his free Ouija Board.

Several years ago Los Angeles campuses were brought to an idiotic standstill after Kobe Bryant was arrested. "Free Kobe" signs and t-shirts were worn en masse. The problem was that Kobe was free the whole time. He was never in jail.

A friend of mine recommended that we just start combining issues to confuse these simpletons. I now maintain that Israeli settlements combat climate change.

Speaking of change, if ever there was a vacuous, meaningless slogan that got so much traction, it was "change."

I would love to see campuses for once try something different. Maybe students could yell, "Hey hey! Ho ho! We support the status quo!"

I do not mind people being passionate. All I ask is that they know what they are talking about. Either be loudly intelligent or silently imbecilic.

I think about this because I had to deal with a Code Pinko protester at the 2008 GOP Convention in Minneapolis. Code Pink, which dislikes Republicans and Israel in proportionate amounts, saw that I was a Jewish Republican and offered me an unsolicited potential monologue.

"Can't you see that we are living in a police state, and that the police are using excessive force?"

I felt like holding up a big sign that said "Kent State, 2008," but this was no time for wishful thinking. There was no hope for this young girl, but using her as a foil for the reasonable moderates in the middle was my intention. I offered my rebuttal.

"Miss, I can prove to you in sixty seconds that we are not living in a police state."

She was curious, and inquired as to my reasoning.

"Simple. Do you see those police officers over there? Five minutes ago I begged them to use indiscriminate deadly force against all of you, and they wouldn't do it. They said we have a Constitution, and that I cannot borrow their batons or rubber bullets. I tried to be bipartisan, but I am sorry to disappoint you. Neither of us will get what we want since none of you or your friends will be beaten within an inch of your lives today. I will try better in the future in the name of coming together."

Things got worse. Despite empathizing with me, the police officers told me that it was illegal for me to return the next day and try to shave the protesters' underarms without their consent.

The young Pinko was attractive, so I left her some final thoughts.

"Your group dislikes Jews and Republicans, but you don't know. Spend time with a Jewish Republican like me and the only thing that will be Code Pink is your backside, and you'll thank me for it. Shall I get my tennis racket?

Oh good, your upper cheeks are blushing bright Code Pink. Play your cards right and your lower ones will join them."

She was speechless. The sacrifices I make for public service. You are all welcome.

The legal solution for college protesters is twofold. First, they should all be forced to watch a movie called *PCU*. *PCU* stands for *Politically Correct University*. In getting the students to chill out, the lead character has them all chanting loudly "We're not gonna protest."[45]

Secondly, no student should be allowed to protest anything until they show that the money spent on their education to that point will yield a respectable return on investment. The ROI on most protesters makes the 2008 financial crash seem like boom times.

I say raise the fees on those not contributing to the California economy rather than tax businesses that are leaving in droves. The bleeding red ink has to stop.

If leftist college protesters don't like it, they can head down the wrong path and one day get free lodging at taxpayer expense. That is why we are spending on more prisons now.

Now that is status quo I can believe in.

eric

Turning into Lou Dobbs

One issue that I do not touch is the issue of illegal immigration. I also do not deal with illegal immigration's sister issue, outsourcing.

I stay out of this contentious fight over Americans and jobs because it is one that splits the Republican Party. I prefer to focus on issues that unite Republicans, such as taxes and the War on Terror. At the risk of enraging many (If you're not enraged by now you died a couple years ago and nobody told you), I just can't force myself to care.

People who obsess about the borders cannot understand how I don't care. I simply cannot force myself to feel passion about something that does not bother me. That does not mean I think they are wrong. It just is not my primary fight. People who obsess about abortion or global warming…in fact, activists in general…do not understand that many people just do not care about their pet cause. The rebuttal is that their issue "is of vital importance." Everybody feels their issue supersedes what others worry about.

Normally I do not obsess about illegal immigration and outsourcing, because the Mexicans did not blow up the towers. The Florida border is vulnerable to Cubans, but they vote Republican. The only Cuban I know who seems to vote differently is Mark Cuban, and he is here legally. The real Florida threat is from South Carolina, where New York liberals keep coming unchecked, determined to screw up Florida as they did New York. Arizona is under siege from native California liberals, and we do nothing.

Despite my normally being fairly blasé on this issue, two events had me turning into the evil twin of Lou Dobbs.

Lou Dobbs used to be the head of a CNN program called *Moneyline*, where he spoke about financial markets. Fox News did not exist at the time. *Moneyline* was intelligent, insightful, must-see television for young stockbrokers like me. The current Lou Dobbs is a raging populist who rails against illegal immigration and outsourcing.

Being against illegal immigration does not make one a racist or a brownbasher. Wanting to defend the border is a legitimate concern. Some people on this issue are racists, but not the majority. Conversely, being dispassionate about this issue does not make one an open-borders, amnesty-loving liberal, as some right-wingers have called me. Me, a liberal?…ummm…no. Respectful people can disagree on how serious this issue is in a civilized manner.

Yet I am on the verge of being uncivilized. I got to a point where I wanted to get rid of all foreigners. The moment passed, but for about thirty minutes, I wanted everybody who did not speak perfect English in an American accent to get out of my existence.

Two separate incidents put me in the Dobbsian corner.

First of all, when I ask for "no tomato" on a burger, I mean no tomato!

I hate tomatoes. I hate them less than al-Qaeda, but I hate them. I hate the seeds. I hate the way the whole tomato slice comes out when I try to bite only one piece. I do not care what nation you are from. If you mess up my lunch, I detest you and your lineage. If you are a white male, you get no slack on this matter.

If I was allergic to tomatoes, you could be killing me. It is not my responsibility to struggle to understand you. You are in America. You will speak clearly. You will grasp that I do not want that red monstrosity on my burger. I do not care if you are a limey with an aristocratic accent saying "tomahto." I want to call the whole thing off on your existence the next time you mess with my taste buds.

I can survive one bad lunch, but if you mess with my financial well-being, I want you to be violated by a goat. If you are from a country that enjoys this, I want you waterboarded instead. This is directed at people in call centers that think they understand me. Delta Airlines had a call center in India and a call center in Texas. I have zero problems with the Texans.

I have a deep respect for the Indian people. They are bright people. The ones in America are as close to the best and brightest as anybody else in this world. I refuse to accept that they are related to the people who work for Delta or HSBC in overseas call centers. If Americans can have recessive genes in the form of liberals, even India, a nation of one billion people, can have several thousand incompetents.

Picking vegetables does not require an MBA. However, I want my heart surgeon to know a few factoids or more. I want MENSA bright. If people are handling my money, they had better know what is going on.

My credit card company outsourced their call center tasks to people in India. One day I almost screamed into the telephone my love for Pakistan, and that Pakistan deserves Kashmir.

I overreacted. I am human. My credit card was blocked. I asked them to unblock it, insisting that there was no fraud on the card. The charges made were mine, and I accepted them. They could not figure out why the purchase I was trying to make online still would not go through.

I repeatedly asked the guy a yes or no question. "Is my card now unblocked?"

He said it was an issue of fraud and...

"Sir, it's a yes or no question, is my card unblocked?"

After several minutes of this, he explained that while the card was unblocked, it could not be used the way I was using it.

The way I was using it? The way I had always used it? Did this guy work for the Hillary Clinton campaign? Was this Indian John Kerry for unblocking my card before he was against it? Unlike Hillary, he was allowed to send me to his supervisor.

After almost an hour, they asked me again to confirm my address.

"Eric Tiger, 123 Main Street, # 111, Los Angeles, CA 90000."

They asked me if I was in an apartment. I again stated I was in # 111. They asked if I meant Apartment 111. I said yes, # 111. They finally explained that because my card says "Apt" instead of using the # sign, I have to type in "Apt" instead of "#."

I could not make this up if I tried. Blvd is not the same as Blvd. with a dot on the end. Street is not the same as St. abbreviated.

Have we really gotten to the point where an hour of my life I will never get back hinges on somebody unable to understand that their own computer needs to be shot and replaced with a dolphin? According to animal rights activists, dolphins are capable of logical reasoning.

This transaction should have taken sixty seconds, not sixty minutes. I could have been stranded on the highway somewhere, while this company kept telling me everything was fine and that I should understand their lack of an intelligible explanation.

I had a six week war with Earthlink and their call center in India. My DSL was not working. They could not figure out the problem, insisting it was on my end. I was truly ready to beg Pervez Musharraf to unload his nuclear weapons on India, and am thankful I was not a blogger at the time.

I remember once calling an airline and getting a guy who spoke perfect English. I replied, "Wait, you're not from India." He laughed and said, "Oh, you went to Delta. Yeah, I understand you."

All I ask is that my right to exist not be infringed. On a macro level, this means do not fly a plane into towers. On a micro level I want to come home, watch television, surf the Internet, and eat my dinner. Unlike my request that Elizabeth Hurley show up naked, declare she is Jewish, and spend the night fanning me and dropping grapes into my mouth, my other requests are reasonable.

I do not hate immigrants or foreigners. I hate people who contribute to the decline of my sanity. To quote an ex-girlfriend who had bohemian overtones, I can't stand people who "harsh my mellow."

Am I going to join the Lou Dobbs militia and take up arms at the border? No. My gripes are selfish. They are overruled by my positive view of some immigrants for equally selfish reasons.

Some people want to keep Hispanic people from reaching American shores. If you are male, you should be reported to ICE immediately. If you are female, between eighteen and thirty-six, and from Cuba, Mexico, Caracas, Venezuela, or any other nation where even the average women are hot, I want you imported here en masse. I know a Guatemalan masseuse who calls me "poppy." Actually, it is more like, "ayyy, Popppeeeeee." Anyone who tries to deport women like this will get a fist full of me (unless they are bigger than me, at which point we can negotiate). "Fist full of me" is not an innuendo. Take it literally so my mother does not throttle me when she reads this.

Some of the best people in this country came from elsewhere. Maria Conchita Alonso still looks good, but go back twenty years...my lord, bring her whole village over!

The problem is when worlds collide. What if a gorgeous Latina masseuse messes up my lunch order? As much as I hate tomatoes, if she forces me to eat the burger off her belly I will be too busy to notice that awful vegetable. I will be more concerned with animal (myself) than vegetable.

157

I take illegal immigration and outsourcing seriously. I just cannot solve every problem. I really am better at helping others when I am happy. Taking care of me should come first.

California has been wrecked, but it is not Mexicans destroying this place. As of now, they cannot vote. Unfortunately, liberals in San Francisco can. Perhaps we can do an exchange similar to Al Bore's carbon offsets. For every illegal alien caught, we deport one liberal Democrat. Many of them are wealthy, so perhaps Mexico would accept them until they started speaking.

I guess I can be more tolerant of others, at least until somebody gives me tomatoes when I ask for potatoes. Who the heck gets a side order of tomatoes with a steak?

The real threat is from Canada anyway. How can Mexicans sneak across? They look different. They are a different color. Canadians look like Americans. If anybody can sneak across and blend in, it is the scourge of the north.

Somebody call Lou Dobbs and let him know that the local cafe is serving Canadian bacon.

I want American bacon. Sheesh! Next thing you know I will get French toast and Belgian waffles with my all-American meal.

My father is a Holocaust survivor, so German Shepherds should no longer be pets. Shepherds pie is fine for lunch, but not German Shepherds pie. That is vile.

Now I can sleep peacefully on my comfy bedspread. From my home in America, I bought it on eBay from a firm located in…well…never mind. It is a comfy bedspread.

eric

No More Heblish

I have had it with Israeli and Jewish spokespeople communicating in a fractured linguistic mess known as "Heblish."

For those that have not been paying attention, Islamofascist terrorists declared War on America in the 1970s. In 2001, we finally declared war on them. The terrorists began their jihad against Jews and Israel fourteen hundred years ago. Israel has fought back brilliantly from a military standpoint. From a public relations standpoint, it pains me as a Republican Jew to see the two worst marketed products on the planet be the Republican Party and Israel.

A badly marketed Republican Party is frustrating. Israel losing a public relations battle during a war is a life and death matter.

America won the Vietnam War on the battlefield and lost it on the evening news. America routed the Taliban in Afghanistan and thrashed Saddam Hussein in Iraq. We lost the battle at home by failing to forcefully rebut the editorial idiocy of the *Jayson Blair Times*.

With Republican Americans, the issue is one of public speaking. Ronald Reagan was that rare breed of human being that had a goodness of heart and a brilliance of communicating. George W. Bush had a noble heart, but his lack of articulateness hurt the party. He was content to let his deeds do the talking. This is commendable from a decency standpoint. Unfortunately, politics is about perception. It does not matter that Bill Clinton and Barack Obama offer vapid words that say nothing and mean even less. They sound good saying nonsense, allowing them to persuade people.

In the long run, the only thing that matters is if the message is communicated. It is in this vein that Israel is flailing, trailing, and failing.

I have enormous respect for the Israeli Defense Forces. The IDF are military geniuses. They are not speakers. Nobody is perfect. Michael Jordan was unimpressive as a baseball player.

Israel is locked in a life and death struggle for its very existence. Israel has many opponents, from some Arabs and Palesimians to their many sympathizers. Israel wins militarily but gets crushed in front of the cameras.

Saeb Arakat, Hanan Ashrawi and Hussein Ibbish all speak perfect English.

Israel offers Hebrew and English mixed together in a gibberish that only Israelis can understand.

I know this comes across as insensitive. We are at war. I am not interested in feelings. I am interested in keeping Jews from being blown to Kingdom Come. If that means ruffling some feathers, the ends more than justify the means.

I am tired of listening to Shimon Peres talk about the "p*ss process." Unless he is filming a commercial for prostate cancer, there is no p*ss process worth discussing.

Even the great "Bulldozer," Ariel Sharon, failed to achieve diplomatically what he spectacularly achieved militarily.

The bottom line is unless one's name is Benjamin Netanyahu, stay the heck away from the cameras. When the television cameras come, show them a picture of a test pattern.

Israelis are bright people. You don't survive surrounded by enemies without lots of brains. Yet these same people that built a nation from nothing but orange groves, and created the Middle East version of Silicon Valley…they have not spent enough money and time on English training classes. The results speak badly for themselves.

Americans want to hear crisp, clear English. That is what opens up checkbooks.

The annual Chabad Telethon raises millions. They don't speak Heblish. They understand that doing good deeds sometimes requires money. People give money to people they like and trust, which means people they identify with.

The best example of this was my trip to Israel in 2008. I was a tourist. Israel relies on tourism. The people that drove me around spoke perfect English. They knew that this was their best chance of getting me to spend money. It worked.

The good news is that all is not lost. Israeli soldier Benjamin Anthony formed an organization called "Our Soldiers Speak." He is British educated. He passionately delivers the message of Israeli soldiers in a crystal clear voice. We need more guys like him.

I will never be qualified to serve in the IDF, nor will I ever advise them on military strategy. As somebody who speaks publicly on a regular basis, I implore Israelis to put aside their pride on this one and just learn perfect English.

I am trying to save Jewish lives. The enemies of Israel have figured out how to play the game. Israel must do likewise. The fractured Heblish must stop.

Israel will succeed at this if they put in the effort. How do I know this?

They are me. They are you. They are us. They are our fellow children of Isaac.

eric

Chapter 11: Musical Idiocy

Only in America could barking like a dog be considered a musical ritual. Kids wear their pants on backwards. This is not a style. It is a sign of lesser intelligence. If Helen Keller were alive today around American youth in public schools, she would thank God that she could not see or hear them. She would still have her sense of smell, which would be a problem when the great unwashed showed up fresh off a marijuana party. Just when things cannot get musically stupider, Ellen Degeneres invites Barack Obama to get down and funky. I do not even know what that actually means, but it sounds bad.

Yakkety Yak, Don't Talk Barack

Rush Limbaugh has a satirist named Paul Shanklin, who has come up with brilliant parodies. His best was a takeoff on the famous 1950s song by The Coasters entitled "Yakkety Yak, Don't Talk Back."[46] His version, at the height of the initial Iraq War was, "Yakkety Yak, Bomb Iraq."

It is in that spirit that I offer a satire of Barack Obama, who should guest host "*Saturday Night Live,*" since he is simply not ready for prime time.

I have nothing against Mr. Obama. He is irrelevant and pleasant enough. I feel he is simply not up to snuff. His comments on several issues reveal him to be a lightweight. With that, I present the song, "Yakkety Yak, Don't Talk Barack."

You've only been around two years…

You are still wet behind the ears…

You need to listen to your peers…

Before you spout off big ideas…

Yakkety Yak…Don't Talk Barack!

Nobody cares that you are black…

It's not your race that we attack…

It's your ideas and what they lack…

An ounce of substance, that's a fact…

Yakkety Yak, No Beef Barack!

You move so fast, you are so deft…

Yet you can't hide from the hard left…

Despite your style, gab is your gift…

Again of substance you're bereft…

Yakkety Yak, Enough Barack!

The USA's military might…

Cannot be given to a neophyte…

Read the foreign policy books on your bookshelf…

And then (don't) come back in 2012…

Yakkety Yak, Not Now Barack!

America's worried about Osama…

Yet what would you do Obama…

Hey do you even have a plan…

Oh yeah you want to bomb Pakistan…

Yakkety Yak, Shut Up Barack!

Barack I say this with respect…

I wish you nothing but the best…

You had a most impressive ride…

For a man who's just not qualified…

Yakkety Yak, So Long Barack!

At some point in the future, when Barack Obama is a trivial pursuit question on par with Kristin Shepherd (She shot J.R. Ewing), this will all be something we can laugh about. Given that we are fighting World War III, it is no laughing matter that a man with so little to offer in terms of anything tangible can be so highly ranked.

It is not the audacity of hope. It is the audacity of thinking that hope by itself is a replacement for actual solutions, and that waxing eloquent equals understanding.

eric

El Dorko's Chicago Trip to Temples...Jesus, Moses and the Almighty (B.B.) King

While visiting Chicago, I had the experience of thirty-eight degree snowy weather in April. To quote rock group Poison, "I wanna go. I wanna go home now."[47]

To take my mind off of everything that makes this city appreciate my trips everywhere else, I decided to go to temple, or as we Hebrews call it, synagogue (also known as Shul). While Passover normally makes me cranky because matzoh tastes like cardboard, I figured being in a new temple could only have positives.

Something seemed wrong right off the bat. For one thing, the service started on time. Perhaps Jews in Chicago want to start early so they can get home before it gets even colder. The singers were high above the congregation. Then the rabbi came out, and he was wearing all black with a white collar. While this did not seem right, it was a reform (liberal) service. I figured it was interfaith night. The rabbi then thanked the crowd for attending services on Friday night, which seemed odd given that Jews have Friday night services every week.

On this Passover, why was this night different from all other nights? For one thing, it was Good Friday. The rabbi then mentioned services on Sunday. Jews pray on Saturday, but with daylight savings time, anything is possible. Yet he mentioned Easter Sunday. Why was that relevant? Then the rabbi crossed the line and asked the crowd to love Jesus.

I am not a fan of Jews for Jesus. This rabbi had better have had a good explanation for deviating from the Old Testament. At that moment out of the corner of my eye I noticed that this synagogue had a deep resemblance to a Presbyterian church. My biggest clue was the sign that said "Welcome to (Insert name here) Presbyterian Church."

I was about to yell "What the Hell?" but realized that this would have been as productive as going to a NOW meeting and demanding that the attendees cook me dinner. I turned around, and the woman behind me asked me "Wrong place?" I nodded, grabbed my coat, and left. As I walked toward the exit, and out the first door, I approached one of the elders. I told him that I did not mean to go to church. My swashbuckling, black-clad, alter ego superhero "El Dorko" brought me here.

The High Priest (He could have just been a random Christian doorman, but he was quite tall. This is as close to a High Priest as I know.) was not judgmental. There were no threats of eternal d@mnation.

I told him that I did not belong there, and he empathetically replied, "Many people feel that way initially. God loves us all." I then clarified what I meant.

I explained to him that I was Jewish. While I have a deep respect for Christianity, it is not my faith. I do not normally walk out of a service five minutes in (unless I am bored and there are no hot women at temple. Like young single guys go to pray for prayer's sake…come on). He then kindly asked me where I was trying to go. Apparently the Jewish temple was across the street.

He explained to me that he thought I was simply an honored guest. I asked him what he meant, thinking that finally I had proof of how much Christians love the Jews. Apparently wearing a Yarmulke (skullcap) meant I was a visiting Roman Catholic dignitary from the Vatican. My Yarmulke was the same red color as the one the pope wears. I was wearing a bright blue Israel necktie with a Star of David on it, which meant only one thing to the churchgoers…I was a Christian supporter of Israel sent from the Vatican to show solidarity with the people of the book.

I then explained to the elder that while I also respected Catholicism, I was simply a Jewish fellow with a lousy sense of direction and apparently an even lower sense of common. My people had wandered lost in the desert for thousands of years, and now the Diaspora was keeping me so close to a synagogue but so far away. For those of you who think crossing the street is easy, this was Chicago in April. I did not have Pharaohs chasing me, but it was incredibly cold outside.

As someone who does not attend church often for obvious reasons, the parishioners were warm and friendly. They were not angry zealot bible thumpers. If helping your neighbor means anything, it meant something to the several people who helped me go exactly where I needed to go. Across the street sounds simple, but the synagogue was inside a mall, between Macys and some CPA firm. No wonder people convert to Christianity. It is easy to find a temple when the letters are written in big bold letters to the point where everyone except me can find it.

There are several ways confusion can be avoided. Reform temples could stop acting like churches. Get rid of the band, the orchestra, and the opera singers. It is a violation of Jewish law. Synagogues should look like synagogues.

Christians should stop wearing Yarmulkes. It is a violation of something undefined somewhere.

Some would suggest that I should just be more alert. Blame the Jew for everything. I got to the synagogue, saw the lack of a crowd, and did not even walk in. I went to the king. I turned to where any other individual facing a crisis of faith would go…no, not Islam…the one place where people in Chicago of all stripes can hear the music of the lord…the House of Blues. B.B. King was there, and he said "Baby I was wrong, to ever let you down, but I did what I did before love came to town."[48]

It was a lovely service, and many in the crowd were too drunk to notice the beauty of the singing. Given the amount of alcohol consumed, maybe this was not a restaurant bar at all. Hallelujah! I had made it to the synagogue. I think it was a Chabad (Orthodox Jewish) house, which would explain the mass quantities of alcohol.

It was another beautiful Friday Night Shabbos at the House of Jews. Chicago truly is a beautiful magical city. Actually, no it isn't. April and thirty-eight degrees…I wanna go…I wanna go home now.

eric

Barack Obama, Meet Mike Tramp

Awhile back I recommended that Hillary Clinton meet Joey Tempest, the lead singer of 1980s hard rock group Europe.

Once again it is necessary for an '80s hard rock band to explain a Democratic politician.

It is time for Barack Obama to meet Mike Tramp, singer of White Lion.

This is not about the great remake they did of the Golden Earring classic "Radar Love."

It is not even about their hit song "Tell me."

It is about the White Lion ballad that should be the official anthem of Barack Obama and the entire Demagogic Party.

The song is called "When the Children Cry."

The left throws temper tantrums due to their own inability to actually accomplish anything.

They blame Rush Limbaugh, Fox News, insurance companies, and everybody else except the people that they should blame…themselves.

I know some liberals have not figured it out, so let me explain it again.

Rush Limbaugh did not cause 9/11. Fox News is not responsible for the Holocaust. Neither Glenn Beck nor Sean Hannity have ever cast a single vote against Obamacare, because no bill even came up for a full vote when the attacks against them began. Even if it did, they could not vote.

People on the left despise George W. Bush, but there is no denying that he was effective. If he was ineffective, they would have no reason to despise him. Liberals love conservatives that fail to accomplish their goals.

President Bush had a 50/50 Senate, yet he got his tax cuts through.

Barack Obama had sixty Democrats in the senate, and could not get them to agree on anything except to blame Republicans.

"When the children cry, let them know we tried."[49]

The Pelosiraptor referred to the voters opposing her as Astroturf. The St. Louis Rams and Indianapolis Colts won many games on Astroturf. Maybe she is blaming Republicans for the recent failure of the Rams. Then again, her opposition to Limbaugh buying them means she wants them to fail.

The first time I heard Nancy Pelosi mention Astroturf, I thought that another woman had just admitted to spending time in Bill Clinton's pickup truck.

I don't have time for irrelevant people like the Bubbahound or the Pelosiraptor. Islamofascist terrorists are trying to kill us all. Conservatives care about this. We don't have time for the absolute nonsense that consumes the left.

We do not have time to hold full-time jobs in the private sector and come home to babysit screaming liberal children neglected by the nanny state the left loves.

The left has two options. Either accomplish something, or don't.

Just quit crying. Quit railing against other private citizens.

George W. Bush did not complain about MSNBC, which truly does exist to spread left-wing bile. He did not complain about the *Jayson Blair Times*. He did not make Gunga Dan Rather and Mary "fake but accurate" Mapes commit fraud and cover it up.

Barack Obama has not and will not ever encounter 10 percent of the criticism his predecessor did for merely existing and breathing air.

It is nobody else's fault but his own that he is seen worldwide as a likable wimp. His predecessor was hated by those who hate this country no matter what.

Barack Obama and the left can either put up or shut up. Until they do the first, they may wish to try the second.

I am recommending that Gerber create a new line of baby food for Democrats. Perhaps the makers of castor oil can give them some before bed.

Until then, they can enjoy some White Lion songs.

The adults will be back in charge soon enough. The children will be sent to their rooms again. Naturally, they will learn nothing from their experiences.

Perhaps Nancy Pelosi can join White Lion. They can rename the band "Lady and the Tramp."

Just kidding. She is no lady. Ladies are adults.

I am off to work, because that is what productive people do. I am hesitant to leave the Obama spokespeople at home alone. At least if we give them a few pacifiers to suck on, the rest of America can get some peace and quiet from their bellyaching for awhile.

eric

Chapter 12: Educational Idiocy

The cliché is that those who cannot do, teach. We are becoming a nation of imbeciles because it is impossible to learn when the instructors are bastions of uselessness. One professor told me that they face the pressure of publish or perish. The only downside is that I am not the one that gets to decide their fate. They would all perish. We could then do something useful with schools, like turn them into prisons. School is jail anyway. Junior high is maximum security prison. High school is medium security. College is minimum security, where occasional conjugal visits can be snuck in. Graduate School is like probation. The only consistent thread is that while there is hope for a precious few students, the professors are like a 1987 Oldsmobile Cutlass. There is no salvage value.

The Indefensible vs. the Incomprehensible

A seminar put on by the Middle East Studies Department at UCLA was entitled "Invasion is a Structure, not an Event: Settler Colonialism Past and Present."

Given that past conferences at UCLA have devolved into overt anti-Semitic propaganda events, I covered this event with a careful eye.

UCLA professors are aware they are being monitored, so they are being much more careful. This particular conference had some Jewish participants in an attempt to give it "diversity." As is typical on campuses, there was no intellectual or ideological diversity. The "Jewish" perspective was a left-wing offering that was barely distinguishable from the Palesimian/Arab offerings.

Making matters worse, the Arab speakers communicated in crisp, perfect English. The main Jewish professor offered a fractured linguistical hybrid known as "Heblish."

One piece of good news for decent human beings is that the "crowd" was small. About thirty people attended. Fifteen of them were professors. Of the fifteen "students," about five of them were over fifty. The rest were a mixture of Arabs and other leftist groups completely disjointed from the actual topic.

Even better news was that the professorial desire to glorify Palesimians and condemn Israel was overridden by the more powerful professorial desire to glorify themselves. Throughout their presentations, they spoke to each other, forgetting that students were even in the room.

The best way to title the conference in terms of "debate," would be "the indefensible vs. the incomprehensible."

Both of these traits were in display from the beginning. Zach Lochman began with the indefensible. He referred to the "Zionist entity," or as I call it, Israel. He also referred to Israel as the "Zionist project." He also claimed that "the Zionist entity has engaged in mass displacement of Palestinians." Palesimians were referred to as the "indigenous people," which would be true if indigenous referred to Jordan and Egypt. He stated that "Israel can be compared to South Africa. Israel uses coercion." He concluded his bile with the statement that, with regards to land and labor, "colonialism is Zionism."

Zach Lochman was educated at NYU, which made his message as perfectly communicated as it is awful.

Offering the incomprehensible was the "rebuttal" of Gershon Shafir, a professor at UCSD. His defense of Israel was as embarrassing as his communication skills.

He started by saying that he "didn't expect such a large crowd. I only brought five handouts."

He was self-deprecating and praiseworthy of his opponent, who was neither.

"I'm not from New York. I can't speak as quickly."

In looking at his own notes, he said, "I can't read this."

He combined Heblish with professor-speak. His jargon could have been taught in a mathematics class.

"Antecedent conditions lead to a critical juncture which leads to structural persistence which leads to a reactive sequence which leads to an outcome."

Perhaps he was saying that Palesimians don't need a homeland. They need a non-Chomsky linguistics class.

He almost managed to offer a Pro-Israel sentiment, but backed away.

"I have all kinds of things to say about (Palestinian) violence, but I would get some ugly looks if I do."

He then looked at the other professors, who glaringly motioned for him to sit down. This is campus diversity.

Australian Professor Patrick Wolfe spoke next on this panel. He stated that he had no stake in the Israeli-Palesimian conflict, which led me and reasonable people to ask "Why are you here?"

He was there to offer the Marxist position. There were no professors offering any conservative or capitalist points of view. Professor Wolfe offered what he promised.

"Black labor and red people's land has been used for white people's benefit."

"The primary goal is not the exploitation of labor. It is the seizure of land."

"Half of the Jews are Arabs, so the Jewish/Arab conflict makes no sense."

It makes plenty of sense. Arabs are murdering Jews, and Jews are against this.

Making less sense was Joel Bienin, who began by praising Lochman before saying that, "It is extraordinary to have such a rich discussion of the issues."

This was false, because only one side was represented. It was also telling that a professor would find an honest discussion on a campus to be extraordinary. Campuses are supposed to offer this.

Bienin also distinguished the current Israeli leaders from their elder founders of Israel.

"The young Turks are militarizing the conflict to advance themselves."

Gaby Piterman opined that "increased settler movement is meant to spread Judeo supremacy at all costs."

Lochman offered that "In 1948 Jews succeeded in getting rid of many indigenous Palestinians, but they can't kill them all. This is the logic and contradiction of the Zionist project."

Patricia Larson, a woman over fifty, spoke about sexuality in colonial Algeria. She managed to unite Lochman and Shafir, initially because they were glaring at her black leather miniskirt and fishnet stockings, and eventually because they badly wanted her presentation to end. It was a distraction from bashing Israel.

Gabriel Piterberg, who was supposed to discuss Israeli writer Amos Oz, offered bizarre thoughts.

"Israeli settlers are running around like R2D2."

(I guess that would make C3PO a colonizer, since he was British.)

"Israel looted Palestinian land after 1948. It was colonial sexual excitement."

"Like an adulterous woman, the nomads moved forward."

"Picture an Oriental Jewish woman fantasizing about a man with a mustache."

(Oriental is a politically insensitive word, and I was not clear if the Asian woman lusted after Saddam Hussein or Inspector Clouseau.)

"A proper white woman must become a Moroccan slut to experience true physical pleasure."

Joel Benin added that "Amos Oz is the Israeli author I most love to hate. We need an extra five minutes to expose his racism and misogyny."

Patricia Larson added that "Sexual anxiety creates a fear of Arabs and Muslims."

(I always thought it was because of bombings and other senseless forms of genocidal lunacy.)

Sondra Hale, the "brains" behind Middle Eastern "studies" at UCLA, asked "How does that relate to settlers?"

Without missing a beat, Ms. Larson replied, "Demographic promiscuity."

She also opined that "Sexual anxiety leads to the politics of this moment. Periods of calm mean that there is no need for 'Frenchness.'"

(I am not sure if she was bashing or praising the French, but it was no less ludicrous than anything else said.)

Gabriel Piterberg offered that "Likud policies are about exerting sexual power."

(I think it was Yassir Arafat who sexually violated everything in sight, not Israelis.)

Joel Benin left the sex talk behind and continued the program by accusing Israel of committing genocide.

"The logic of settler colonialism is eliminationist."

(That is not an actual word, but campuses have nothing to do with grammar.)

He cited as fact Rasheed Khalidi, who said that "in 1884, violence occurred two years after Zionists arrived in Palestine."

"The 'Nachba' (mistake) occurred in July, 1948. Yitzchak Rabin expelled fifty thousand Palestinians."

(Jordan murdered one million of them. This is why they want to stay in Israel so badly. Far from being oppressed, they are allowed to live.)

He then said that "I am not here making a pacifist solution." This remark was followed by loud laughter.

When somebody asked about problems with the Palesimian leadership, Bienin replied, to more laughter, "Some things I don't discuss in black and white."

The conclusion of this bizarre conference was stunningly and unintentionally honest.

Gabriel Piterberg stated that, "We all write about the settlers, but none of us write about the indigenous population. This could be for a variety of reasons."

Sondra Hale replied that "We are only interested in the settlers because we are careerists. That is unkind, but true. There is plenty of material on the indigenous people, we just ignore it."

She is wrong about material. There is no material on Palesimians because they are not indigenous. There is nothing in history, and they know this. She is totally right in admitting that none of them care one bit about Palesimians. Criticizing Israel on campuses is good for business, and easier than original thought.

Joel Bienin concluded by saying that "The Zionist argument is that there were zero Palestinians before 1948. Palestinians are a result of the Nachba. Rasheed Khalidi has a fine book."

The worst bile actually occurred during a break when the professors took their barely civil masks off.

Sondra Hale had a conversation with attendees Carol Smith and Karen Pally. They showed their true agenda.

"'Stand With Us' are the White Citizen's Council without the sheets. They are McCarthyists."

(The actual word is McCarthyites, but why let academics get in the way of a professorial argument.)

"The ZOA are Nazis."

"Zionists are more despicable than Baathists."

(I am surprised they disliked Baathists at all.)

"If we could just use the courts, we could make the Zionists feel the financial sting."

To truly understand what these people actually care about, one has to know that nothing in this conference galvanized anybody to do anything. It had a shelf life of an Arabic *Star Wars* Conference, which Gabriel Piterberg may be working on next. One issue did spur a call to action, and the ladies discussed it passionately.

"These are expensive coffee cups. They are not biodegradable. I am going to say something and write letters."

Jewish people should be relieved that the few attendees not eligible for an AARP card found the indefensible aspects of the conference overrun by the incomprehensible.

eric

A Teachable Moment About Useless Symbolic Photo Ops

Barack Obama held a meeting.

Liberals everywhere should celebrate.

What was the meeting about? It does not matter. What was discussed? Irrelevant. Were any tangible agreements reached? Immaterial. Were there any safeguards or enforcement mechanisms to make sure that agreements are not breached? To even ask this is totally inappropriate.

There was a meeting. That is a victory.

For those who do care, the meeting took place between Barack Obama, Joe Biden (who was invited because apparently his schedule was clear from whatever it is he does), Professor Henry Louis Gates, and Sgt. Jim Crowley.

(On this White House version of Gilligan's Island, Sgt. Crowley played pure as can be Mary Ann. President Obama was Thurston Howell III. Vice President Biden was either Lovey or Gilligan, with the Professor being the Professor.)

For those who do not know, an arrogant gasbag Harvard professor (redundant, I know) locked himself out of his house. This makes me qualified to be a Harvard professor, since I have done that as well. The professor then compounded his idiocy (it is idiocy when I do it too) by trying to break into his own home.

A concerned neighbor saw a man breaking into the home and called the police. Professor Gates might consider this racism. Others call it being a good neighbor. The police officer then showed up. Professor Gates might consider that racist as well. Others call it doing one's job.

The matter could have been completely avoided had Professor Gates not tried to play the race card from the bottom of the deck. Being polite to police officers defuses many situations. Being belligerent escalates them.

I understand that in decades past, police abuse against minorities occurred. Like everything from sexual harassment to hate crimes laws, the pendulum has swung to the other end of the illogical spectrum.

This was a situation of a racially obsessed minority heaping abusive behavior on a law enforcement officer who had no racial animus whatsoever. This was about more than race for Mr. Gates. This was about class. How dare a blue-collar whitey question a man who is friends with Obama! How dare a Harvard graduate be questioned by a plebeian commoner!

President Obama then pulled "a Biden." He claimed that he did not have the facts of the incident, but that the cops "acted stupidly."[50] Even some liberals understood that this was problematic. Naturally their concern was for how it would appear, rather than what was actually said...liberals and substance, oil and water, etc.

President Obama invited Sgt. Crowley and Professor Gates to share a beer at the White House.

This was nothing more than a useless symbolic photo op designed to stop the slide in President Obama's polls.

President Obama wanted this to be a "teachable moment."[51]

What President Obama means is that he can lecture us in a high-minded manner. We should be forced to understand Professor Gates. Whitey can learn from this, and be more sensitive.

Sorry, Mr. President. The only person that should be speaking at this gathering is Sgt. Crowley.

Barack Obama and Henry Gates have nothing to teach me. There is nothing valuable I can learn from them. One is a Harvard Professor. The other is a Harvard academic that community organized his way into the White House.

The only thing people who develop Harvard syndrome know how to do is talk...and talk...and talk. They teach. They don't listen or learn.

Harvard is not an institution of higher learning. It is a left-wing house of elitism where ideological discussion is forbidden. Liberals are good, conservatives are bad, end of discussion.

That does not cut it with me. I don't need a toilet paper-sized piece of fancy parchment with letters next to it to teach me common sense or right from wrong.

President Obama screwed up. He issued a namby-pamby, half-hearted, half-baked, too little, too late non-apology apology. The words "I'm sorry" never occurred.

As for Professor Gates, I have very little sympathy for a grievance-monger that earns three times my salary. In his "nothing has changed since 1863" world I am the oppressor. Make no mistake about it. His behavior was no different than what police used to do before Miranda. The professor was the one who abused his power and connections, for no other reason than he thought he could.

The professor was delighted by this controversy. It kept him in the news, which is great for book sales. He had a tome coming out, and his "street cred" for standing up to "the man" went through the roof.

The only thing worth teaching about this moment is that accusations of racism need to be shot down rapidly and unequivocally. Sgt. Crowley did not back down. He did not give an inch. He was right.

The system is not rigged against black people. Anybody who thinks otherwise should learn about what happened to a coworker of Sgt. Crowley. The coworker sent a mass email that referred to Professor Gates in racially inappropriate terms. The officer who sent that email was justifiably suspended. The system can work.

That is a teachable moment. Don't put bad stuff in emails. Email is forever. Also, don't be a racist. Is it really that hard to wake up and not be a bigot? I think not.

The media spent endless hours discussing the different flavors of ale each man consumed. At some point they had Joe Biden fetch them some cigars and then leave the room so that the adults could have a conversation without it being leaked incorrectly to this very same media.

Nothing of substance came out of this, exactly as intended.

The only thing that improved were Obama's poll numbers. He got credit for healing a nation when the truth is all he did was exacerbate a situation with his own bungling.

Maybe he does need a teleprompter to speak eloquently. If he really wants to make things better in America, he could do what liberal academics simply refuse to do.

He can stop teaching, pay attention to others, listen, and learn.

This is called being quiet and doing one's job without excuses.

Perhaps Sgt. Crowley can teach him. That is a photo op worth seeing.

eric

Chapter 13: Community Organizer Idiocy

Community organizers are basically unemployed people that are well dressed. It is easy to look sharp when earning a living by leeching off of less educated and less fortunate people under the phony guise of help. Barack Obama is the First Social Worker-in-Chief. The world is one giant caseload. If he could just love every person, he could get every case closed with a happy ending. Like many social workers, President Obama is going to see violence and carnage before he goes to sleep at night. Aggressors, be they drunken spousal abusers or homicide bomber Islamists, will not be stopped with hugs and love therapy. Barack Obama has the solution. He just doesn't care.

Barack Hannah Montana Obama

Gerard Baker of the London Times masterfully lacerated the myth of the Obamessiah. The anointed one spaketh, and Mr. Baker brilliantly satirized. I hope to one day reach his skill level.

For those looking for some politically liberal gifts for loved ones, Eau D'Obama Anus perfume can now be purchased on eBay. Rumor has it that Chris Matthews bought several bottles, which might explain the tingling sensation on his leg.

I suspect that Barack Obama bought a few bottles for his own bathroom, given that he absolutely loves the smell of his own rumpus. He is a built-in air freshener because his (redacted) simply don't stink.

We can all celebrate that society has come so far that a black man can succeed in politics by being as much of a vapid gasbag as the white man. Having said that, I believe we have been too tough on Barack Obama. He is a sweet young kid, and should be given a lollipop and a pat on the head.

It is in that spirit of loving our little cherubs that his new nickname is now officially being rolled out.

Barack Obama is now forever BHMO: Barack Hannah Montana Obama.

Think about it. Both Barack Obama and Mylie Cyrus are loved by young preteens around the world. Both of them fill up amphitheatres and fill them with sweet sugary pop. With Obama, it is more pap than pop. Either way, there is pep. He is a sweet young pup for a little pip.

Both Obama and Mylie have been filmed in provocative clothing that may not have been appropriate for such young angels. Mylie did a photo spread that proved embarrassing. Obama was caught with his shirt off after swimming.

Both Obama and Mylie are lighthearted fun, far away from the real problems that exist in this world. They are an escape hatch from what truly matters.

The stock market? Iraq? The Global War on Terror? Come on. Stop bothering these kids. They have plenty of time to worry about that when they grow up.

Mylie Cyrus is warmhearted. She is simply a nice kid. She seems to truly believe in goodness. Her songs are friendly.

Barack Obama sings songs about hope and change. We can hope to have change, and change to hope. It is a beautiful circle, and may it never be unbroken, by and by lord, by and by.[52]

All we have to do is look to the heavens and everything will be great.

I can even picture Obama and Mylie singing, "Sunshine, lollipops, rainbows, and everything that's wonderful."[53]

Don't tell Obama or Mylie's Achy Breaky Heart that things are not sweet. I just don't think they would understand.[54] Billy Ray Cyrus has had pain, but he has done a great job of shielding Mylie from the darker aspects of life. As for Barack, he just has the gift of ignorant bliss. May this adorable cherub never lose his naiveté.

I just hope that the real world does not swallow them up. I pray that Mylie Cyrus never turns into Britney Spears, Paris Hilton, or Lindsay Lohan. I pray that Obambi never becomes as cynical as most politicians by relying on obscure concepts such as reality and facts.

Both of them speak in words that show a refreshing innocence, unspoiled by actual life experience.

Both of them get to frolic around the world, playing to adoring audiences. Both of them have unlimited bank accounts, and most likely spend it on frivolities.

The cheerleaders in junior high schools across America are preparing their routines.

Heck, no! We won't go!

We love BHMO!

Cuter than the Dali Llama!

Barack Hannah Montana Obama!

Good little girls! Hug your momma!

It's Barack Hannah Montana Obama!

No more crying, no more trauma!

Here's Barack Hannah Montana Obama!

Hot Hot Hotter than a Sauna!

Barack Hannah Montana Obama!

Past our bedtime? We don't wanna!

We want Barack Hannah Montana Obama!

No more school! No more drama!

Smiles from Barack Hannah Montana Obama!

Period, semicolon, question, comma!

Exclamation Barack Hannah Montana Obama!

Raise 'em high! Raise 'em low!

We love BHMO!

Yyyyaaaayyyyy, Barry!

The bottom line is that children need love. They need a steady hand of an adult parent to guide them.

Mylie Cyrus has her father Billy Ray, and her mother. She will be fine.

America will be okay as well. We have adult Republicans like George W. Bush and Dick Cheney to deal with the many serious adult challenges that our nation faces. He worked to defeat the bad guys so that kids of all ages could sleep safely and snugly in their beds at night, whether they be girls such as Mylie Cyrus or boys such as Barack Obama.

Goodnight sweet Barack Hannah Montana Obama. Don't worry my little one. Daddy Republican will take care of everything. You just smile, rest up, and get some sleep.

eric

Toddler Thursday–President Obambi Turns One

America's adorable lil Cherub-in-Chief turned one. The day is therefore Toddler Thursday.

Happy birthday young President Obambi.

I have observed this sweet little boy try to enter an adult world with as much success as most liberal children. Like parents, conservatives are always the bad guys. We are hated for not giving away free candy that belongs to somebody else and is not really free.

As we prepare to celebrate his presidency birthday, I am amazed by the similarities between Mr. Obama and my close friend's baby son. "The boy," as we affectionately call him, is two years old. Apparently age comes with maturity.

It is tough to get mad at the boy for acting like a two-year old. He is one. When President Obama acts this way, it is tiresome.

One similarity is that both Obama and the boy are gasbags. The lil el gaso bago (The boy, not the president) is being potty trained, and soon will not be a little gasbag. As for the president, he continues to spew nonsense.

My unofficial nickname for the boy is "3M," after the Minnesota Mining and Manufacturing Company. I call him 3M because some of the first words he learned were "me," "mine," and "more." The president is an expert with these words, especially the word "me."

Whenever he says, "this is not about me," he means it is completely about him. The boy is too young to know what a narcissist is, but at age two it is okay to be one.

The boy likes to stare at himself in the mirror with fascination. I suspect Obama does likewise.

(I have no evidence that Obama bathes with a rubber ducky.)

The boy likes to watch a children's program called "The Wiggles." He gets up and dances, zigs, and zags, and contorts himself into various shapes.

So does Obama, when asked a question he does not want to answer. He wiggles and wriggles, and uses big words to make it look like he answered the question. He has a bigger vocabulary than the boy, but he says less in terms of substance.

The boy also watches Charles Krauthammer with his father, although that is more about being with Dad. He would rather watch the Wiggles. President Obama would rather watch anything else but Charles Krauthammer. We would all be better off if he did.

When the boy gets cranky, his parents count to three. Reaching three means he sits in the corner and takes a "timeout." In all the times I have been at their house, the last number was two, and a timeout was averted.

Obama pressed the reset button with regard to the rest of the world. Now he needs to reset himself. He needs a do-over. First he needs to take some deep breaths and take a timeout. He is not getting his way, since the punishment for defying him is absolutely nothing.

Come to think of it, Obama has as much influence over the world as the boy. The boy at least doesn't claim otherwise.

Beneath all the jokes is the fact that while Obama talks about the future, the boy is the future. The president is on the verge of being irrelevant. The boy is as relevant as it gets.

If Obama does not keep America safe, the boy may not have the same joys in life that his father and his de facto uncle have. It is a scary world out there. The boy will probably not worry about anything in the coming years more sinister than monsters under the bed. Obama has to worry about real monsters that want to kill us all.

The boy lives in a pre-school world where the kids care, share and play well with others. There are adults to make sure that the kids are nice to each other. Obama does not have somebody to make the bad guys behave. He has to be the one to do it.

The main difference is that the boy should act like a child. He should be allowed to believe in rainbows and lollipops and all that other good stuff.

Obama needs to grow up in a hurry. He needs to lead by example. He needs to stop demonizing fellow Americans and start going after our enemies hard. If he gets this stuff wrong, there might not be a world for any of us.

Both the boy and President Obama came into our lives with stars in their eyes. The boy will try to remain this way. Obama needs to snap out of it.

186

It is time for Obambi to grow a pair. He needs to stop whining, end his toddler temper tantrums, and fulfill his job responsibilities. My friend will do his part. He will make sure along with his wife that the boy has a loving mother and father, food on the table, clothing on his body, and a roof over his head.

As for Obama, he seems to be a good father. Unlike my friend, he is having trouble balancing work and family. Given that his wife and mother-in-law help with the kids, Obama needs to start focusing on his job.

Even though he will only be two next year from a presidential standpoint, he needs to start acting above his age. Unlike the boy, who should grow and learn at his own leisurely pace, President Obama must grow up right now this minute.

Children grow up way too fast. Some adults never grow up at all.

May Toddler Thursday be about the boy, and not about our Peter Pan president.

eric

The First Blatherer-In-Chief Spaketh

I am promoting President Obama from First Gasbag-in-Chief to First Blatherer-in-Chief.

In a speech that will last forever or a few minutes, whichever comes first, President Obama gave America another teachable moment.

(I remember a skit of Conan O'Brien when Bill Clinton had to have his State of the Union on the same night as the O.J. Simpson civil verdict. The Clinton character claimed that he was glad his speech was interrupted. "Don't you see Conan. I'm glad it happened. I had nothing to say.")[55]

The lesson…when one is known as all talk and no action, continuing to talk is not the best option.

Like health care, I prefer Obama choose the private option over the public option with regards to his speeches. He should keep his thoughts private. That is what got him elected. People like him as long as he does not try to do anything. This is what happens when one is basically likable but completely wrong.

Hillary Clinton smiled. I still think that she wants to leap on the stage and explain why she would handle the issue better despite the 1994 avalanche contradicting this.

As for President Obama, I looked to see if he did his fifty-four degree angle head tilt to convey seriousness, as pointed out in *The Onion*.[56]

For those who wonder how many times he head tilted, I am sure that some enterprising college students made a drinking game out of it already. "Hope," and "change" are the new versions of "Hi Bob (Newhart)."[57]

He really does look and talk like Dr. Spock, except with less emotion.

"I will not let up until those Americans who seek jobs can find them."[58]

He took credit for pulling the economy back from the brink.

I now take credit for landing a man on the Moon.

"We did not come here to clean up crises. We came here to create a future."

Now that is a platitude.

"I am not the first president to take up this cause (health care), but I am determined to be the last."

That means he will mess it up so no future president will want to go near it.

He then praised John Dingell for repeatedly presenting a bill that never got passed.

I then gave myself a gold star for trying at things regardless of the results. This liberalism stuff is not half bad sometimes.

"Thirty million American citizens cannot get coverage."

Notice he did not say the forty-five to fifty million figure this time. He also said "American citizens" to take into account illegal aliens.

He then went into a couple of sob stories. These stories are touching. It could be me one day. Stories are not solutions. He pointed out that rising costs are a problem. Mosquito bites are a problem. The solution is ointment. Mr. Obama would rather restate the problem. Maybe he just likes stating and restating.

"Our health care problem is our deficit problem. Nothing else even comes close."

Fair enough.

He then, as I predicted, turned into Bill Clinton. He began triangulating.

"Build on what works, fix what doesn't."

Platitude! Drink a shot!

Charles Rangel paid very close attention, thrilled that health care reform was taking headlines away from his possible indictment for financial crimes.

He used the word "details" regarding "his" plan. I listened intently.

"Nothing in this plan will require you or your employer to change the doctor you have."

He then restated this. He really does like stating and restating, as I previously stated.

"It would be against the law for insurance companies to deny you coverage in case of a preexisting condition."

What happens when insurance companies go bankrupt? He is offering us good news, but how will he pay for this?

Maybe he will bring me a chicken in every pot.

"No one should go broke because they get sick."

Platitude alert! Drink a shot.

I mean who could disagree with this?

He then endorsed wide-reaching legal reform and tort reform.

Just kidding.

"We will create a new insurance exchange...a marketplace."

We already have this! It is called the "marketplace."

Next Mr. Obama will invent electricity so that Al Gore can invent the Internet.

"This exchange will take place in four years, so that we have time to get it right."

(We can saddle his successor with a nightmare.)

He pointed out that some young people will refuse to take coverage. He called that "irresponsible behavior." He is right. Will he mandate them or not? He says he will. What if they don't? Are they arrested?

Why does he not apply this same logic to irresponsible mortgage owners?

"There are significant details to be ironed out (the crowd laughed), but significant consensus exists."

No it doesn't. If it did we would have passed a bipartisan bill.

As for "death panels," he said, "it is a lie, plain and simple."

Everything with this guy is plain and simple except the details of his plan.

He emphatically stated that illegal immigrants will not be covered. Some people booed this in the chamber. He also stated that abortion rules would not be affected. There was stone silence.

"My guiding principle has always been that consumers do better when there is choice and competition."

He accused companies of "cherry picking individuals," yet he actually admitted that they did this "because it is profitable."

This is an example of him going out of his way to acknowledge opposing views in words while completely discounting them in deeds.

"I have no interest in putting insurance companies out of business. I just want to hold them accountable."

I do not want to fire Barack Obama (Okay, I do). I just want him held accountable.

He insisted that taxpayers would not be subsidizing the public option. He actually claimed that there would be less bureaucracy with the public option.

I really need to start drinking so that the pink elephants I am seeing make more sense.

"The public option is only one part of my plan."

What is his plan?

"We should remain open to other ideas that accomplish our goal."

Platitude alert!

"Republicans, work together so we may address any legitimate concerns you may have."

Platitude alert!

"These are all constructive ideas that we should consider."

Before being discarded.

If I was playing the platitude alert drinking game I would be blitzed right now.

Forty minutes into his speech, he discussed that he was going to discuss how to pay for it.

"I will not sign a plan that adds one dime to our deficit now or in the future."

He then spoke about a part of the plan that enacts spending cuts if savings don't materialize. These spending cuts never ever happen. It is called congressional budgeting. Give breaks now. Ignore spending cuts.

He then bashed George W. Bush for the "Iraq War and tax cuts for the wealthy."

This is the man who wants to work with Republicans. Child, please (I saw that on a sitcom).

He will not touch the Medicare trust fund.

He will eliminate waste and fraud.

Just because I can tell you that sugar is not in a diet soda does not mean I can tell you exactly what is in a diet soda.

Mythical savings from combating waste and fraud will fill the gaps. That is like releasing a three hundred pound linebacker and replacing him with a one hundred-fifty pound backup.

"I will protect Medicare."

(Grabbing a bullhorn:) "What is your plan?"

Maybe he does not even know.

This would be laughable if it were not so sad. I could have been watching sitcoms where the laughter is intentional.

He will charge insurance companies for their most expensive policies.

"This modest change could help…"

He alluded to Republican support for tort reform.

"I don't believe that malpractice reform is a silver bullet."

"I do believe that defensive medicine takes place."

He then stated that he would direct his HHS person to begin an "initiative." That was not the same thing as actually endorsing tort reform.

He then mentioned Iraq, Afghanistan and tax cuts for the wealthy.

This guy can't stop campaigning.

His plan reduces the deficit by $400 trillion in the long term. He is the one that is creating this ridiculous deficit.

He again created the straw man argument that his opponents want to "kill the plan rather than improve it."

"If you misrepresent what is in this plan, we will call you out. I will not accept the status quo as the solution."

Call yourself out Mr. President. The issue is not doing nothing. It is saying nothing, which is what you do.

"We cannot fail because too many Americans are counting on us to succeed."

Platitude alert!

Then came the obligatory story about Ted Kennedy.

Is the president so crass as to use Ted Kennedy to get a plan passed? No way, that would be like using children as props. Never mind. He does that too.

"At stake are not just the details of policy, but the fundamental policies of social justice and the character of our country."[59]

Those words from Ted Kennedy are exactly why this plan must be killed. Social justice is code word for destroying productive people.

Mr. Obama then acknowledged Ted Kennedy's critics before discounting their opinions in his typical polite but dismissive way.

Ted Kennedy was "concerned about the plight of others."

Except when he was driving them over a bridge. That should never be forgotten.

He then went into the beauty of how government can get things right, such as Social Security and Medicare. He left out that they are both going bankrupt.

"Government could not and should not solve every problem, are not worth adding constraints on our freedoms."

Platitude alert!

He bemoaned the lack of civility in politics, forgetting that he blames his predecessor for his own personal failings on the political front.

"We did not come here to fear the future. We came here to shape it."

Platitude alert!

"I still believe we can replace acrimony with civility."

Start with yourself and Professor Gates, Mr. President. Then work on Van Jones.

I have only one question about his plan.

What is it?

We still have no idea. The details need to be worked out.

If it was mathematically possible, had his speech been twice as long he would have said half of less than nothing.

All hail the First Blatherer-in-Chief. If he promises to stop talking and actually do something, I will demote him back to First Gasbag-in-Chief.

Louisiana Representative Charles Boustany delivered the Republican rebuttal. He is a heart surgeon, which means he actually has something to say. He began by citing the Congressional Budget Office. He pointed out that he actually read the bill that creates "fifty-three new bureaucracies."[60] This is what we call specifics.

"I performed surgeries on many people who could have been healthier had they made better choices earlier in life."

He pointed out that real reform must include tort reform.

Mr. Boustany said more in five minutes than President Obama did in an hour.

He was short, sweet, and to the point.

Mr. Obama can't do it.

Let's end this on a positive note.

His necktie is still perfect. If it comes undone, it will be his predecessor's fault due to Iraq and tax cuts.

eric

The First Gasbag-In-Chief Spaketh

I was going to cover President Obama's remarks to the nation, but then I decided only to cover the substance. Figuring that a blank page would leave readers cheated, I realized that the speech can be declared substantive simply because President Obama said so.

I expected him to cover familiar themes, ranging from his own fabulousness and heroic nature, to saving America from everything in this world, which was all George W. Bush's fault. I also expected him to declare that he was bipartisan simply because he said he was, and that Republicans were not bipartisan because they disagreed with him.

I also expected environmentalists to praise him despite the fact that the gas from his speeches is killing the Ozone Layer, assuming that anybody really ever cared about that.

I was right. He began his speech by mentioning that in the first few weeks of his administration, quick and decisive action was taken to save this economy.

No, Mr. Obama. That was George W. Bush and Hank Paulson. You and Timothy Geithner had no idea how to handle the problem, and you still don't. The idea that everything bad belongs to your predecessor while anything good is all because of you is more tired than me at a mattress testing convention.

(Nordstroms should not have thrown me out. I may have bought that hammock.)

He then continued by spouting nonsense, but with his head tilted at an angle to convey seriousness.

"The recovery act we passed has already saved jobs and created new ones."[61]

Are you kidding me? Only a liberal could expect to lose ten jobs, "only" lose five, and call that job creation. These are the same liberals that think that if a program grows by 5 percent instead of 10 percent, that money is being saved. This is how Republicans were accused of "cutting" Medicare when they were merely slowing the growth rate. Liberals make stuff up.

Mr. Obama needs only sixty seconds into a speech to remind me that he is full of cr@pola.

Just level with America sir. Stop telling us that anything you have done so far has worked. If you want to say you need time, and that in time things will work, I can listen. Do not say you have already succeeded. The facts contradict this.

He then stated that he provided Americans tax relief. Who are these people? What tax relief?

Then he stated that "our economy was not ready to compete in the twenty-first century." He mentioned green jobs. Enough with the Deepak Chopra gobbledy gook. Steel workers and coal workers are being decimated while the First College Professor-in-Chief lectures us about going green.

If he wants me to go green, make stoplights friendlier so I don't have to see red every morning on the main road.

Then he lied about forty-seven million Americans not having health care. This is the most fraudulent statistic the Democrats use, which says a lot for Democrats. The number is a bald-faced lie.

He then lied about how people would not be forced to give up their private insurance. With a public option, government will undercut private companies. The same liberals who criticize Wal-Mart for successfully lowering prices to drive competitors out of business deliberately ignore that government is like Wal-Mart to the hundredth power. At least Wal-Mart plays by the rules.

He declared that the AARP "endorsed his reform efforts," as if that actually means something. The AARP are partisan Democrats.

He criticized one anonymous Republican strategist for saying that Republicans should "go for the kill" and reject compromise. Apparently Mr. Obama had no problem with allowing Rahm Emanuel to say that "a crisis should never go to waste."[62] Mr. Obama truly believes that compromise means cramming a liberal agenda down conservative throats with no dissent in the name of bipartisanship.

On the one hand Mr. Obama is tired of businesses being hit with tax burdens. Then he says he wants to raise taxes on businesses. Unlike George W. Bush, apparently when Mr. Obama raises taxes it will be an investment and not a burden. Problem solved.

Once again, the Associated Press got to ask the first question, because they are a liberal organization posing as a neutral one.

They asked him if he would offer specifics as to what he wanted from congress. He would rather let Nancy Pelosi succeed so he can take credit, or fail so he can shift the blame. Of course he does not want to leave any fingerprints. He is lazy. He likes campaigning, but has no interest in doing the actual work.

He never answered the question.

"There are a number of different ways to raise money. I preferred my proposal."

How modest of him.

He thinks that there are enough rich people to pay for this.

"I am not for closing other ideas."

My lord this man is generous of spirit.

He does not want to hurt the middle class. Instead he will harass rich people, and they will lay off or refuse to hire middle class people. President Obama will then blame George W. Bush for this as well.

President Obama was asked, "What's the rush?"

While the answer is because he wants to ram things through before his polls slip further (the reason George W. Bush could not bomb Iran), he cited the need to help families.

He always makes one or two valid but meaningless points per press conference. He says things nobody could disagree with that don't matter. This speech featured the line that "inertia is the default option." He also mentioned that "it is important that we get this right." Who could argue with that?

"I will not sign a bill that I don't think will work."

Then no bill should be signed until he is out of office.

In the interest of moderation, the president asked MSNBC to ask him a question. Chuck Todd asked if everyone would be covered.

President Obama said unless we had a single payer system, only 97 to 98 percent would be covered. During the campaign he said 100 percent of Americans would be covered.

"You haven't seen me out there blaming the Republicans."

For the love of God Mr. President, that is your entire political platform. Sheesh! Everything in life that is wrong is your predecessor's fault. He left you with a mess, but you are not blaming him. You need to stop bathing in that shower gel that mixes ginseng extract with Obama adoration beads.

In President Obama's world, Republicans play politics while Democrats act on principle. The president even brags that he has "seen Republican ideas." Then he rejects them out of hand.

For those who think I am always against President Obama, let me give credit where credit is due. His necktie was perfect. I think he uses a Windsor knot. Like his necktie, his words are contorted into a twisted shape that fits him perfectly but benefits nobody else.

"Americans have to give up things that won't make them healthier."

President Obama is a smoker and a hypocrite. His smoking habit does more to raise premiums than anything I do.

I was only halfway through when I decided to throw in the towel. Health requires a good night of sleep, which I cannot get if I stay up all night listening to this windbag.

(Windbag is a better term than gasbag due to his hostility toward the oil industry.)

He then went on to blame George W. Bush again, before taking credit for a stimulus package that George W. Bush passed.

President Obama then stated that he saved $2.2 trillion for America. I will not be getting a check in the mail, because these savings are as mythical as the jobs he saved.

He then blamed his predecessor again. The theme here was to cry, blame, and protest.

This is our leader. I think the start of any health care plan should be pre-natal. We can start by giving the First Baby-in-Chief his bottle and a nice long nap, or at the very least, a timeout.

eric

The World's Least Interesting Man

"Stay thirsty my friends."

With those words, a beer company created a legend.

"He lives vicariously through himself.

He once had an awkward moment, just to see how it would feel.

The police often question him, just because they find him interesting.

His blood is made of cologne.

His personality is so magnetic, he cannot carry credit cards.

Even his enemies list him as their emergency contact.

He is…the most interesting man in the world."[63]

He now even offers advice on various important topics.

"There is a time and place for pick-up lines. The time is never. You can figure out the place on your own."

While discussing the most interesting man in the world with coworkers, we joked that this Colombian adventure seeker and life of every party in real life was probably a boring average guy.

Sadly enough, he is just some Jewish actor who is most likely not even South American.

Although his identity was revealed, I will not say his name. Let people do their own research.

What I take away from this is that beyond commercials, there are so many people that we put on pedestals that have no business being there. One of the main reasons is political correctness.

One example of this is Tiger Woods. Just to be clear, Tiger deserved every ounce of success he achieved. He is one of the greatest golfers of all time. Yet the fascination with him was bizarre. Golf itself is colossally boring. Even if one rejects that assertion, there is no denying that Tiger Woods is duller than dishwater. Listen to him give a press conference. He is boring. This is not a criticism. Again, the man is a golfer.

(He also deserved the consequences of his conduct. His wife beat the tar out of him in the same way Brenda Richie took down Lionel. The only surprising aspect of this story was that a golfer actually had sex with anybody.)

The media fawned over his every move because he is multi-racial. He is racially all of us. Despite trying to turn this man into a unifying factor, he repeatedly stated that he just wanted to keep quiet and golf.

This is ironic. Most celebrities refuse to shut up, despite nobody of any relevance wanting to hear what they have to say. Tiger never publicly expressed an opinion on anything. He spent all day hitting a little white ball into a small hole. For this he was treated like the second coming.

If Tiger Woods was projected onto others, his hero worship was nothing compared to how the media treats Barack Obama. Unlike Mr. Woods, Mr. Obama has not done anything yet. He won a popularity contest. Great. That is equivalent to being drafted. He barely stepped onto the field, and already the media had him in the Hall of Fame.

While his being bi-racial and getting elected was a first in American politics, outside of that President Obama is a fairly dull guy being held up as a fascinating individual.

He is beyond normal. He is ultra-conventional. He is Al Gore, John Kerry, and Michael Dukakis all rolled into one. His beliefs are ordinary and non-descript. His family is typical.

This is not an indictment of the man. It is a criticism of the media that holds him up as if he were some suave South American folk hero.

The man killed a fly with his hands, and the media celebrated it.[64] A crowd even once cheered at a campaign rally when he announced that he had to blow his nose.[65]

I remember when David Letterman made a joke about Joseph Lieberman in 2000.

"You know what the really interesting thing about Joseph Lieberman is? Actually, there's nothing interesting about Joseph Lieberman."[66]

Why are these jokes about Barack Obama not coming?

Picture him in the beer commercials.

"His face is tilted at a fifty-six degree angle to convey seriousness that mere mortals cannot understand."

"He is a world-class athlete who can jump twenty feet just to reach his nose."

"He can get Iowa corn farmers to grow arugula, while others cannot even spell the word."

"His teleprompter has a teleprompter."

"He once killed a fly with his bare hands, leading to a media holiday."

"His trips to the restroom are the hottest selling items on eBay."

"He made Joe Biden vice president and Hillary Clinton secretary of state to successfully get them both out of government."

"His prime time news conferences are dedicated to his own popularity in prime time news conferences."

"He is…the least interesting man in the world."

I think I would rather hang out with the fictional Dos Equis guy.

Stay thirsty my friends.

eric

Barack Obama–Meaningless Words Celebrating a Meaningless Milestone

A meaningless milestone in the form of an unrealistic artificial timeline was celebrated with a meaningless speech by an artificial leader specializing in meaningless words.

His chin was tilted to the perfect angle to hide the lack of meaning. He looked downright authoritative and serious with his meaningless proclamations.

Then the evening went downhill when President Obama stopped doing his "wow, I look important" pose and began the lecture.

The Blatherer-in-Chief let us know that the flu virus situation was "serious."[67] The government is "doing something about it." He told us to wash our hands and cover our mouths when we cough.

He claimed that his recovery package "saved or created one hundred-fifty-thousand jobs, and gave a tax cut to 95 percent of all working families."

The guy makes up numbers out of thin air and the media blindly accepts them, but let's be fair. His suit looked good and his shirt was crisp. The *Jayson Blair Times* will be doing a three-part expose on whether he prefers rice, fries, or baked potato with his steak. His speeches should be in *Vegetarian Times Magazine* because there is no beef.

He even claimed that his housing plan led to a spike in refinancing, which in Obamaland, "is the equivalent of another tax cut."

Sure. When a doctor just puts on the rubber glove and checks for testicular cancer, it's the same thing as when my girlfriend visits, except it is completely different. It depends what the word "equivalent" is. Equivalent is a word that lying politicians and makers of diet soda use. The equivalent is just as good, except not.

"We have to lay a new foundation for growth."

He is just brilliant.

He bragged about closing Gitmo, without addressing whether he will actually work on a plan to place the detainees.

He claimed to be against torture "without exception," which I thought meant he would end his speech right there. Unfortunately, he continued.

He thinks he is doing a good job. He is pleased with himself. There is a surprise.

He acknowledged that projected deficits were still too high, without acknowledging that he was the cause of the projected increases.

He would continue scowering the budget for savings and eliminate programs that don't work. The man is a genius.

The first question belonged to *AP* reporter Jennifer Loven, who is a left-wing hack married to a former John Kerry campaign staffer. Oh, and she is unbiased. She asked about closing the Mexican border and possibly quarantining people. This allowed him to come across as "compassionate," as if there was any chance he would say yes.

He actually said that "the Bush administration did a good job" regarding the bird flu epidemic in 2005. He should get some hate mail from leftist lunatics for that remark.

He reiterated washing hands and covering the mouth when coughing. He then admitted that what he was talking about "sounded trivial." He then told people to stay home from work if they are sick, and not to fly when they are sick, as if that will ever happen. Then again, maybe he can change the behavior of the entire human race.

For some bizarre reason, the *Detroit News* was allowed to ask a question. President Obama spoke about Chrysler and General Motors. He said nothing of consequence, but nothing harmful.

ABC News asked if waterboarding was torture, with the obligatory war crimes accusation against President George W. Bush. President Obama insisted that we could have gotten vital information "in other ways, in ways that are consistent with our values." He did not elaborate because that would have meant having a solution. He then rambled about Winston Churchill in World War II, and how Churchill did not torture.

Churchill would have taken any steps to win, but let's not confuse facts with President Obama.

Shockingly enough, President Obama was comfortable with his decision. President Obama would not commit to pursuing war crimes charges against President Bush. He wanted no part of that powder keg.

I found it ironic that the conversation was about terrorism, especially since the next questioner looked like a terrorist. It turns out the fellow with a beard scruffier than most vagrants was actually Mark Knoller of *CBS Radio*. I have nothing against Mr. Knoller, but when entering a room with the president, even I would shave, or at least trim.

Mr. Knoller asked if President Obama would use coercive interrogation methods if there was an "imminent threat." President Obama insisted that we could have gotten the valued information without torture. Apparently Khalid Sheik Mohammed disagrees with President Obama.

President Obama then said, "I will do whatever is required to keep the American people safe, but…"

There is no "but." That is where President Obama goes off the tracks.

He then said, "There is no information I have seen that makes me second guess the decision I have made."

Surprise, surprise. When a guy makes up his mind before the question is asked, there is little room for reflection.

Naturally, MSNBC got to ask a question. Chuck Todd asked President Obama to promise to secure loose nuclear weapons in Pakistan. Barack Obama crossed his heart and hoped to…well, not die.

He is confident on the issue, a recurring theme.

CBS News asked if the Arlen Specter switch would lead to "one party rule, where he runs roughshod over the Republican Party."

He replied, "I am under no illusions that I will have a rubber stamp Senate."

He meant to say that he would *not* have a rubber stamp Senate. That was an interesting Freudian slip that the leftist media ignored. With regards to Republicans, "reaching out to them has been genuine."

Inviting them to a Super Bowl party is not reaching out. Reaching out does not mean politely listening to opposing views and then dismissing them. Nobody questions his politeness. His (lack of) sincerity is the problem.

He then reminded America that he won a historic election.

Ed Henry of CNN asked if the president would keep his promise to sign the Freedom of Choice Act.

This allowed Obama to be at his most weaselly. He went out of his way to say that he respects those with an opposing view. That is not the same as actually offering an ounce of compromise on an issue. He should have just said, "I am pro-choice, so yes." He tries so hard to sound moderate that one could believe he actually is a moderate, if one was a media lapdog.

He then said that the Freedom of Choice Act was "not my highest legislative priority." NARAL will find a way to take that dismissal and claim that he supports them.

The *Jayson Blair Times*, never one to show an ounce of humility or ask a tough question of a liberal, asked what surprised, troubled, enchanted, and humbled the president about his office.

The surprise came in the form of the number of issues coming to a head at the same time. President Obama did not anticipate "the worst economic crisis since the Great Depression," despite talking about it on the campaign trail repeatedly. He claimed arbitrarily that "other presidents have two or three crises, while he has seven or eight."

He was troubled by partisanship, which is odd since he is a driving force behind it. For one thing, he will not rein in the Pelosiraptor.

He likes our troops. He claims that they are "really good at their job." Now if only he would let them do it.

He is humbled by the power of the presidency, and the patience of the American people.

Black Entertainment Network got to ask a question on what the president would do to lessen the impact of the recession on black people. President Obama smartly responded that he was trying to help all people.

Time Magazine asked about the State Secret Doctrine. President Obama wants it "modified," which is a fancy way of saying, "mend it, don't end it."[68] This guy really is not Jesse Jackson. He doesn't even rhyme.

He didn't want to reveal covert information which might compromise our safety. In short, he will do exactly what President Bush did without saying so.

The *Wall Street Journal* asked him what kind of shareholder he would be, regarding auto companies. Then Barbara Walters asked him what kind of tree he would be.

President Obama claimed that he did not want to own auto companies or banks. At the same time, he was refusing to let banks pay back the TARP money.

He wants to "help these companies make tough decisions."

The banks that are screaming that they do not want or need his help are being ignored.

I have to concede that his five minute speech was not dreadful. The remaining fifty-five minutes were inconsequential.

Those who want substance should wait for his Republican successor.

eric

Mr. Obama, Enough Press Conferences

President Barack Obama is officially more overexposed than the Geico Gekko.

Whenever he speaks, the stock market suffers. The market had a nice rebound, and I really wish he would just leave well enough alone. He again spoke to the nation.

He praised himself for saving jobs of certain people. How does he know that somebody did not lose their job because of anything he did?

He spoke about the "equivalent" of a new tax cut. Would it kill him to give me an actual tax cut? I know, 95 percent of people, blah blah blah. Not gonna happen.

He wants to make sure that we do not return to the cycle of bubble and bust. We will keep cycling because speculation has existed since the beginning of time. He wants to make sure we do not face an economic crisis ten or twenty years from now.

Will somebody please at least admit that Barack Obama cannot defeat the business cycle? We will have good and bad times in the future.

As for the rest, there were some basic themes.

1) Nothing is his fault. It was like that when he got here. His predecessor was 100 percent at fault.

2) We are all in this together, except when it suits him to blame the other side and absolve himself.

3) We should not demonize investors trying to make profits. What the heck does he think a corporation is?

One troublesome aspect of Obama press conferences is that he chooses in advance who gets to ask questions. As always, he started out with partisan liberal activist and John Kerry campaign hack Jennifer Loven of *AP*.

She basically, in the form of an AIG question, asked why we should trust him. This allowed him to answer why we should.

President Obama pointed out that unlike banks, which were regulated by FDIC, AIG as an insurance company had no regulatory oversight. While there is no federal insurance commissioner, insurance is regulated at the state level.

MSNBC naturally was allowed to ask a question. The president was asked what sacrifices were expected of the public. Shockingly enough, he replied that the public has sacrificed enough. These were astonishingly ridiculous questions, even for liberal shills. The president also offered platitudes about how we have to make tough choices, and that we cannot ignore the long term. He also reminded people that AIG contracts were put in place before he took over. Nothing is his responsibility in this era of shared responsibility.

When ABC asked if him if he would promise to veto any budget that did not include cap and trade and a middle class tax cut, naturally the president bobbed and weaved. Apparently he feels that the middle class already received their tax cut. I never got mine. He shifted to health care, energy, and education. These things have nothing to do with the question, but the president answers questions the way he wants to answer them.

When CBS asked him about increasing the debt $9.3 trillion in the coming ten years, he passed the buck without stating he was passing the buck. He inherited the problem. Yet he is going to drive down the deficit in half in the next five years. Only after that does it absolutely explode.

He claimed that the CBO forecast 2.2 percent growth, while he assumed 2.6 percent. He claimed that without fixing health care, energy and education, there will be no growth at all. Perhaps he fails to grasp that spending does not equal growth. He claimed that the GOP had no alternative budget. The minority has proposed ideas. The Pelosiraptor rejects them all. The president then blathered on about cutting out wasteful spending, and going through the budget line by line. Does he know he already won the election?

A reporter from Univision asked if he was taking Mexico seriously. Shockingly enough, of course he is. I know this because he intoned this in a serious voice.

When *Stars and Stripes* asked him if he was going to find savings in the defense budget and money allocated for veterans, Mr. Obama explained that of course everybody would agree that savings could be found in procurement. John McCain agrees with him.

Several times he mentioned that every credible person agreed with him.

Ed Henry of CNN finally offered something valuable from a reporter standpoint. He pointed out that Obama did nothing on AIG, and has blamed Bush. Will Obama leave a mess for his successor to blame him for?

Mr. Obama claimed that his job was "hard."[69] He then used a straw man by claiming that the alternative was to stand pat and do nothing. He did state that he held a fiscal responsibility summit, as if that meant something. He truly does believe that words equal deeds. He does not want Chinese and Indian kids to surpass American kids, as if anybody in America does. He ducked the AIG aspect of the question.

Major Garrett of Fox News brought up the fact that the Chinese were worried about the dollar and Europe was worried about our spending. The president then claimed that we need to increase job growth, but that the dollar is strong and that investors see the strongest economy and political stability in the world here. When President Bush and Senator McCain said the same thing, Obama pilloried them. Did he praise President Bush for the strong economy he inherited? This man is a pretzel, yet unties himself because he is not challenged.

When asked if he regretted trying to eliminate the mortgage interest deduction, he said no. He then offered a stinging and completely false justification of his absolutely dreadful proposal to raise taxes on charitable giving by lowering the deduction.

He claimed that if people were truly charitable, the deduction would not matter. Comments like that are why he occasionally disgusts me. This man will not get off of his moral high horse. When asked what he thought about charities claiming that giving will lessen, he simply stated that the charities were wrong. Either this man knows everything, or he is a gasbag.

Ebony magazine asked him what he thought about one out of every fifty children being homeless. No evidence of this statistic was cited. President Obama bravely pointed out that no child should be hungry, and that having homeless children in America was not acceptable. He then shifted to homeless veterans. Proving himself the king of courageous stands, he is against veterans being homeless.

Ann Compton of *ABC Radio* wasted time by asking him if he felt he was still being judged by his race. He correctly pointed out that people were worried about the economy and that the glow of a black man being elected ended about one day after the last inaugural ball.

The *Washington Times* wanted to know if he had any ethical concerns about embryonic stem cell research. This allowed him to state that of course he thinks issues through. He is against human cloning. He claimed that he was only in favor of using embryos about to be destroyed. This is untrue. That was the Bush position. Obama is in favor of destroying perfectly healthy embryos. If science offers solutions that avoid controversy, that is great. He is not interested in ideological rigidity, except that he is. He respects different opinions, which means listening to people without ever altering his position.

A French reporter acted like a French reporter by asking an anti-Semitic question about how the Israeli-Palesimian issue could possibly be resolved with Bibi Netanyahu and Avi Lieberman in the Israeli government.

The president lamented that it will "not be easier." He stated that the status quo was unsustainable. He left out that Hamas are terrorists.

He then praised George Mitchell and actually compared the peace in Northern Ireland to the situation in the Middle East, as if there was any basis for comparison.

He again reminded us that he inherited knotty problems before going on a tangent about economics, and insisted he was right about Timothy Geithner. He defended his video to Iran, and considered it progress despite their rejectionist response. In liberal minds, symbolism actually is a victory regardless of any benefit.

He is confident we are moving in the right direction, and that in four years we will be better off.

If we are not, he will just hold a press conference and blame his predecessor, all the while telling us things are fabulous anyway because of him. He will not cite specifics, nor be asked any.

eric

Chapter 14: Religious Islamofascist Jihadist Idiocy

Jihadists are not intelligent people. They do not have to be intelligent. They have bombs. Margaret Thatcher was a strong, bright woman, but put her in a ring with Mike Tyson and she will lose. At the very least, she might lose an ear. The terrorists are smart enough to know that some Americans do not have functioning ears. We call them liberals, and the tin things hanging on either side of their faces do not seem to allow them to pick up on things the way most people and animals can. Terrorists scream "Jihad," and liberals hear a ringing through the tin things that translates as "dialogue." I don't mind liberals going to talk in terrorist nations. I just mind their being like Palesimians and insisting on a right of return.

From Disneyland to Damascus...Nancy Pelosi and Bashar Assad Sitting in a Tree

Nancy Pelosi, you've just won the house of representatives and become house speaker. What are you going to do next?

(In an incredibly over-the-top voice that would make the Spice Girls seem like rocket scientists) "I'm going to Damascus!"

At this point the fellow shooting the commercial yells "cut" and explains to her that the line is Disneyland. Betty White's character on the *Golden Girls* learned the difference between a Lebanese and a lesbian. The Pelosiraptor seems to confuse a pleasure trip for the entire family with a nation that sponsors worldwide terrorism.

Initially I was unconcerned about Nancy Pelosi becoming speaker. Since Democrats at this point in history stand for nothing, I was under the illusion they would not disrupt society by actually doing anything. They could make bombastic speeches. They could conduct endless investigations on Republican non-scandals. They could even claim that their supporters that have nothing to do but attend protest rallies do not represent them. The one thing Democrats were not supposed to do was actually try and govern. They were not to enact actual policies. When they do this, they lose elections.

Nancy Pelosi is going to find out what Newt Gingrich found out over a decade ago. There is only one president. Nancy, you are no Newt Gingrich. Newt had ideas. He had core beliefs in sync with the American people. When he rolled up his sleeves and got to work, he dragged Bill Clinton kicking and screaming into a balanced budget. When he tried to become a de facto prime minister, Bill Clinton clobbered him in the court of public opinion. The reason for this is simple. The president is the Commander-in-Chief. There is no other.

President Bush rightly told America that Syria is a terrorist nation. It is illegal...yes illegal...to do business with them. What gives anyone the audacity to take a trip there? I would expect this type of behavior from Jesse Jackson and Al Sharpton, because they do not actually work for a living or have any responsibilities. Nancy Pelosi is the speaker of the house. She has work to do.

Nancy now understands her fate. Presidents get to ride on Air Force One, meet foreign dignitaries, and make world history. Nancy is simply the tallest member of four hundred-thirty-five legislative grunts who have to sit in subcommittee hearings and read multi-thousand page documents that no one seems to care about. This can be tedious when there is a complex legislative agenda such the 1994 Contract With America. It is even more boring when there is no agenda at all. Having meetings to determine what to actually believe, say and think is not for people who want more out of life than keeping C-Span employed.

Ms. Pelosi, as much as you enjoyed your visit to Syria, the cold hard reality is that nothing you did on that trip was consequential. George W. Bush was president. You were not. Once you leave the shores of the USA, your status ranks between Paean and nobody. This is not to demean you, but to remind you that an overblown sense of self-importance does not go over well with voters. You are a congresswoman from San Francisco. Period. That is it. Taking junkets to Syria for the sole purpose of undermining President Bush bordered on sedition. When Jimmy Carter does it, it is not as bad. Nobody took Jimmy Carter seriously when he was president, so his proclamations mean even less now. You however are seen by a dwindling precious few as relevant. Disagreements with the president must therefore stay within the confines of the USA.

Some people focused on the fact that the trip was a failure. She made promises to Syria regarding Israel. Israel rapidly contradicted those promises. This made Ms. Pelosi look foolish. The real issue is that a president banning people from doing business with Syria issued an executive order. If General Motors or IBM or Coca-Cola had been caught doing business with Syria, the CEOs could have gone to jail. Nancy Pelosi's visit to Syria was plain and simple… again…a crime. What makes it even worse than that is that the third most powerful person in the USA actually believes that dialogue with Syria works. Has she ignored their history? Did she not notice that putting on that head scarf was submitting to Sharia law? Did Bashar Assad promise to stop funding Hezbollah? Did he turn over the murderers who killed the former Lebanese prime minister (of course not, he would be turning in himself)?

What Nancy Pelosi fails to grasp is that it is easy to be a revolutionary. Governing is harder. She led the Democrats to victory in 2006 (It can be argued that if they had lost, she would have been the reason why. She is a liability). Then came the time to govern. If George W. Bush is the enemy, then Nancy Pelosi should stay the course. Most clear thinking Americans believe that having tea and crumpets with Islamofascists is a bad idea for America. If she believes this, she should do what liberals do best when they want to be popular…go on vacation and hope Republicans self-destruct.

Disneyland awaits you Ms. Pelosi. It is the friendliest place on Earth. They employ Rosie O'Donnell. You could have tea and crumpets with her and discuss Iranian President Armageddonijad. What you cannot do is give aid and comfort to America's enemies. Despite being speaker, you need to do what is right for America and politically smart for Democrats. You need to stop speaking. You are a good misguided kid. It is time for the adults to handle the business of governing. Take a time out and go play with Mickey, Obambi and friends. Republicans have work to do.

eric

Talk to the Taliban? Are You Kidding Me?

Maybe Barack Obama thinks he truly is God almighty.

Even worse, maybe I am wrong and he actually is God almighty. He is every bit as good as he thinks he is.

Short of him being naive and clueless, I cannot think of another explanation for him wanting to talk to the Taliban.

What the hell is there to talk about?

I will explain this slowly so that even an eighteen-year-old Facebook friend of Obama who finds him dreamy can understand.

The Taliban gave aid and comfort to Osama Bin Laden. The Taliban know whether he is alive or dead, and where he is located. Osama Bin Laden and Khalid Sheik Mohammed planned the horrific terrorist attacks of September 11th, 2001. Three thousand people were murdered in New York. President Obama wants to have dialogue with those that are every bit as complicit as the hijackers.

For eight years, liberals complained that Iraq was the bad war and Afghanistan was the good war. Conservatives knew that the leftist peaceniks were against all war. By pretending to want to get tough on Afghanistan, they could criticize George W. Bush endlessly on Iraq.

We now all know the truth that conservatives have known from the beginning. If we had never invaded Iraq, liberals would have criticized the war in Afghanistan.

Now that Iraq has been secured thanks to Republican President George W. Bush, Democrats are less inclined to prattle on about how Iraq was "his war." Well it was his war. He won it without the sniveling little brats on the other side. He won it with plenty of help from Senator John McCain and General David Petraeus.

For those who forget General Petraeus, he was the honorable fellow that was called a liar by Senate leftists.

These same people that slandered President Bush and General Petraeus want to simply take the Taliban at their word.

Liberals point out the successful counterinsurgency strategy that they violently opposed. The only time liberals get violent is when condemning Republicans or conservatives. Liberals gush about how dialogue with Sunni Muslims saved Iraq.

What liberals cannot and will not grasp is that first we went in and leveled everything. We used hard power, and captured Saddam Hussein. Then we leveled every area in Iraq that contained large amounts of bad guys. Only after military successes did we speak with low-level, low-hanging fruit. They surrendered and got down on their knees. Then we spoke to them.

After we took down Saddam, Libya's Khadafi surrendered. He turned over his weapons. We did not just trust him. We verified. Only after he surrendered did we talk to him..

What is it going to take for President Obama to separate himself from every Democrat in the last four decades to become president, or get demolished trying? When is he going to develop a spine?

Barack Obama took an oath to protect America from our enemies. He also piously and pompously wanted to strengthen our friendships, which in his uninformed world were globally frayed.

He refused to meet with the British prime minister. This act of discourteousness had England steaming. Yet he will meet with "moderate" members of the Taliban.

I love the way liberals decide that even the most bloodthirsty and murderous elements contain moderates.

Moderate Taliban members are as fictional as moderate Palesimian leaders.

Afghanistan is not Iraq. Iraq was a secular dictatorship based on Stalinism. The Taliban are religious fundamentalists. They are true believers. What does one discuss with them?

Will they apologize for hiding Bin Laden and disclose his whereabouts?

Will they stop beating women in the town square for walking without their husbands?

Will they allow Jews and Christians to live in peace? Are non-Muslims infidels?

Exactly what will we negotiate away?

If Barack Obama truly wants to motivate himself to toughen up and stop being so bloody effeminate, maybe somebody should tell him that the Taliban are Republicans. Better yet, tell him they are employed by Fox News. Let President Obama have classified documents showing they have Rush Limbaugh and Sean Hannity bumper stickers in their caves.

What is it going to take for this man leading America to drop the smug attitude, and stop being so aloof and detached? What makes him think he is so special that his words will get religious genocidal wack jobs to develop human empathy?

Does he plan on offering up seventy-two virgins?

The Taliban are murderers. You do not bond with them. You defeat them. You kill them.

On the one hand, the left claims that Afghanistan was neglected all of these years. Then the left simultaneously decides to talk to them. Do they plan on sending John Kerry or Al Gore to Afghanistan to bore the enemy to death?

Will Hillary Clinton nag them into submission? Men in those parts of the world do not fear women, not even Hillary.

"Asked if the United States is winning the war in Afghanistan, Obama said 'no.'"[70]

I wonder if the military appreciates their Commander-in-Chief taking this ridiculous approach.

"Given that remark, Gary Berntsen, a former CIA officer who led CIA forces in Afghanistan after 9/11, said Monday that it could be difficult to get members of the Taliban to work with the United States.

'If you keep saying the Taliban are winning, what incentive is there now for individuals who are fighting against us to come over to us?' he said on CNN's 'American Morning.'"[71]

What a complete and utter shock. A military man knows more about a military conflict than a civilian gasbag that knows nothing about the military.

Maybe Barack Obama can get real tough and treat the Taliban like they were stockholders. He can confiscate all of their wealth with a few harmful utterances.

The Taliban do not have wealth. They live in caves. They have nothing to lose. They will never surrender until they are beaten, battered, and bloodied. Even then, they might prefer death.

Mr. Obama, you talk too much and say too little.

You accomplish nothing and embolden our enemies.

For once, just be quiet. I have given up asking you to do anything positive.

Just stop making things worse.

Pretend the Taliban are Republicans. Then pretend to talk to them but really give nothing.

We are in the middle of World War III.

It would be nice if Obama actually wanted to win.

eric

Terrorist Armageddonijad Interviewed By Apologist Larry King

The terrorist and the apologist joined hands and started a love train.

The murderer vowed to continue murdering. The Zionist victim interviewing him thanked the murderer for his graciousness.

The Jewish newsman gave the Holocaust denier the platform to spread his bile.

As my friend Evan Sayet has said on many occasions, *Larry King Live* is an oxymoron. I have said that Larry died twenty years ago, and nobody told him. In the spirit of the movie *Weekend at Bernie's*, Larry King's corpse was wheeled onto the stage, where his spirit asked warm and lighthearted questions of a mass murderer.

Iranian Terrorist and President Mahmoud Armageddonijad spent the day in New York attending an anti-Semitic rally, known as a United Nations forum. While the world leaders did not chant about death to America or Israel, they did sit silently and allow Armageddonijad to spread his lunacy.

Armageddonijad then decided that he needed a forum to air his views where he would not be challenged. While nobody has hard evidence that Larry King ever asked Adolf Hitler if he preferred the Whopper or the Big Mac, he did have a chance to share warm fuzzies with the man who dreams of inflicting the next Holocaust.

Below is the best of the worst of the interview.

LK: "Do you like being in New York?"[72]

He could not say he liked coming to New York. Larry never got to ask him if he preferred the Yankees or the Mets, or what he thought of the Joe Torre situation.

MA: "Hostility is not coming from our end. We want friendly relations. Hostility is one-sided from American politicians."[73]

LK: "Are you controversial?"

Larry at that point was handed a memo indicating that water is wet, bears actually do take care of their business in the woods, and despite rumors to the contrary, the pope is a practicing Catholic. Larry then debated whether to consult with Barbara Walters and ask the madman what kind of tree he would be.

Armageddonijad should go on *The View*. The imbeciles can all talk and laugh together in their hatred of George W. Bush. He can let them know how terrible it is that women are oppressed in America. Joy Behar will indignantly agree at the top of her leftist lungs.

MA: "Never has the Iranian nation taken a misstep against another nation. We are for peace and are friendly with others. The only war against us was Saddam Hussein, and the U.S. supported that."

We played both sides well. I was disappointed the day in 1988 that the Iran-Iraq war came to an end. Thank you Ronald Reagan for keeping Israel safe, by allowing the enemies to murder each other instead.

MA: "Defending our nation does not mean we infringe on the rights of other nations."

He could not say he was happy the U.S. took out Saddam even though he hated Saddam.

He and Palin were both mayors. How charming. He did not state he would meet with her.

MA: "The U.S. incited Saddam to attack Iran."

The left really should give this warm furry fella a big socialist hug. He keeps reciting the talking points of the Democratic Party.

MA: "Our religion teaches us to be against weapons of mass destruction. The atomic bomb has lost its use in political affairs. The bomb did not keep the Soviet Union intact. It did not help America win in Afghanistan and Iraq. Can it save the Zionist regime?"

At this point Larry King donned his Captain Obvious superhero outfit.

LK: "What do you mean by wiping Israel off the map?"

Somebody please buy the man a dictionary for his birthday. The phrase is rather literal. This is different from a less literal sentence, such as the fact that nobody watches CNN. I really did have nothing to do that night.

MK: "We oppose the Zionist regime because of peace and justice."

I oppose the Iranian president and wish that we would shove a grenade up his hide and pull the pin while he is visiting the world's only simian ophthalmologist, Bashar Assad of Syria.

He then pretended to care about the Palesimians.

MA: "Three big wars were started by the Zionist regime, the last one in 2006 when they attacked Lebanon. Our solution is a humanitarian one. The Palestinians must determine their own fate."

LK: "Why not sit down and talk with Israel?"

Larry then taught Armageddonijad the lyrics to "Kumbaya."

MA: "The Zionist regime is an uninvited guest in the Middle East."

Somewhere at a violent peace rally Medea Benjamin orgasmed and ruined her new Code Pink protester panties.

MA: "The Apartheid regime of South Africa, the Soviet Union, where are they today? It was not talking, it was resistance. This Zionist regime is fundamentally illegal."

LK: "You don't want to see Israelis die. Do you?"

I am thrilled my grandfather and father escaped Nazis to see another liberal Jewish apologist share cookies and milk with a murderer of Jews.

MA: "When we speak of disappearance, crimes, murder, and terror must disappear. Our solution is humanitarian and Democratic."

Only a naive fool working at CNN could believe such nonsense.

LK: "Does Israel remain Israel?"

MA: "Let the people decide."

I am a person. I decide we turn Iran and Syria into 50,000-hole golf courses.

MA: "The root cause of the problem is the others that came and harmed the Palestinians."

This guy wants to explore phony root causes of crime. Maybe he is a liberal. I wonder if Democrats would vote for him over George W. Bush. I wonder who they hate more.

MA: "We must allow for free elections in Palestine."

We had them, and terrorists were elected.

LK: "Do you wish the Jewish people harm?"

MA: "There are Jews in Iran. Zionists are not Jewish people. They have no religion. They wear a mask of religiosity. How can you be religious and occupy lands of other people?"

LK: "Do not Zionists come from persecution?"

MA: "No one is allowed to freely discuss the history. Let more research be done on that history. Even if it did happen, it did not happen in Palestine, it would have happened in Europe. Why should the Palestinians be victimized? The Jews can be given Alaska."

Now we know that despite protesting to the contrary, he dislikes Sarah Palin. After all, he hates Jews and wants them to be placed in her state. This guy might be leading the current demagogic party in secret. How come we never see Armageddonijad and Nancy Pelosi in the same room at the same time? Khalid Sheik Mohammed turned out to be Rosie O'Donnell. Stranger things have happened.

LK: "Do you have any concerns about the future of your country?"

MA: "I have no concerns. The worst thing the U.S. government can do is attack us. Israel is much smaller. Have you visited Iran?"

LK: "I am planning to visit next year."

Isn't it illegal for American citizens to visit Iran? I am nevertheless delighted that Jewish Larry King would bypass Israel, which depends on tourism, for Iran, which finances terrorizing tourists.

LK: "Do you have human rights problems in Iran? Do you deny that there are homosexuals in your country?"

MA: "God's rules are to improve human life. In our religion, this act is forbidden."

So is murder.

LK: "What happens to gay people?"

MA: "Are you concerned for seventy million Iranian people or a few hundred homosexuals?"

MA: "It will benefit everyone if the U.S. leaves Iraq. The U.S. must limit its excursions to the United States alone."

LK: "If you could go anywhere, what would you like to see in this country?"

MA: "California and Los Angeles."

The land of fruits and nuts would welcome him. Perhaps UCLA Hillel could invite him for an interfaith dinner (I attended USC).

After being asked about his family, Armageddonijad announced that he sired three future terrorists.

LK: "You don't look old enough to have married children."

Yes he does. Larry King has not been the same since Martha dumped him at the altar for George Washington.

Larry King found the interview "illuminating."

The only thing that should be illuminated is the part of Tehran containing the mullahs.

Larry then had a heart attack on stage. Armageddonijad let him die before harvesting his organs. He took Larry's heart and lungs, had them coated in steel ball bearings, and used them as miniature bombs to be dropped on Israel. Armageddonijad then blamed the Jews for the attack since Larry is Jewish.

My sentiments are no more nonsensical than the idea of this interview.

The moment this animal steps on American soil, well placed sharpshooters should be ready to take him out. This man was one of the animals responsible for the taking of American hostages for four hundred-forty-four days in 1979. Given that a Democrat was in the White House at the time, we did nothing to respond to the terrorism.

Now those on the left do less than nothing. We interview terrorists on television and treat them like Hollywood Celebrities. That would explain Susan Sarandon and Tim Robbins planning a fundraiser for A-Jad's 2010 Democratic congressional primary. Barbra Streisand will sing for him. That may be the one thing that might make him finally crack.

Sean Hannity interviewed Ambassador John Bolton that very same night, proving that intelligent discussion does still exist...just on Fox News, not CNN.

eric

Chapter 15: Religious Leftist Jihadist Idiocy

We should take the leader of every liberal activist group and lock them all in a steel cage with instruments of death. Animal rights activists, environmentalists, feminists, and every other group could fight for the right to have their agenda advanced. The surviving group gets everything. Every other group gets eliminated. This is what they do now anyway. Animal rights activists are against animal testing for AIDS because letting people die will save an extra bunny rabbit. At least they do not test on dolphins. After all, if we got rid of dolphins, liberals would have nobody to bond with and understand them.

Getting Gay at Guantanamo Bay

From Perez Pelosi to Nancy Hilton, left-wing bullying against mainstream America is now back in that dance that Madonna sang about Marilyn Monroe.

It does tie together since Perez, like Rita Hayworth, gives good face.[74]

The Pelosiraptor has every right to twist and Vogue herself into a metaphorical pretzel with extra salt. This is America. Lying is not really lying when you're a Democrat, especially if under oath.

Perez has every right to twist himself into a sexual pretzel. Who he fornicates with is his own business.

Apparently the tolerance does not extend in both directions. People with traditional values are under assault by fringe offshoots that have hijacked legitimate minority groups.

Miss California Carrie Prejean was not attacked for attempting to pass any legislation that could limit anybody's freedom.

She was not even lambasted for volunteering an opinion that certain freedoms should be limited.

She was brutalized for answering a question that was asked of her by a questioner that already knew the answer. She was punished for her thoughts and beliefs.

While we already know that the Perez-Pelosi marriage of convenience exists solely to torture conservatives (they do support that kind of torture), there is a solution that could benefit the Republican Party and still offer a bone to the leftist zealots.

First, the terrorist murderers at Guantanamo Bay should immediately be placed in the Pelosiraptor's San Francisco district.

Some people will rightly complain that they might be too moderate for the district. After all, the only thing more dangerous than a violent jihadist is a violent peace activist. Also, the ACLU might block the move because relocating them there might be considered cruel and unusual punishment under the Eighth Amendment, even for terrorists (Thank you Thaddeus McCotter).

Excellent points, but importing moderates is good for the one kind of diversity that leftists hate, that being ideological diversity. Diversity of values is important. Lumping warriors in with peace activists could balance the district into a tranquil oasis of violent centrism.

Secondly, upon relocation, the enemy combatants of America (the detainees, not the unshaven leftist Friscotics) should immediately be given gay marriage rights.

I normally stay out of the culture wars, preferring to focus on cutting taxes and killing terrorists. However, San Francisco appears to be against both, and this would be a great test of how sincere the Friscotic inhabitants are in their activist lunacy.

Think about it. This is the perfect wedge issue to use against the Demagogic Party. If Speaker Pelosi says no to giving terrorists gay marriage rights, she will further enrage the hypertolerant leftist crowd that thinks storming into churches and defacing sacred property is free speech. If she says yes, she will further enrage the Islamists, who coincidentally also enjoy destroying churches. Islam forbids homosexuality, and as Armageddonijad of Iran told his soulmates at a Poison Ivy League university, "There are no gay people in Iran. This is an American phenomenon."[75]

By forcing Pelosi to choose between the two groups that despise America most, leftists and Islamists…that is her entire base. We have just fractured her coalition.

What if the detainees do not want to be part of gay marriages? Then we just force them.

Since gay marriages do not lead to pregnancy, pro-choicers can embrace this program. A lack of pregnancy means no chance of abortion, making it wonderful for the pro-lifers as well. Who knew that terrorist gay marriages could solve the abortion debate?

Sanity far aside, Perez and Pelosi should immediately embrace this new program entitled, "Getting Gay at Guantanamo Bay." For those who love acronyms, we can call it "Getting Gay at Gitmo," or G3 for short.

Perez and Pelosi have a common natural ally in the detainees, who also wish to assault Middle America.

If the detainees don't like it, they can just blow themselves up. That was their original plan anyway. Locking people up for life that want and deserve the death penalty is cruel and unusual punishment.

Human Rights advocates, who apparently nobody listens to anyway, will argue that not all of the detainees are Muslims. Well in that case those heretics should immediately be forced to convert to Islam. The Muslim detainees want to establish a Caliphate, and they were going to forcibly convert these people anyway. At least if we do it, we can make sure to be nice about it.

Like most liberals, I am tired of Gitmo killers not being given the same rights as you and me. Speaker Pelosi must immediately come out in favor of gay marriage for Guantanamo Bay inmates, even if it means desecrating their beliefs.

Somebody besides Christians have to have their beliefs and rights violated daily.

Perez Hilton should immediately start drawing X-rated drawings of these Radical Muslim gay marriages. What could possibly be done to somebody just for drawing a cartoon, especially if the cartoonist is also a cartoon?

I just hope that America never finds out my true hidden agenda. I want the ratios reversed so that straight men make up only 10 percent of Americans. Any man that is richer than me, taller than me, or driving a nicer car than me, should immediately be gay. This reduces my competition for women.

Lesbianism shall be outlawed. They are selfish, never thinking about my needs.

That is for down the road. For now, in the name of tolerance, Islamist detainees should immediately be sent to San Francisco and married to each other.

Some people kill others with kindness. We can torture our enemies with love.

Support the Perez-Pelosi-Prisoner Plan.

Support Weddings for Wahabiists.

Support Nuptials for Nutcases.

Support the San Francisco chapter of Getting Gay at Guantanamo Bay.

It's the forcibly tolerant thing to do.

eric

Joe Piscopo and other (angry) mob(ster)s

I am now officially a mobster.

This is surprising to me. I am not Italian. Most Italians I know are not mobsters anyway.

I like Italian food, but found the Sopranos colossally boring. For those who said "Bada-Boom!" and "Bada-Bing!" I responded with "Bada Yawn," also known as "Bada who the hell cares?"

Yet in the health care debate, town hall attendees are now part of an angry mob.

This is apparently less about mobsters than mob(ster)s.

Being part of a mob requires only one qualification. One has to disagree with President Obama and refuse to be silent about this.

When George W. Bush was president, dissent was patriotic. Leftists ran wild. Were there reasonable Democrats that protested in a civil manner? Sure. Yet the lunatics were celebrated. Every organization from "Lesbians against Bush" to "Hillary's hags and harpies" to "Bush lied, the music died" was out in full force.

Cindy Sheehan engaged in behavior toward President Bush that can only be described as stalking. Medea Benjamin and the rest of the Code Pinkos engaged in verbal bombthrowing that bordered on terrorism.

Despite accusations that President Bush was clamping down on free speech, those accusations from Hollywood celebrities and other leftist nitwits defied logic. Leftists love yelling about censorship at the top of their lungs. They never face repercussions...sounds like a police state to me.

As for Barack Obama, anybody disagreeing with him is a concern. Leftists are constantly complaining about Gestapo tactics, but seem to enjoy inflicting them. What else would one call collecting evidence of conservatives critical to the president, and then emailing the White House to inform them?

Despite having the White House and both houses of congress, the left is more enraged than ever. They still have not grasped what election after election has told the rest of the civilized world.

Leftists don't matter. They are, were, and will always be irrelevant.

Conservatives get elected by saying who they are and what they believe. Liberals get elected only by denying who they are, and when conservatives mess up. They make up phony terms like "progressives" because they are too gutless to admit they are liberals.

Because of this, there is no mandate for liberalism in America.

For those that point out the 2006 and 2008 elections, think again. Democrats won in 2006 by not discussing anything remotely resembling a policy or a program. They stood for nothing, which was good enough when the Republicans were seen as less than nothing. Outside of non-binding resolutions and hating President Bush, they did nothing.

Then they got the White House in 2008, and they claimed a mandate for liberalism. This is false because Barack Obama denied who he was from day one of his campaign. He had a mandate to fix the economy, not to remake it in the tradition of FDR.

Democrats had a few brief months where blaming Republicans for everything from killing puppies and kittens to hating seniors and children worked. Then a funny thing happened.

The voters wanted results. They wanted the blame game to stop. The liberals were incapable of stopping.

Liberal hatred of conservatives is pathological. They need hatred the way normal human beings need oxygen.

With no Republicans to blame, the liberals had no choice but to blame somebody. It was tornado temper tantrum time. First the Democrats lashed out at each other. The Blue Dogs correctly understood that allowing the Pelosiraptor to dictate legislation would not affect her. She has a safe seat. She would not care if they all lost their seats once the legislation was passed.

The Blue Dogs eventually turned into lap dogs. There was just one problem. Nancy Pelosi, Barack Obama, and even Rahm Emanuel ran into the one group of people that could not be bullied…voters.

First the Democrats got shellacked at town halls. Then they simply decided to stop holding them. They began a ruthless assault on ordinary Americans like Joe the Plumber.

They then verbally attacked people attending tea parties and town halls as either lunatics, or plants. Liberals are experts in having planted questioners in their midst, to ensure favorable coverage.

I remember attending a press conference by Barbara Boxer where the questioners were required to write the questions on pieces of paper, and she would choose which ones to answer.

The liberals once had complete domination of the media. Then conservatives found outlets, including talk radio. The left came unglued, knowing that dissenting conservative opinions were even allowed.

This led to citizens getting more politically active. This is not a threat to democracy. This is democracy.

The left then demonized people attending town halls for simply disagreeing with the president.

The left is determined to find people that act badly. In the same way Palesiminans are having a tougher time recruiting new homicide bombers, leftists are posing as hateful conservatives because mainstream conservatives refuse to act like bat-spit crazy nut jobs.

When Senator Boxer complains that the protesters are fake because they dress well, she is conceding that most liberal protesters are unshaven creatures that should be profiled at airports.

I attended a strategy session, and we were told as conservatives that we were to be polite and civilized. We were told not to hold up any crazy signs or yell any bad words. One incident of bad behavior allows liberals to present all conservatives as wack jobs.

Conservatives do not even need this advice. Unlike liberals, we do not need to experience extensive training in civilized behavior. We do not throw objects or celebrate those who do. We would never throw shoes at Barack Obama or a pie at a liberal commentator.

The left has become so unhinged that they actually accused senior citizens in a town hall audience of grandstanding so that they could be on You-Tube.

It was at this moment that a liberal mobster had to settle down other liberal mob(ster)s, even though he agrees with them politically.

I never thought I would witness this, but the voice of reason in this discussion was Joe Piscopo.

As a political blogger, I never thought to ever write his name. He is an actor or comedian who was famous for something awhile back. I mean no disrespect. He seems nice enough. Yet his appearance on Hannity was brilliant.

I still do not understand why he was on Hannity, but again, for a Hollywood celebrity, he actually spoke like somebody thoughtful. When the You-Tube issue was brought up, Piscopo deadpanned that "These are senior citizens. They don't even know what You-Tube is."[76]

That is hilariously accurate. They call it "new media" for a good reason. It is mainly the tool of young people.

I do not know what Joe Piscopo knows about new media, but Joe Piscopo knows about mobsters. He and Danny Devito were hilarious in *Wise Guys*, when Dan Hedaya hired each of them to kill the other one. Ray Sharkey was killed, but Piscopo bungled his way into survival.

He knows comedy, and apparently he knows seniors as well. They are not looking for Internet glory. That is a young thing. They do not know You-Tube from MySpace to the space race to the *Great Space Coaster*.

My father is a bright man, but he has no idea how to do most things on a computer. He is old and set in his ways. He dictates letters, and my mother types them. I taught him how to download music, and he got angry when nobody else had the songs he liked. My mother wakes up at 3:00 AM to handle his eBay auctions. Again, this man is no dummy. He is just old, and not interested in Twitter and Facebook. My mother checks his email.

Many seniors are angry because they truly love America and see liberal policies wrecking the nation they inherited.

These people are not fake plants. The assertion is ludicrous.

The Pelosiraptor claims that insurance companies insuring these people are "carpet-bombing"[77] this country. Many of these seniors belong to the World War II generation. They know more about carpet-bombing than the Pelosiraptor ever will.

These are not political agitators. They don't put on war paint like Code Pink. They are not college kids that wouldn't know fact from opinion if it was drilled into their skulls.

The seniors simply want the truth. They want congress to read the bills they vote on. They want congress to level with them. They want honesty.

They are not an angry mob. I have seen angry mobs. During the LA Riots of 1992, I saw a city put on lockdown. It was not Republican senior citizens burning and looting. It was young people with a sense of grievance and entitlement. Why would seniors steal VCRs back then? They did not even know how to program them (I let mine blink 12:00 because twice a day, every day, it was right).

The left can kick, scream, cry and hurl epithets. What they cannot do is govern.

They control everything, and are repeating their mistakes of 1992.

The louder they yell, the more they will be rejected and the more desperate they will become.

They could try reaching across the aisle, but if they did this they would not be liberals.

When hatred is a religion, it is difficult to let reason trump emotion.

I will continue to exercise my right to free speech. I will engage in democracy.

I may attend some protests. I am sure the crowds will be filled with decent and civilized human beings.

I will also hang out with other great Americans.

The annual Freedom Concerts offer Charlie Daniels, Lee Greenwood, and of course, Sean Hannity.

I never thought I would say this, but if Joe Piscopo is there, that would be cool as well.

We will be portrayed as angry mob(ster)s, but thousands of people singing "God Bless the U.S.A."[78] along with Lee Greenwood sounds like a love-fest to me.

eric

Black Eyed Perez

Homosexual blogger and leftist bully Perez Hilton, fresh off of his successful ideological bigotry of sweet Miss California Carrie Prejean, decided to try and pick on somebody his own size. He mouthed off to members of the music group Black Eyed Peas, and they responding by deciding to "get retarded."[79]

For those who need a translation, getting retarded is the equivalent of getting medieval on somebody's buttocks.

While those that love to stir up conflict will try to turn this into a conflict between blacks and gays, the truth is that it seems that Mr. Hilton is simply one individual that has a tendency to act ignorant, or as my hip-hop friends say when music comes on, "ign'nt."

While many people will see this as a fight between people that do not matter, Mr. Hilton's behavior does matter.

What is not in dispute is that the situation between Hilton and Peas lead singer Will*i*am escalated when Hilton referred to Will*i*am (Don't give me a beat-down hippity-hoppers, but I am going to be lazy on my keyboard and call him William) as a word that begins with the letter "f" and rhymes with maggot.

You read right. Homosexual Hilton used an anti-gay slur against heterosexual William.

When asked why he called William that slur, Hilton responded that "it was the worse (sic) thing he could think of to call the singer at the time."[80]

The idea that a gay American should be allowed to use that word when Ann Coulter got in trouble for referring to John Edwards the same way is hypocritical. This follows the asinine argument that a black person can use the n-word.

This is not about context. It is about bigotry. Any person in any culture can be bigoted, even against their own community. It is called self-hatred. Perez Hilton used a disgusting slur, and mostly was given a free pass by the politically correct media.

(To their credit, the Gay and Lesbian Association Against Defamation [GLAAD] condemned the slur in what might be a "Sister Souljah" moment for the movement. This gives new meaning to the slogan "Don't get mad... get GLAAD." GLAAD did a great job taking out the trash on this one.)

Even worse than the slur was the reaction of Mr. Hilton after the incident. Rather than go straight to the police, he decided to Twitter about his experience first.

I admit my hostility toward celebrity Twit(terer)s (although I am softening my anti-Twitter posture due to its usefulness in following the Iran situation). Yet think about this. After being allegedly punched in the face, Hilton went to the Internet to blather about it.

"I was assaulted by Will.I.Am of the Black Eyed Peas and his security guards. I am bleeding. Please, I need to file a police report. No joke."

"Still waiting for the police. The bleeding has stopped. I need to document this. Please, can the police come to the SoHo Met Hotel."

"I spoke to my lawyer. I really need to talk to the authorities. Please come to the SoHo Met Hotel. Have called the police. Need them here."

"The Toronto police are here now. Thank you. Please stop calling them."

I am going to make an assumption that despite Mr. Hilton's eccentricity, he is actually descendant from a mother and father like the rest of us. At some point one or both of them, or whatever raised him, probably taught him how to dial 9-1-1. Ironically, it was Flavor Flav that pointed out that 911 was a joke, which means that maybe Perez Hilton has more in common with the hip-hop community than he realizes.

The cynic in me wonders if this entire event was staged. Whether it be *Bruno* vs. Eminem, or Morton Downey Jr. and Tawana Brawley, people in the news have been known on occasion to resort to strange behavior to get attention.

Our culture has become so desensitized that what would have been shocking behavior now makes us yawn. A rapper got angry and had a member of his entourage punch somebody? A gay activist tossed out a slur in the name of tolerance?

Next thing you know Hollywood celebrities will get real wild and start mocking Republicans. I am convinced that this fight was a plot by heterosexual Republican PBWGs to keep the man (whoever that is) down.

This celebrity spat matters because unlike me, some people do care about the existence of these participants. They emulate them. Right now in a nightclub somewhere, kids are "throwing down," "representin'," and "keepin' it real." This is often followed by somebody getting beaten, stabbed, or shot.

This should not be seen as anything other than what it was. A leftist bully who uses his homosexuality to verbally mouth off to others mouthed off to the wrong person. A member of the aggrieved group, rather than walk away, decided to turn into the modern equivalent of "Bad, Bad Leroy Brown." At least nobody got kicked in their Jim Croce.

The Black Eyed Peas turned Perez Hilton into Black Eyed Perez.

Sadly enough, nobody involved learned an intelligent lesson from this. Even worse, the participants decided to not only get retarded, but spread their retardation throughout the information superhighway.

eric

Be Gay and Shut Up

I was going to call in gay recently, but I was out of days off. Instead I came in straight and earned my paycheck. I would like to think that if I was gay, I would have still gone to work and honored my responsibilities.

For those who were lucky enough to not know, the gay community declared December 10th to be "Gay Day."[81]

This is not to be confused with "Dre Day," the Gangsta Rap album by Dr. Dre that launched Snoop Doggy Dogg on the way to starizzledom (or as we say in the mother tongue, stardom).

Gay Day is the next angry protest against California Proposition 8, which bans gay marriage.

Gay Americans vowed to skip work, and "call in gay." This would be the equivalent of "calling in sick."

This is ironic since many anti-gay people say that gay people are sick, while gay people have argued that they are normal and healthy. Adopting an approach of "I am gay, I am sick," is about as intelligent a marketing ploy as the old wives' tale about Chevrolet marketing the Chevy Nova in Mexico, unaware that "Nova" means "doesn't go."[82] At least Chevrolet was being truthful. Gay Americans are not sick, and are therefore lying by claiming they are. Calling in sick is also quite unethical, but that is for another time and place in case my boss reads my blog.

Did "calling in gay" revolutionize America? Did the economy notice? Is orange the new blue?

In order, no, no, and I have no idea what I just said. I am not a fashionista. I am your stereotypical unkempt straight guy with jeans and sneakers.

Why did gay day fail?

The reason that gay day fell flat is actually a successful, optimistic reason for all Americans.

Dear gay America…listen to me closely…there is a word to describe you.

Gay people…I am officially declaring you…

(Grabbing a bullhorn): NORMAL!

That is right. You are normal. You are not special. You are boring and generic. You are "been there, done that." Being gay is soooo 2007 the same way that being black was all the rage in 2006. I hope I live long enough for everybody to be Jewish Republicans, but I will not hold my breath.

I am tired of listening to gay people because I am tired of listening to everybody. I keep emphasizing my favorite holiday of "Shut the hell up and go to work" Day. It crosses all of the human strata. Everybody should try it at some point. Many people feel I should shut up. They do not read my blog. I survive.

For boycotts to work, there has to be a special skill set.

Police officers have been known to have massive sick days that are known as a "Blue Flu." Blue Flu has a chance of succeeding because being a police officer requires a certain skill set. Donut jokes aside, police officers do things that many of us are not qualified to do.

Being homosexual is not a skill set. It is a lifestyle.

Most people are not pro or anti-gay. We are pro-productivity.

I don't care who my CPA sleeps with. I just want my taxes done right. My oil change was done by a guy at Jiffy Lube. Now as much as I am tempted to make an infantile remark on how I do not like getting a Jiffy Lube because I prefer she take her time, the bottom line is when I bring my car in I just want my oil changed.

Gay activists are fighting for gay marriage to become the law of the land.

I personally stay far out of the culture wars. My attitude toward gay people has always been, "Be gay, but don't raise my taxes or fly a plane into the towers." Coincidentally, that is also my attitude toward heterosexuals.

The gay community must accept that any movement lives or dies by the number of disinterested moderates it persuades. The Civil Rights movement needed white moderates. Dr. King understood this. The Jewish community needs support of Christians.

There are not enough gay people in America to influence the law on their own. They need straight people to show solidarity. They need people like me. I am a moderate on gay issues. I can be persuaded. What I really despise more than many things in this world is traffic congestion.

I love President Bush, but I got mad even at him when his motorcade blocked traffic. I live near a federal building, and every week it is something different. One day it is "anti-animal rights activists and feline eugenics." The next day it is Chinese television executives trying to pitch the "Falun Gong Show." The day after brings "Birkenstocks for Bush." One protest group wanted to hang Luke Perry for breaking up with Shannon Doherty on *Beverly Hills, 90210*. A counter protest came about with the group chanting, "No Noose Lukes."

Americans are a tolerant bunch. We just like order. We dislike chaos. Disrupting traffic and skipping work are bad approaches.

This is not about gay marriage. It is about tactics and strategy.

Boycotting work at best will have no effect. The gay receptionist can be replaced by the straight receptionist. Temp agencies have tons of workers looking for assignments. With the economy the way it is, slacking off from work is unwise. If the boss fires any of these people, it will not be because they are gay, but because they disrupted the workplace.

At worst, such tactics lead to a backlash.

Americans are reasonable people. We are like data. 99.7 percent of us fit within three standard deviations of normalcy. Beyond those parameters are the extremes. These include yelling "We're here, we're queer" at innocent bystanders to yelling anti-gay slurs. The very worst extreme is physical violence, such as what happened to Matthew Shepard.

Most Americans do not see the struggle for gay marriage as a struggle for gay rights. This is not Selma, Alabama. Gay people are not having fire hoses turned on them.

This is not the Holocaust. They are not being sent to concentration camps, unless one considers wealthy enclaves in San Francisco and West Hollywood to be punishment. While not all gay people are wealthy, many of them are financially successful. They are getting high paying jobs somewhere. This is not because they are gay, but because they have marketable skills as all people do. This is another example of being less different than some think. They are the same.

The bad news for America is that Gay Day was a flop. What the gay community called Gay Day, I referred to by its given name…Wednesday. At least nobody made a comment about why they chose "hump day."

(At the risk of a completely irrelevant tangent, *Law and Order* just came on. A gay guy was killed. I am guaranteeing that a straight person did it. *Law and Order* has a clear political agenda.)

A tree fell in the forest, and it may or may not have been gay. It made not a sound.

Gay people should be happy about this. Most Americans did not even know about Gay Day. We did not bash gays. We did something that we consider better and they might consider worse. We shrugged our shoulders.

(Second and last irrelevant tangent: *Law and Order* just ended. Naturally, a gay man was wrongly convicted. The actual murderer was a heterosexual hard-charging business executive. This show is as predictable as it is politically disgraceful. Corporate executives do not go around committing murders. In real life, poor downtrodden people accused of things actually did them.)

If gay people want to be accepted the way everybody else is, they should do what everybody else does. They should fight the good fight, pursue the noble struggle, but avoid causing moderates to move away from them.

They need to do what I and many others are forced to do. They need to celebrate "Shut the Hell up and go to work" Day.

We all do.

eric

William Jefferson–Still Innocent By New Jersey Standards

While one William Jefferson was frolicking in North Korea with an adorable warm fuzzy dude that you just want to pat on the forehead, another William Jefferson was finding out that Louisiana Democratic corruption is no longer as acceptable as Arkansas Democratic corruption.

In a shocking verdict that actually seemed to represent upholding the rule of law, William Jefferson was convicted of crimes due to bizarre concepts such as evidence, and the fact that he actually did it.

Yes, he took bribes. Yes, the FBI found $90 thousand in his freezer, giving new meaning to the term cold hard cash.

I pointed out awhile back that William Jefferson was innocent by Louisiana standards.

I also predicted that people would try to make this about race, when it was about corruption. Many of the people Mr. Jefferson cheated with his behavior were black. The non-reactions of Jesse Jackson, Al Sharpton, and yes, Barack Obama, were priceless. With Obama, being thrown under the bus is expected. When Jackson and Sharpton do it, you know you are alone. The last time a liberal black congressman was abandoned by black leaders was Mel Reynolds, and he committed statutory rape.

(In all fairness to black America, they have a point about unequal justice since Ted Kennedy roamed free.)

When thinking about Mr. Jefferson, I feel bad for Mrs. Jefferson. I don't mean the congressman's wife. I feel bad for the late Isabel Sanford. Sherman Hemsley never would have pulled a stunt like this. Ask yourself…what would Weezie Do?

Louise Jefferson would have straightened George out in a hurry and moved on up to the Eastside and that deluxe apartment in the sky with or without him.[83]

William Jefferson ran for reelection while under indictment. He proclaimed his innocence. This was the coolest customer on the planet. To the credit of his district, he was kicked out after nine terms.

He could have resigned, but liberals never resign or surrender. Only Republicans are told they must leave.

Will William Jefferson one day be a punch line? Worse, will he become an acronym?

I can see the t-shirts that read "Free Will-Jeff now."

(Can one guy on these shirts actually be in jail for the sake of accuracy already?)

Perhaps the Photoshop people can combine William Jefferson with his legacy.

The story would be "Cash and a clunker."

I am willing to admit that I was wrong. With Governor Bobby Jindal in power, this is not your father's Louisiana. Apparently they have discovered the rule of American law, despite being infected with French law in some areas of the state.

Even by Louisiana standards, William Jefferson has been found guilty.

Maybe the swamp truly is getting drained.

There is only one thing for William Jefferson to do.

He needs to move to New Jersey.

He is still innocent by New Jersey standards.

Mayors…governors…clergy people…no corruption is too much for New Jersey.

I have often maintained that New Jersey is not a state. It is a province of New York, with a small slice of it belonging to Philadelphia.

New Jersey truly represents diversity. A homosexual governor with a corrupt financial scandal disguised as a sex scandal was succeeded by a heterosexual governor with a corrupt financial scandal disguised as a sex scandal.

William Jefferson would fit in perfectly. Black officials are as equally corrupt as their white counterparts.

Washington, DC, is not an option. Mr. Jefferson does not smoke crack.

Plus, DC is amateur hour compared to New Jersey.

Think about it. When state officials can make the United States congress pale by corruption comparison, then lofty status has been achieved.

Chicago is not an option because the only available job was filled by Roland Burris. Rod Blagojevich is not available to spread any more graft. President Obama is busy in DC. At least he is not smoking crack, although Joe Biden and his comments still defy explanation.

The only hitch to this plan will be the issue of New Jersey being a New York province. Charles Rangel might already have his corrupt congressional empire covering that area.

William Jefferson has what it takes. The voters of New Jersey are…well, even they know. People get the government they deserve.

Rather than send William Jefferson to jail, force him to live in New Jersey, the garbage state.

(A girl I had a crush on twenty-five years ago lives there, so stop trying to think this is some deep-seated vendetta.)

The weather is cold, the factories would make an environmentalist cringe, and Six Flags Great Adventure is more twisted than even the most tortured explanations of New Jersey officials.

William Jefferson was not given a jury of his peers. The jury were law-abiding citizens. Therefore, he needs to be judged by his contemporaries. Only New Jersey qualifies.

Tony Soprano lives in Joisey. He is fictional, but so is most of New Jersey law and order.

For those who feel that forcing William Jefferson to live in New Jersey amounts to cruel and unusual punishment, liberal sissies need to stop being soft on crime. It is time to crack down.

Make the man shovel snow. He has shoveling experience, piling it high and deep.

Budget problems may make the transportation issue a problem. It looks like these Jeffersons will not be moving on up to the state neighboring Jefferson Cleaners.

Mr. Jefferson deserves to be governor of New Jersey.

Weezie, rest in peace. George is doing fine, although William is in a heap of trouble.

Next time he will know better. He will launder the money to a New Jersey freezer. That way it will not be a crime. It will just be business as usual.

eric

Chapter 16: Rancher Idiocy

Liberals love to refer to Ronald Reagan and George W. Bush as cowboys. Had these elitist leftist mental midgets taken their noses out of the air and into a dictionary, they would learn that cowboys roam around from place to place. The Gipper and the Dub have homes. They are ranchers, which is the opposite of the cowboy lifestyle. There are so many critics of these men, but none of them are useful enough to dignify a response. A few brief moments lambasting the worst of the worst is sufficient.

Krugman, Arafat, Gore, Obama, and Carter–Nobel Prizes Remain Worthless

The Nobel Peace Prize has long been worthless, as evidenced by Jimmy Carter and Yassir Arafat.

Al Gore is proof that the Nobel Prize might be the only thing worth less than an Academy Award, which he also won. As for Barack Obama, his victory means that the only way he could be more insufferable is if he received another honorary doctorate.

Further proof that the Nobel Prize for Economics is a useless piece of garbage is the rendering of the award to Paul Krugman, who writes an economics column that has absolutely nothing to do with economics.

Paul Krugman never murdered anybody in the tradition of typical Palesimian Yassir Arafat, but Krugman should now be considered a potential murderer.

I say this because a madman murdered Dr. George Tiller, who performed third-trimester abortions. When one read the left-wing media, the blame was placed on Bill O'Reilly. God forbid George W. Bush, Dick Cheney, or any other prominent conservative gets murdered, Mr. Krugman should therefore be blamed. He has done more to foment hate than anybody in America not connected with the *Daily Kos*, Moveon, or *Huffington Post*.

This leftist bully thinks that bashing any economic policies to the right of Leon Trotsky is worthy of making him qualified to write about economics. It is true that he writes for the *Jayson Blair Times* and not a real newspaper, but he should not even be doing that.

Some will point to his Nobel Prize, which as anybody knows is given to those that either despise Jews, Republicans, or both. A self-hating Jewish leftist is the ideal candidate.

Paul Krugman's affront of everything decent and right in this world comes in the form of his umpteen-thousandth attack on Ronald Reagan.

I am not sure if Mr. Krugman belongs to Moveon.org, but this is not a man capable of moving on. Some of his drivel is below, as he blames a man unable to fight back for the current financial crisis.

"Indeed, Reagan ushered in an era in which a small minority grew vastly rich, while working families saw only meager gains."[84]

My parents headed up a working family. They did very well under Ronald Reagan. They were public schoolteachers. They taught inner city kids. They never owned stock. Their middle class experience under President Reagan was the rule, not the exception. Paul Krugman can lie, but his manipulating the numbers to his own liking makes him worthy of a career as a CEO of a liberal government-owned General Motors.

Perhaps Mr. Krugman truly believes that up is down, but most people have their head above the waist and their hide below it.

"On the latter point: traditionally, the U.S. government ran significant budget deficits only in times of war or economic emergency. Federal debt as a percentage of G.D.P. fell steadily from the end of World War II until 1980. But indebtedness began rising under Reagan; it fell again in the Clinton years, but resumed its rise under the Bush administration, leaving us ill prepared for the emergency now upon us."

Ronald Reagan incurred debt because Tip O'Neill and George Mitchell kept rejecting his spending cuts. Additionally, we were in the middle of a Cold War, which Reagan won. Bill Clinton did not lower deficits. Newt Gingrich did, with Clinton being dragged kicking and screaming. George W. Bush faced 9/11.

Barack Obama is spending more than all of them combined, but Krugman remains silent. The reason for this is because he does not care one leftist iota about deficits. He is all in favor of spending provided it is spending that he agrees with. If we slashed the defense budget and quintupled welfare benefits, he would be dancing in the streets. This notion that he focuses on actual issues is an illusion. He looks at who is in power, decides if he loves them (liberals) or despises them (conservatives) to the point of fury that conservatives reserve for al-Qaeda.

"We weren't always a nation of big debts and low savings: in the 1970s Americans saved almost 10 percent of their income, slightly more than in the 1960s. It was only after the Reagan deregulation that thrift gradually disappeared from the American way of life, culminating in the near-zero savings rate that prevailed on the eve of the great crisis."

Mr. Krugman should immediately take any capital gains he has ever earned from any stock sales since 1982, and donate those proceeds to either the Reagan Library or the Republican National Committee. He complains about our low rate of savings, yet refuses to acknowledge that actual wealth creation skyrocketed under the Gipper.

Mr. Krugman also hates the lower tax rates Reagan enacted. He should immediately pay more. Like any other Lear Jet Leftinistra, he wants me to give more, while he pontificates from his ivory tower at the *JBT*.

If he really wants to criticize a man who let ideology bankrupt something, he should go after human cancer Arthur "Pinch" Sulzberger Jr. The *JBT* has been outsourced to Mexico. Does Krugman care about his coworkers losing their jobs? If he did, he would target the real culprits. His own company has the worst CEO in America, and that includes GM.

(He sees the collapse in stock prices as proof that Reaganomics failed. I wonder if the subsequent surge in stocks will be because of Ronald Reagan as well. He has to call it an Obama rally because liberals would never praise any kind of "surge.")

Paul Krugman is a man who insists that every single day of Republican rule will bring rain. It could be sunny for seven years, which the economy was from 2001 to 2007. On the day it rains, Krugman will be there to bash conservatives. When Republicans rule, it is also acid rain. Thankfully Barack Obama cured this as well.

This is not about Paul Krugman being a liberal. It is about him being the journalistic equivalent of a toxic asset. Given the balance sheet of the *JBT*, he is a toxic liability.

The man is a terrible human being not fit to be in the same room as Ronald Reagan. Ronald Reagan treated his opponents with dignity. Paul Krugman carries himself with as much dignity as Gore, Arafat, and Carter.

He has the Nobel Prize to prove how little he knows.

Perhaps he could use the prize money to buy himself some decency.

eric

Chapter 17: 2012 and Future Idiocy

For those wondering why I left Sarah Palin out of a discussion of 2012 contenders, it is because she should not run for president. This is for the same reason that I will not run for political office. It is a pay cut and a loss of prestige. Politicians have to be diplomatic and calculating. I love being a private citizen. I lambaste people that deserve it with abandon because I can. Private citizen Sarah Palin can destroy her critics. Besides, the 2012 nomination has already been decided.

Meeting Governor Mitt Romney

At the California State Republican Party Convention in Sacramento, I had the pleasure of meeting and speaking with Massachusetts Governor and presidential candidate Mitt Romney.

One word that must be used to describe Mitt Romney is "likable." Politics involves plenty of glad-handing, and Governor Romney truly enjoys shaking hands and meeting people. Unlike some politicians that try to walk out the door as soon as their remarks are finished, Governor Romney is known to stay for long periods of time, all the while taking pictures with people.

The first time I saw Governor Romney was at a previous California State Republican Party Convention. That one was only blocks from my home, and Governor Romney wowed the crowd.

"Some say that Governor Arnold Schwarzenegger gets along better with Democrats in the state legislature than I do in Massachusetts. Of course Arnold gets along well with the Democrats. He is sleeping with one."

"After I helped turn around the Salt Lake City, Utah, Olympics, Sports Illustrated wrote about me and featured me. My sons turned to me and said, 'Dad, in all our lives, we never thought we would see you on the cover of the sports pages.'"[85]

At that event I asked him, "Governor, why is Massachusetts having trouble passing tough drunk driving laws? Is there political resistance?"

Governor Romney did not miss a beat.

"Yes there is, but I am not going to elaborate."

I then saw Governor Romney speak at the Republican Jewish Coalition 2008 Candidates Forum. His full throttled defense of Israel left zero ambiguity. His best line came with regards to the War on Terror.

"Forget closing down Guantanamo Bay. We shouldn't close Guantanamo. We should double it."[86]

I briefly ran into him at the 2008 Republican Convention in Minneapolis. He was in a hurry, but still took time to shake hands with people.

At this current state party convention, he was there to show support for California gubernatorial nominee Meg Whitman, the founder and former CEO of eBay.

Throughout the weekend, Governor Romney would speak, and introduce Ms. Whitman. This time, they decided to reverse roles. Ms. Whitman got the crowd revved up, and Governor Romney kept up the excitement.

Due to the crowds, I was pushed so far forward that I was practically on the stage. I managed to find a crevice so that I was one to two feet from the governor. He was in fine form right from the start.

"You see, Meg builds crowds, and I take credit for it."

"There are three issues in the 2010 campaign. They are jobs, taxes, and schools. JTS."

(Despite being a staunch and unwavering supporter of Israel, Governor Romney was not referring to the Jewish Theological Seminary when he referenced JTS.)

"In California, your schools are a real problem."

"Do you Twitter? Tweet, Tweet, Tweet. Look, I am an old person by comparison."[87]

Somebody in the crowd then yelled out "Romney in 2012!" The crowd chanted "2012." When that died down, I decided to interject my own comment.

"2009 when Obama is impeached!"

The governor and the crowd cracked up. It was a joke, and I am glad it was taken as such.

When I got to speak to Governor Romney again, I asked him only lighthearted questions. He is so incredibly quick. Nothing I asked him will change the world, but he was affable as always.

It was not an official interview.

"Governor, I saw you in Century City. I loved your comments about Arnold. That was hilarious."

He thanked me, and I continued.

"Governor, do you feel that you have been the subject of bigotry? Isn't it true that the media has hostility against you because you belong to a sect of people that is constantly inviting hatred, that being people with absolutely perfect hair?"

251

The governor laughed heartily, expecting the question to be about his religious faith.

MR: "Absolutely they are jealous."

"Governor, aren't you living proof that a man can have perfect hair without being vapid like John Edwards?"

The governor's response will remain off the record since this was not an official interview. With John Edwards, fixing his hair is a religion.

"Governor, thank you for your strong support of Israel. I am always apologizing to Christians for the 80 percent of my community that does not get it. Do you ever want to go up to Harry Reid and tell him to stop messing things up for the rest of your (Mormon) community?"

MR: "Absolutely. I have tried my best. There is nothing I can do about him."

"Lastly Governor, you have ties to Michigan. Do you think General Petraeus and the United States military have what it takes to take back, secure, and turn around Detroit?"

MR: "That is a good question. That I do not know."

Governor Mitt Romney is great at "working" a room, but that should not be seen as bad or insincere. Mitt Romney genuinely does like the crowds. He feeds off of the energy, and gives it back in abundance.

California is a mess. We would do well to heed the advice of a man who turned around the state formerly known as Taxachusetts.

Governor Romney, as always, it was a pleasure.

eric

Meeting Norm Coleman–A Mensch Among Men

I had the pleasure of Minnesota Senator Norm Coleman.

Senator Coleman was locked in a tight recount battle for his senate seat. He was fighting for his political life, and I prayed for him.

(As my friend Burt Prelutsky, a former writer of *Mash*, told me, "God answers every prayer. Sometimes the answer is no.")

I have met Senator Coleman before, and will see him again many times. This event in Los Angeles was blocks from my home, and it was a truly special event. This is because Norm Coleman is a truly special man.

I have taken great pride in his career, since he is a Jewish Republican. While I agree with him on issues, my affection for him goes beyond politics. It is personal.

Senator Coleman has taken an interest in the issue of Guatemalan adoptions. My close friend and his wife were in the process of adopting a baby from Guatemala in 2007. Despite following all the proper procedures, the adoption became bogged down in bureaucracy. On the day after Thanksgiving, Senator Coleman flew to Guatemala. He worked with the Guatemalan government to help the process flow more smoothly for families that were already far along in the process. On Valentine's Day, 2008, my friends got the official word that the loveliest boy on the planet would forever be their son.

"The boy," as we affectionately call him, was in my home watching the Super Bowl. He knows how to raise his hands after a touchdown. I am trying to make him a Raiders fan. If Senator Coleman requests it, the Vikings will get positive mentions in his toddler ears.

When I look in the boy's eyes, I see the great work that Senator Coleman did to make my friends' dream become a reality. When I looked into Senator Coleman's eyes, I could not thank him enough. When I told him how much his work on the issue was appreciated, he responded in a way that was warmer than I could have possibly expected. Before getting to that, here are some of his remarks from the event itself.

"I have been in public service for thirty-two years, and these are challenging times. They might be the most challenging times I have seen in my three decades of public service. Times are challenging regarding Israel, and regarding the economy."

"We cannot live through a Jimmy Carter time again."

"The Republican Jewish Coalition brings out the best in us. The commitment to Tzedakah and Mitzvahs are important values. They are the values of our caring for our fellow man. Our commitment to entrepreneurship is important. People can take away our land. They can take away our property. They cannot take away what is in our head and our heart. What is between our ears and inside our heart cannot be taken away."

"Times have been tough. 2008 was a tough election. Yet tough times like these is when we define friendship. A friend is someone who walks in when everyone else is walking out. Thank you all for being here."

"My heart is with those that support Israel, and support economic growth."

"The other day I was talking with Bernie Marcus, who founded Home Depot. He told me that he does not think he could start Home Depot today."

Senator Coleman then shifted to the Minnesota recount battle that was underway.

"For those who need to know where we are, they are still counting."

(laughter)

"I have been counting and recounting my blessings."

(more laughter)

"You really shouldn't have more votes than actual voters."

"The Democrats wanted to stop as soon as they got ahead. It would be like in the Super Bowl if the St. Louis Cardinals…excuse me, I am dating myself, the Arizona Cardinals…The Cardinals went up 23-20 when Larry Fitzgerald, a good Minnesotan by the way, scored that touchdown. Yet they were not allowed to just end the game at that point."

(Senator Coleman moved on with grace and class, but I as a private citizen know that Stuart Smalley stole that seat. If Smalley tries to dispute this I will quote his lack of decorum by saying "I object.")[88]

Senator Coleman then offered more political analysis.

"In baseball, there is a game every day. Football is once a week at a specific time. The Masters Tournament and Wimbledon are annual, at specific times. Yet foreign policy is a tug of war. It is 24/7."

Senator Coleman then offered opinions on the Middle East and other foreign policy issues.

"Israel should bring me in as an adviser on close elections."

"In the United States, we build coalitions, and then have elections. In Israel, they have elections, and then build coalitions."

"There should be concern if President Obama talks with Iran. What is the starting point? They will begin with demanding that we get out of Afghanistan, get out of Iraq, and stop supporting Israel. Where can we go from there with that as a beginning?"

"Bernard Lewis said that 'Strength in the Middle East is how people judge you.' Jimmy Carter does not understand strength."

"For some people, a handshake is a deal. With others, if you offer a hand, they will slap it away. Hugo Chavez is a thug. If we act nice to him, that does not mean he will be nice to us. John Bolton points out that talking does not work if the other side does not have the same mindset."

"People should read what (the late) Tom Lantos had to say about Durban I before considering Durban II."

"Negotiating with despots and terrorists gives them credence."

"I met Mahmood Abbas. He told me that Hamas are extremists. Jimmy Carter met with leaders of Hamas while Hamas is throwing Fatah people out of windows."

"Your support for the RJC helps the senate stay strong on Israel."

"God's miracles stop when we stop doing our part. Israel is a miracle. America is a miracle."

"We must stand strong for Israel and stand strong for America. These are tough times, but better times will come. By standing strong during the tough times, we will then be able to celebrate the good times."

Senator Coleman then took questions. The first question dealt with the Israeli election, which the senator spoke about.

"We don't control Israel. Israel is a sovereign state. We think we know people, but things change over time. Benjamin Netanyahu may be different from what we remember. Our focus should be on keeping Iran from getting nuclear weapons. Otherwise, it does not matter who is in charge."

Somebody else asked about the bailout of 2008 and the 2009 stimulus law. Senator Coleman gave a thoughtful answer.

"We are in uncharted waters. Nobody has the answers. I voted for the bailout. I took plenty of heat from conservatives in Minnesota for voting for it. I would have voted against the stimulus. People took advantage of the current climate to enact a transformation that will burden our kids. Two-thirds of the spending will have zero impact until 2011. The question is whether we get through this, or become like Japan in the 1990s. I believe we will come back, but not quickly. Real estate will come back, but not the way it was between 2001 and 2005. I voted for the bailout because I believed that we needed to do something. There are no geniuses on this. Not Ben Bernanke, Hank Paulson, or Alan Greenspan. Nobody knows."

Senator Coleman, unlike many Republicans, has a spine. When one questioner asked if he could and would defend President George W. Bush, he did not cower.

"President Bush called me the Friday before he left office. He said that we were part of a very special group that has been through recounts. He said that he 'felt my pain.'"

(laughter)

"President Bush has a legacy. When Joe Biden had Iraq divided into three parts, President Bush stayed strong. Others said that al-Sadr would win. In the recent Iraqi elections, the secularists defeated the religious parties. Iraq without Saddam Hussein has made the world safer."

"President Bush also has a legacy with regards to helping fight diseases including AIDS in Africa. I went with Senators Bill Frist, a licensed heart surgeon, and Mitch McConnell and Mike Dewine to Africa in 2003. The actions that were taken these past few years have resulted in millions of lives being saved."

Senator Coleman concluded his formal remarks with what he said near the beginning of the event.

"A friend is one who walks in when everyone else is walking out. Thank you for your friendship."[89]

After a standing ovation, I had the opportunity to ask Senator Coleman a question about the recount. I wanted to know if the Minnesota Supreme Court was fair and honest, or if it was a kangaroo court. Since the U.S. Supreme Court decision of Bush vs. Gore was established precedent, was the Minnesota Supreme Court going to adhere to it, or act like the Florida or Massachusetts Supreme Courts?

When I cited the activism of the Ninth Circuit Court of Appeals, Senator Coleman assured me that this was not the case in Minnesota. He would know better than me. I hoped and prayed he was right.

The real highlight of the evening is what gave me the most insight into the character of the senator. Before his remarks, when I first spoke to him, I informed him that my best friend had adopted a Guatemalan baby. I told him the very condensed version of events.

Senator Coleman then surprised me by asking me for my friend's phone number. I gave him the number, and he promised me that after his remarks, he would call my friend. After he was done speaking, I was on the other side of the room. I heard a voice call out, "Eric." I turned around, and Senator Coleman said to me, "I am calling him now."

When my friend picked up the phone, the senator asked for him by name, and then said, "Hi, this is Norm Coleman."

I am very grateful that my friend knew that this was not a prank. I would have been mortified had he hung up on the senator. They spoke for a few minutes, and I deliberately wandered just out of earshot so I would not hear the conversation. I wanted it to be private, even from me.

That phone call encapsulates the kind of man that Senator Coleman is. My friend lives in Los Angeles. He has never even been to Minnesota. His wife is not even a Republican. Politics should be about policy, not elections. It should be about making the world a better place and taking joy in helping others.

After all he has done, I am forever grateful to Norm Coleman.

Whether one is Jewish, Republican, both, or neither but just supportive of what is decent and right in this world, please help

Norm Coleman in any of his future endeavors.

He stands strong for what is right. He himself is right. Let us all stand strong for a true friend of America and Israel. Let us stand strong for a fine man. Let us stand strong for a true Mensch.

Thank you Senator Coleman. I am proud to stand beside you. So are the people I know best, who are also the best people I know.

eric

All Hail Michael "The Real Deal" Steele

Let us celebrate the beauty of America. A black man reached the top of the political heap. May the confetti rain down. May the next few years be a never-ending ticker tape parade. May we celebrate diversity until every human being on Earth knows that this black man is the answer to what ails us all.

Barack Obama? No, forget him. With all due respect to Evander Holyfield, I am talking about Michael "The Real Deal" Steele, the Chairman of the Republican National Committee.

It is one thing for the president to be black. Now we can say that the president and the leader of the opposition are both black. In addition, with Michael Steele we can celebrate the fact that along with his easy personal style, there is actually substance.

I met and had the pleasure of interviewing Michael Steele at the 2008 Republican Convention.

Unlike the Democrats, who judge people by the color of their skin, my affinity for Michael Steele is solely based on the content of his character. He is a true Reagan conservative that happens to be black.

I would not care if he was as blue as Papa Smurf or as green as Hillary (envy) or Obama (inexperience). Michael Steele wants to cut taxes to grow the economy. In addition to being right on most issues, he has the one quality that has been missing from the Grumpy Old Party in some years...likability.

Go back to every single presidential campaign since the modern era of television in 1960. The guy that people were more likely to drink a beer and watch a ballgame with won the election.

Conservatism works. Liberalism fails. Yet optimism sells. Reagan had the ideology and the affability.

In tough times, delivering harsh messages of responsibility will not work without a true dose of empathy. I believe in "suck it up" as an individual, but that is not a politically sellable message. To do good things, you have to get elected first. The GOP finally removed its head from its elephant hide.

Michael Steele is a good man, and the best choice the party could have possibly made for its leadership.

He also has a great sense of humor. When I interviewed him, I pointed out that the GOP had Michael Steele and the liberals had Barack Obama. Obviously, the left is bigoted against the follically challenged. Mr. Steele pointed to his own head, and vowed that those without the crop on top absolutely could make it to the top. He was right, and as we all know, a fabulous head of hair cannot mask a lack of substance underneath.

We need to rally around Mr. Steele. He was one of the only people (along with me) who had the spine to be against the bailout from the very beginning. He was against the dreadful "spendulus" bill (Thank you Andrea Tantaros for that slogan).

The left cannot exist without despising somebody on the right, and nobody makes for derision like a minority conservative. George W. Bush is gone, and Sarah Palin was the perfect whipping girl. A black conservative is the dream demonization tool. Just ask Clarence Thomas.

Get ready to hear that Michael Steele is the devil. As he has warned us, he will be accused of hating puppies. Well he likes puppies.[90]

Go ahead liberals. Attack him personally. He will smile, and then kick your liberal hides.

President Obama, I am totally comfortable with a black leader. I just want one who is not wrong about every issue that matters to me.

Go get 'em Mr. Steele.

eric

My Interview With Governor Tim Pawlenty

At the 2008 Republican Convention in Minnesota, I had the pleasure of meeting hometown hero and favorite son Governor Tim Pawlenty.

In addition to being a popular governor and rising star in the party, Governor Pawlenty was a finalist to be vice president under John McCain. In fact, I confess to guaranteeing that he would be the pick.

My rationale was simple. He is tall, has good hair, and is inoffensive. He is the epitome of a "safe, do no harm" choice. I suspect he will be on various Republican short lists for some time to come.

I initially met him in South Florida at a Republican Jewish Coalition event honoring Vice President Dick Cheney. Governor Pawlenty was a rock star at this event. The elderly Jewish ladies kept coming up to him and fawning over him as if he were Joe Lieberman. They insisted on showing the governor pictures of their daughters and granddaughters in the hopes of fixing them up with him. He politely and genially insisted that he was happily married and not Jewish. The women did not care. He was simply that telegenic. At forty-seven, the man looked like John Cusack.

At the convention, I ran into him at the very end of the third night. I did a rapid-fire interview with him before his aides whisked him away. Given that he was the governor of the host city, he was under more pressure than most politicians, making sure everything went like clockwork. It did, and he shined.

Here is my interview with Governor Tim Pawlenty.

1) What are the most important issues of 2008?

TP: "The economy and National Security. Both of those are vitally important and require a strong leader who is prepared."

2) Who are your three favorite political heroes?

TP: "Abraham Lincoln, Ronald Reagan, and Teddy Roosevelt."

3) How would you like to be remembered 100 years from now? What would you want people to say about Tim Pawlenty the person?

TP: "I would like to be remembered as a good person who shared his commitment to public service with the people of Minnesota."

4) How did Sarah Palin do in her speech to the convention?

TP: "She did a fantastic job. She introduced herself to America in a powerful way."

Time was short, but if I had more time, I would have asked him about the twenty-four hours following the Minnesota bridge collapse. While it was not 9/11 or Katrina, it was a tragedy nonetheless. His steady and compassionate leadership in the wake of the bridge collapse was what public service should be about.

One other thing about Tim Pawlenty is that while he is a very competent executive, he is also very likable. One can be pleasant and still get the job done. When he talks about "Sam's Club Republicans," he means it. He is a blue-collar guy at heart. He truly does like people. He once got a reporter in a playful headlock and gave the man a "noogie." As governor he even had a "mullet" hairstyle.

Once he became a leading contender for vice president, he had to cut that part of his personality off.

The last thing I said to Governor Pawlenty was, "Governor, I lost money on you. I bet on you for VP."

He laughed, gave me a hearty handshake, and let me know that he appreciated the support, even if it did not put him over the top.

The people of Minnesota are lucky. They have a great governor. I wish the very best for Minnesota Governor Tim Pawlenty.

eric

Cancel the 2012 Primaries

Cancel 2012. I don't mean the movie that I have zero interest in seeing. Actually, cancel that too. Cancel the 2012 Republican primaries. Skip Iowa and those twelve people in Dixville Notch, New Hampshire. They are like Punxsutawney Phil the Groundhog. When they see their shadows, they give themselves fifteen more minutes of self-importance.

Cancel the GOP nomination because the nominee has already been decided. It was decided in 2008. For those of you backing other candidates, you have no say. You don't get to choose. The nominee is decided. Mitt Romney is the nominee.

Whether you like Mitt Romney or not, this doesn't matter. He has been anointed.

Republicans preach conservatism, but when it comes to picking presidential nominees, we are the biggest bunch of socialists on the planet.

Democrats may be wrong on every issue, but at least they have real primaries. Obama is dreadful, but Hillary was not given her coronation. We Republicans are a hierarchy. We always pick the person who is next in line.

I am as thrilled as anybody that Ronald Reagan was given three chances, but this was an aberration. In real life if somebody keeps running for president and losing, and then is handed a nomination as a consolation prize, there is a chance they may lose again. We are not a charity. Just because liberals reward people like Arab sympathizer Helen Thomas for violating the law of averages does not mean we have to do the same.

The entire rational in 1996 for Bob Dole's candidacy was that it was "his turn." John McCain was handed the 2008 nomination because he lost in 2000. This is not summer camp where the last place kid gets a prize. We would all be better off if the last place kid was told that he sucked, but that he may or may not be good at something else. Maybe if Simon Cowell was allowed to screen GOP nominees we could weed out the chaff.

I have nothing against Mitt Romney. He looks like a presidential nominee. He is tall, has good hair, and is inoffensive. That means Tim Pawlenty will be the vice presidential choice. He is tall, has good hair, and is so harmlessly inoffensive that he may be standing in your living room.

Mitt Romney is what we call "acceptable." Rudy Giuliani was loved by the Neocons and other foreign policy conservatives. He was fine with the economic conservatives. The social conservatives were suspicious of him. Mike Huckabee is perfectly qualified to be king of Iowa, but Republicans do not get elected without support from the *Wall Street Journal* editorial pages and Sir Charles of Krauthammer.

None of the three legs of the Republican stool would be in a state of open revolt over Mitt Romney. 2008 was a year where we needed a sexy nominee on the ticket. We had to swing for the fences. After four years of Obama, people will have had all of the sexiness they can handle. Like a hot woman at a bar, sexiness left us broke. In 2012 the social, economic, and foreign policy conservatives will look at Mitt Romney and think, "fine. He's good enough."

We have so many talented people in our party that never get mentioned. One person I love is Mississippi Governor Haley Barbour. Three people helped the GOP take back the congress in 1994. Newt Gingrich brought the strategy. Rush Limbaugh brought the media and the message. Haley Barbour brought the money and the bourbon. The bourbon was used in a late night meeting with Gingrich, resulting in the agreement to get the money.[91] After Hurricane Katrina, some Louisiana lady was crying that she was "so overwhelmed."[92] Haley Barbour was rolling up his sleeves, turning into the Rudy Giuliani of the south, and getting the job done. Never send a liberal to do an adult's job.

Another great choice would be Hawaii Governor Linda Lingle. She is a Jewish Republican who got elected in a state with virtually no Jews and no Republicans. She simply vetoes everything. In one recent legislative session there were thirty-three bills up for veto, and she vetoed twenty-seven of them.[93] One that became law was a children's health care bill. After all, anything for the children has to be good. A few weeks later she did not like how the law was working, so she had it overturned.

I just want the GOP to have a real primary. The media creates tension. George Herbert Walker Bush defeated Reagan in Iowa. George W. Bush stumbled in New Hampshire. It doesn't matter. Mitt Romney is next in line, and his opponents are running for the right to lose and be handed the nomination the next time around. If people want to prove me wrong, that would be fine. Otherwise, let's cancel the primary and give the money back to Republican voters in the form of a tax cut.

eric

Chapter 18: American Idiocy

The American people are not idiots. As Karl Rove has said, "The masses are not @sses."[94] The idiocy comes from those that want to change America from what has worked for over two hundred-thirty-three years. Liberals love to say how much they love America. They love America for what they want it to be. I love America for what it already is. America does have black marks, such as slavery and Vietnam. Those were problems caused by Democrats anyway. So that liberals do not feel like the only cellar dwellers on the logical food chain, they occasionally have some company worthy of being in their comically insufferable presences.

Black Friday

Like many of you, I enjoyed a good Swanson dinner derivative on Thanksgiving and watched nine hours of football plus highlights, or in the case of one game, lowlights.

Thanksgiving Thursday was in the bag, and it became time for Black Friday 2009.

That reminds me...I really hate it when I try to write a column and I keep getting interrupted. Anyway, the interruption is not your concern. It has already passed for now. Back to Black Friday.

(Not to be confused with "*Back in Black* Friday," a pre-weekend party ritual involving lots of rock group ACDC and people in short skirts. Sadly, it is men, and they are kilts.)

I am so sick and tired of these politically correct holidays. Having a holiday for Martin Luther King Jr. is fine. Black History Month is fine, although I have no idea why February was chosen instead of January. Wouldn't it make sense to have MLK Day be during Black History Month?

The truth behind all of this is that racist white politicians made a compromise deal with black leaders. February used to have thirty-one days. To balance the lunar calendar with the solar calendar, three days needed to be eliminated. The compromise gave February as Black History Month, but February was reduced from thirty-one to twenty-eight days.

At some point Al Sharpton and Jesse Jackson need to stop meddling. Do we really need another Million Man March? This whole Black Friday thing is just another feel good ebonics type...

Wait, hold on one second. Somebody just slipped me a piece of paper. Well now, this is embarrassing. Apparently Black Friday has nothing to do with race or politics.

Black Friday obviously deals with Wall Street. Can we all stop whining about the stock market? Trading is always light the day after Thanksgiving. Even a market drop really should not be overanalyzed. Stocks go up and down. Stop being glued to CNBC. It's not like CNBC is the NFL Network or ESPN. Get lives.

Oh no, another interruption and another piece of paper. Apparently those reading the front page of the *Wall Street Journal* can just skip and go to the editorial pages. Black Friday has nothing to do with the stock market or any financial matter (although it did emanate from that world originally).

In sports news, today is Silver and Black Friday. I would like to congratulate the Oakland Raiders on a spectacular victory. The ticker-tape parade is in order. It is about time the team started winning and...

Sheesh, can a guy write a sports column without being bothered. Well apparently another note scribbled in crayon has confirmed that the Raiders lost that game, and that Black Friday is not happening in Oakland or anywhere else due to anything sports related.

If it is not about sports, politics, or business, then a certain individual who is not even close to being well-rounded is unaware of Black Friday.

That's it. It is historical. We are back in the dark ages. Some people worry about bird or swine flu. We should be worrying about the resurgence of the Bubonic Plague. If I recall correctly, it was black. I knew we should have quarantined schoolchildren. Now they will be sick all weekend. I am not an expert on medicine but...

You know, these notes are beginning to make me feel like I don't know what I am talking about. I am even more way off base than usual.

I can't stand the hassle of trying to write this column. I need peace and quiet away from everybody. I need a place where I can be by myself.

I can go to the mall. After all, Thanksgiving is over. People are back at work. The stores should be empty.

Hey, who and where is the person throwing spitballs at me? Oh, they are big notes. Hmm, apparently Black Friday is about soccer moms killing each other over some Furby, Elmo, Garbage Patch Kid, or other toy that is to be given at another holiday celebrating peace and love.

(In a tangent even irrelevant for this column, one hilarious guy's t-shirt I saw had a downward pointing arrow with a sign that said, "Tickle THIS Elmo.")

Do they call it Black Friday because the women give each other black eyes when fighting over the last toy?

I only wish there was a solution.

Actually, there is. Forget swine flu. The only pork product of today is Pig Latin. The word "be," as in "to be or not to be," in Pig Latin is pronounced "eBay."

I don't even have to leave my condo. I can eat my lunch, watch more football highlights, buy sports stuff, and…well, whatever else it is that people do.

I think I will take a nap. I am off to close the shades, close my eyes, and block out all of the interruptions and distractions.

Now that is Black Friday I can believe in.

Now shut the heck up Elmo. I am trying to sleep.

eric

Facebook, MySpace, and Twitter–Dear God No

I am technologically incompetent, with no way of changing.

I believe Facebook and MySpace should be abolished. I am truly convinced that Twitter is the apocalypse. I still refer to the people that use twitter to discuss their mundane existences as what they are…twits.

Although I am still rabidly opposed to these sites, I have decided to use them. I equate them to a monthly social event that takes place one block from my home. Regarding this social event, everybody hates it, but everybody knows that everybody goes, so everybody goes. Social networking sites are no different.

I have books to sell, and I want people to buy them.

Here is how I approached the sites. I post once a day, usually in the morning. The post is a link to my column. That is it. There is nothing more. You don't care what I had for breakfast, what television shows I watch, or what I do on the occasions I leave the computer, which more people should do. If you do care about these things, God help you.

This whole "friend request" thing makes me ill. I have no idea what constitutes proper decorum. Why the heck do I need to be Internet friends with people I talk to all the time in real life? It seems silly. I travel a lot on business, and have found that I am insulting somebody if I do not immediately accept a friend request.

Why can't people just email me, call me, or drop by and visit?

Other people send me "friend suggestions." People I like want me to know other people I do not know. Then if I do not say yes, I am insulting the person who made the suggestion.

What I absolutely have no problem rejecting are requests to play games. I am not on these sites to have pillow fights, mafia wars, or figure out what tree I would be if I were a tree. I don't care.

This then makes people think I dislike people. Quite the contrary…I love people. I treasure real friendships. Forming bonds with total strangers does not seem sincere. If we are trying to advance ideas, such as politics, hearing good ideas is useful. Just don't send me recipes for crying out loud. I won't use them.

For me the Internet is business. eBay is commerce. Purchasing plane tickets is useful. Even JDate was about maximizing productivity, Romance was merely the product.

I say this because I am learning things about Facebook the hard way.

First of all, anybody that I accept as a friend has their life on my page. I could delete their feed, but that might be rude. Others will have "feed envy" if their feed is accepted.

Secondly, I had no idea that everything I type on my wall gets sent to every person on my list. I write a political column. I have friends who disagree with my views. I would never email them my political opinions. Yet my opinions show up on their wall, and they are unhappy. Sheesh!

Thirdly, commenting on anything anybody writes seems to be a death sentence. I commented on one person's wall. I then received an email every time there was a follow-up comment. For the person who owns the wall, I can understand this. Does every commenter care about what every other commenter says? This cannot be the case.

Fourth, I have so many feeds on my page that I miss things. I do not stare at the site twenty-four hours per day. I post my column and then leave, although I am polite enough to return emails. If somebody leaves an offensive comment, I most likely will not see it. On my actual blog, I regulate and monitor all comments. Profanity and personal attacks are banned. Hate speech is deleted as quickly as possible. On Facebook it is much tougher to do this. This leads to "friends" getting offended, when I have no idea why.

People should just comment on my blog. Then they know I will see it.

I know I do not have the right to dictate what others have to say. This is America. Yet when does enough become enough?

I am promoting books. People can buy the books.

I am not discussing my bedroom, bathroom, or shopping habits, or any other private behavior. I certainly do not put up explicit pictures of myself. I did not even have a picture on Facebook until other people posted pictures of me thinking I would be delighted by this.

None of the pictures are harmful, but I cannot imagine that anything in my private life matters. Are we that dull that we have to shout from the rooftops about how interesting we are?

(It really all does tie into the Dos Equis Guy.)

Somebody suggested I should create a fan page for myself. Why the heck would anybody be a fan of me? I am a guy spouting opinions, occasionally with eloquence.

My dreams of going back to the horse and buggy and abacus will not happen. Technology is here to stay, and it will keep rapidly changing.

Twenty years ago when a person talked out loud to nobody with accompanying hand gestures, they were carted away to the looney bin. Now people have earpieces that are telephones. Personally I think it is a cover, and they really are talking out loud to nobody.

So yes, I am on Facebook and Twitter. I will keep my remarks brief and to the point.

I pray that the rest of you do the same. After all, less time on the computer means more time reading.

For those that read, I have a good book I can recommend. I should know. I wrote it.

eric

Idiotic Conclusions

My experiences are based on a simple premise: My critics are imbeciles. Nobody in this world learns anything from feedback from people who never mattered.

In football, the players do not have time to discuss diplomacy. They understand that somebody is coming at them trying to kill them. They either defend themselves or get knocked on their backs. They do not stop to see if the other side wants to dialogue. The Super Bowl is often ruined by people yammering during the game and then demanding silence during the commercials. The rules in my home for football are the same as for politics. If you have no idea what you are talking about, shut up and leave.

Whoever said love is about never having to say you are sorry has never been in love. Love is about apologizing as quickly as possible so that they leave the room. It is hard work trying to balance romance and the ball game. It is easier to just agree with whatever was said and get back to the game rather than argue and miss the action.

Love and sports are pleasures. Real life is about trying to keep a toxic cocktail of Islamofascism and leftism from getting us blown to Kingdom Come. Our choices are to make a sincere effort to understand idiocy, or to verbally shake the stupidity out of these miscreants while yelling, "Knock it off!"

We need to support our troops. The next time a member of congress says that they support the troops and want them to come home, let that soon to be ex-politico know that the troops feel the same way and want congress to go home and stay there.

God created imbeciles, and they begot more imbeciles. All Adam had to do was avoid a tree. He was a guy. He had no interest in trees. He made the mistake of listening to Eve, the world's first feminist environmentalist. Then the snake showed up and we had animal rights activists. Adam was a conservative. He minded his own business. Eve was a liberal activist. She and her liberal descendents of both genders are proof that one can eat from the tree of knowledge, have an inflated sense of intellectual importance, and yet know virtually nothing that benefits anybody in society.

As for me, my battle cry remains the same. *Hineni*. Here I am. Jewish, proud, politically conservative, and morally liberal.

So what next?

I'll be flying down the highway headed west ...

In a streak of black lightning, called the Tygrrrr Express.

On to the next adventure. God bless.

eric

Acknowledgements

My grandparents are gone, but with me always. My parents were never wealthy, but I was raised right.

Without love, there is no life. The love of my life is the current romantic administration.

My friendships are lifelong friendships. They are listed in alphabetical order by last name to avoid any possible (insert nightmare scenarios here).

Leeor Alpern, Gary Aminoff, Seth Arkin, Brian Arnold, Rachael Aron, Richard Baehr, Jane Barnett, Jeff Barry, Billy Beene, Michael and Ann Benayoun, Lara Berman, Arno Berry, Leo Bletnitsky, David Blumberg, Peter Bylsma, Shane Borgess, Sherry Caiozzo, Johnny Ceng, Ligang Chen, Lisa and Bob Cohen, Nim Cohen, Chaim and Tova Cunin, Val Cymbal, Toni Anne Dashiell, Ari and Fini David, Aaron Deutsch, Chuck and Diane DeVore, Susan Duclos, Seth Edelman, Brian Elfand, Sharon Elias, Jason Elman, Chad Everson, Uri Filiba, Ken Flickstein, Deron Freatis, Eric and Jennifer Goldberg, Steve Goldberg, Eugene Grayver, Molly and Leonard Grayver, Meri Green, Elyse and Aaron Greenberg, Larry Greenfield, Celeste Greig, Steve Grill, Moira Gruss, Danny Halperin, John Heller, Micky Himell, Julia and Marc Jaffe, Jason Kenniston, Tarik Khan, Jonathan Klein, Jamie Krasnoo, Jerry Krautman, Jeff Kuhns, Amy and Gene Laff, Elana Landau, Esther Levine, Isaac Lieberman, Lisa Macizo, David Marcus, Jason Margolies, Jersey McJones, Margie and Tom Mergen, Carl Merino, Mike Monatlik, Andrew Nelson, Izzy Newman, Greg Neyman, Erica Nurnberg, Doris Ohayon, Terry Okura, Mare Ouellette, Brian Ozkan, Mike Patton, Stevie Rivenbark, Harold and Sharon Rosenthal, Jeanie and Bernie Rosenthal, Ron Rothstain, Michael Rubinfeld, Peggy Sadler, Beverly Sandler, Pat Saraceno, Daniel Savitt, Evan Sayet, Alan Schechter, Steven Slade, Alicia and Josh Stone, Ryan Szackas, Ruth and David Tobin, Borah Van Dormolen, Dov and Runya Wagner, Adam Wasserman, Doug Welch, Hilarie Wolf, Laura Wolfe, Woody Woodrum, Nate and Janna Wyckoff, Oliver Young, Marc Zoolman.

My extended family includes the Arzillos, the Diels, the Katzs, David Malakoff, the Mouradians, the Rossis, and the Weitzs.

Lara Berman convinced me to start a blog. Jamie Krasnoo provided the technological advice. Eliot Yamini of Hotweazel developed it. Hugh Hewitt, Armstrong Williams, Ward Connerly, Evan Sayet, and Larry Greenfield all have helped my blog expand. Celeste Greig, Ralph Peters, Peggy Sadler, Patricia Saraceno, Borah Van Dormolen, and Toni Anne Dashiell all helped my speaking career. Chabad, USC Hillel, the Republican Jewish Coalition, and the Zionist Crusader Alliance have all nourished and inspired me.

Thank you Ronald Reagan, George W. Bush, and Dick Cheney for your leadership.

Almighty God, thank you for tolerating my nonsense.

eric, aka the Tygrrrr Express   http://www.tygrrrrexpress.com

Endnotes

I am not the *Jayson Blair Times*, Dan Rather, or Mary Mapes. "Fake but accurate" stories are for liberals. Many of my sources are from liberal sites. While I loathe promoting leftists in any way, listing established conservative sites would just open me up to liberal charges of less thorough research. I want the world to see that evidence of left-wing ideological idiocy can be found at dreadful, ghastly excuses for "sources."

(1) Weiss, Michael. Jewish Leaders Meet With Obama. *Tablet*, July 14, 2009

(2) Murphy, Eddie. *Raw*, 1987

(3) Marx, Groucho. *Groucho and Me*, Page 321, 1959

(4) J Street. *http://www.jstreet.org*

(5) Shakespeare, William. *Hamlet*

(6) Weisberg, Jacob. How to Lean on Israel. *Slate Magazine*, June 13, 2009

(7) Guns n Roses. Welcome to the Jungle. *Appetite For Destruction*, 1987

(8) Gordis, Daniel. When Mistakes Are Worth Making *danielgordis.org*, July 1, 2008

(9) Peres, Shimon. Concession Speech. 1997

(10) Piper, Linda. *The Storyteller's Creed*

(11) Reagan, Ronald. Tear Down This Wall. *ReaganLibrary.com*, June 12, 1987

(12) Affleck, Ben. *Boiler Room*, 2000

(13) Brooks, Mel. *History of the World Part I*, 1981

(14) The Chambers Brothers. Time Has Come Today, *The Time Has Come,* 1966

(15) Genesis. No Reply. *Abacab,* 1981

(16) Collins, Phil. Sussudio. *No Jacket Required,* 1985

(17) Peter, Tom A. Israeli proposal: Make Jordan the official Palestinian homeland. *Christian Science Monitor,* June 1, 2009

(18) Gore, Al. Press Conference, March 3, 1997

(19) Colmes, Alan. *Hannity and Colmes,* Debuted 1996

(20) Stewart, Jon. *Crossfire,* October 15, 2004

(21) Stewart, Jon. *The Daily Show,* 2008

(22) Stewart, Jon, *The Daily Show,* 2009

(23) Adams, Rob. Alec Baldwin Photographer News Reveals Assault Incident. *Newsoxy.com,* February 14, 2010

(24) Langella, Frank. *Frost-Nixon,* 2008

(25) Sowell, Thomas. *See, I Told You So,* 1993

(26) Sheen, Martin. *Wall Street,* 1987

(27) Hank Greenberg at war. *Businessweek,* March 27, 2006

(28) Festa, Paul. Coming back to haunt them. *CNET News,* March 24, 2004

(29) Serwer, Andy. Madoff investors burned by SEC. *Fortune,* December 15, 2008

(30) Rivers, Joan. *Celebrity Apprentice.* April 26, 2009

(31) Rivers, Melissa. *Celebrity Apprentice.* April 26, 2009

(32) Young, Neil. Rocking in the Free World. *Freedom,* 1989

(33) Georgia Satellites. Keep Your Hands to Yourself. *Georgia Satellites,* 1986

(34) Petty, Tom. I Won't Back Down. *Full Moon Fever*, 1989

(35) AC/DC. Dirty Deeds Done Dirt Cheap, *Dirty Deeds Done Dirt Cheap*, 1976

(36) AC/DC. TNT. *TNT*, 1975

(37) Powers, Kirsten. Time For a Summit On Sexism. *New York Post*, August 3, 2009

(38) Safire, William. Hillary is a Congenital Liar. *New York Times*, January 8, 1996

(39) Grayson, Alan. Speech on House Floor. September 29, 2009

(40) Radner, Gilda. *Saturday Night Live*, Debuted 1975

(41) Reid, Harry. Press Conference, December, 2009

(42) Green, Tom. Play With Your Balls. *Tom Green Show*, 2000

(43) Jilted Bride Awarded $150K. *WSBTV.com*, July 23, 2008

(44) Clapton, Eric. Forever Man. *Behind the Sun*, 1985

(45) *PCU*, 1994

(46) The Coasters. Yakkety Yak. *The Coasters Greatest Hits*, 1959

(47) Poison. Home. *Hollyweird*, 2002

(48) U2 and BB King. When Love Comes to Town. *Rattle and Hum*, 1988

(49) White Lion. When the Children Cry. *Pride*, 1987

(50) Obama, Barack. Press Conference. July 22, 2009

(51) Obama, Barack. Press Conference. July 24, 2009

(52) Habershon, Ada R. May the Circle Be Unbroken. 1907

(53) Seville, David. Sunshine, Lollipops, and Rainbows. *Chipmunks a Go-Go*, 1965

(54) Cyrus, Billy Ray. Achy Breaky Heart. *Some Gave All*, 1992

(55) O'Brien, Conan. *Late Night With Conan O'Brien*, February 4, 1997

(56) Obama Practices Looking-Off-Into-Future Pose. *The Onion*, May 28, 2008

(57) Newhart, Bob. *Saturday Night Live*, February 11, 1995

(58) Obama, Barack. Speech Before Congress. September 9, 2009

(59) Kennedy, Ted. Letter to Barack Obama. May 12, 2009

(60) Charles Boustany, GOP Rebuttal to speech before Congress, September 9, 2009

(61) Obama, Barack. Press Conference. July 22, 2009

(62) Emanuel, Rahm. *Wall Street Journal TV*, November 7, 2008

(63) The Dos Equis Guy, Beer Commercials, Debuted 2007

(64) Obama, Barack. Interview on *Countdown With Keith Olbermann*, 2009

(65) Obama, Barack. Campaign Rally, 2008

(66) Letterman, David. *The Late Show With David Letterman*, August, 2000

(67) Obama, Barack. Press Conference. April 29, 2009

(68) Clinton, Bill. State of the Union Speech, 1995

(69) Obama, Barack. Press Conference. March 24, 2009

(70) Keck, Kristi. Is Talking to Taliban Right Approach? *CNN.com*, March 9, 2009

(71) Berntsen, Gary. *American Morning*, March 9, 2009

(72) King, Larry. *Larry King Live*, September 23, 2008

(73) Ahmadinejad, Mahmood. *Larry King Live*, September 23, 2008

(74) Madonna. Vogue. *I'm Breathless*, 1990

(75) Ahmadinejad, Mahmood. Speech at Columbia, September 24, 2007

(76) Piscopo, Joe. *Hannity*, February 13, 2009

(77) Pelosi, Nancy. Press Conference, July 30, 2009

(78) Greenwood, Lee. God Bless the USA. *You've Got a Good Love Comin'*, 1984

(79) Black Eyed Peas. Let's Get Retarded. *Elephunk*, 2003

(80) Hilton, Perez. *92.3NOW.com*, June 24, 2009

(81) Craig, David. Why There's a Day Without Gays. *CNN.com*, December 9, 2008

(82) Don't Go Here. *http://www.snopes.com/business/misxlate/nova.asp*, 2007

(83) Dubois, Janet. *The Jefferson's* Theme Song, 1975

(84) Krugman, Paul. Reagan Did It. *New York Times*, May 31, 2009

(85) Romney, Mitt. CRP Speech, 2007

(86) Romney, Mitt. Republican Jewish Coalition Candidate Forum, October 16, 2007

(87) Romney, Mitt. CRP Speech, 2009

(88) Franken, Al. Senate Session, December 17, 2009

(89) Coleman, Norm. Republican Jewish Coalition Speech, 2009

(90) Steele, Michael. Campaign Ad, 2006

(91) Dan Balz and Ronald Brownstein. *Storming the Gates*, 1996

(92) Blanco, Kathleen. Press Conference, August, 2005

(93) Finnegan, Lynn. Special Session Less Partisan. *Honolulu Adv.*, July 19, 2007

(94) Rove, Karl. American Jewish University Lecture Series, 2008

CPSIA information can be obtained at www.ICGtesting.com
Printed in the USA
BVOW011707201112

305964BV00001B/7/P

9 781450 211741